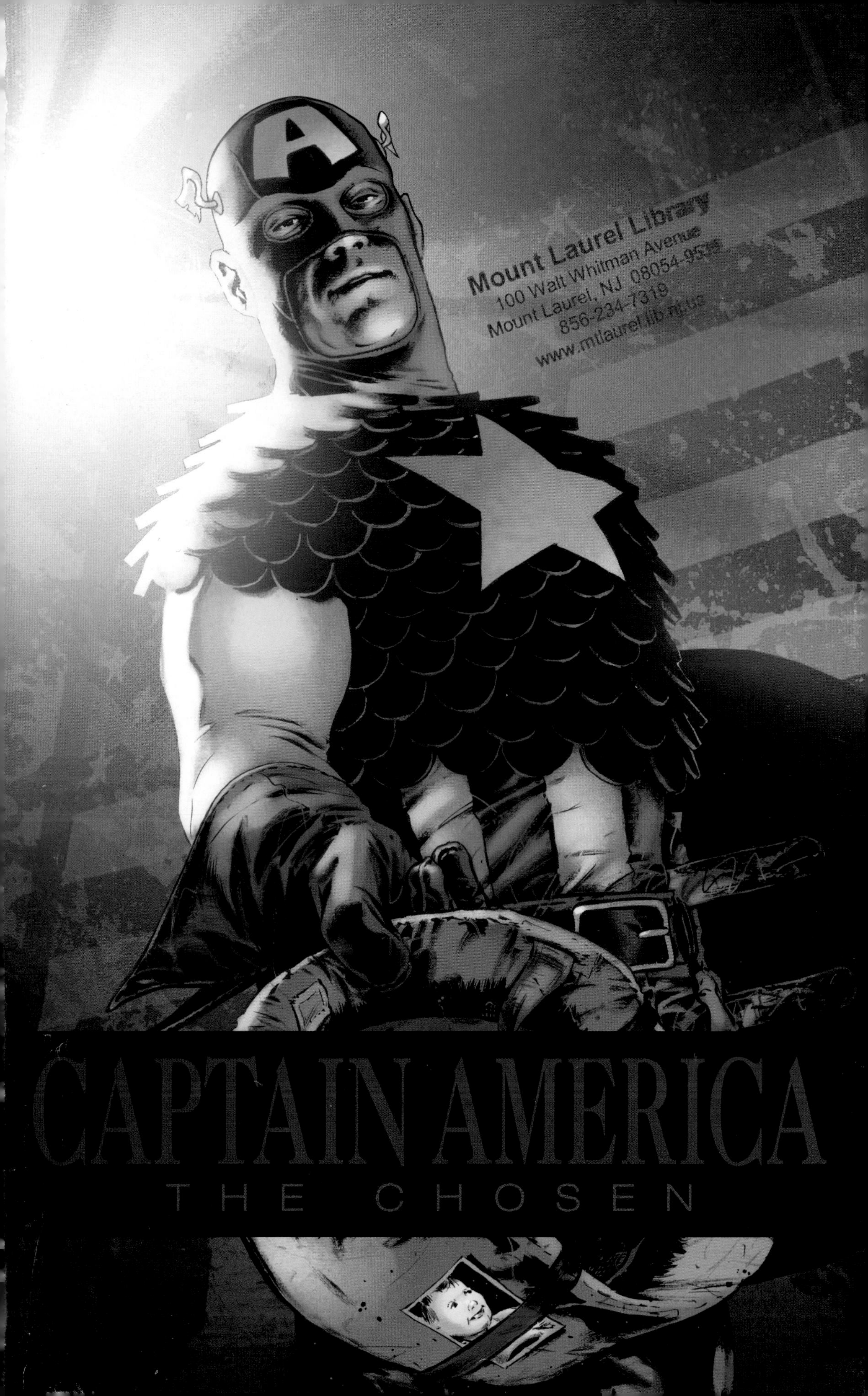
CAPTAIN AMERICA
THE CHOSEN

CAPTAIN AMERICA: THE CHOSEN. Contains material originally published in magazine form as CAPTAIN AMERICA: THE CHOSEN #1-6. First printing 2008. ISBN# 978-0-7851-2905-9. Published by MARVEL PUBLISH-
ING, INC., a subsidiary of MARVEL ENTERTAINMENT, INC. OFFICE OF PUBLICATION: 417 5th Avenue, New York, NY 10016. Copyright © 2007 and 2008 Marvel Characters, Inc. All rights reserved. $24.99 per copy in
the U.S. and $26.50 in Canada (GST #R127032852); Canadian Agreement #40668537. All characters featured in this issue and the distinctive names and likenesses thereof, and all related indicia are trademarks of
Marvel Characters, Inc. No similarity between any of the names, characters, persons, and/or institutions in this magazine with those of any living or dead person or institution is intended, and any such similarity which
may exist is purely coincidental. **Printed in the U.S.A.** ALAN FINE, CEO Marvel Toys & Publishing Divisions and CMO Marvel Entertainment, Inc.; DAVID GABRIEL, SVP of Publishing Sales & Circulation; DAVID BOGART,
SVP of Business Affairs & Talent Management; MICHAEL PASCIULLO, VP of Merchandising & Communications; JIM O'KEEFE, VP of Operations & Logistics; DAN CARR, Executive Director of Publishing Technology;
JUSTIN F. GABRIE, Director of Editorial Operations; SUSAN CRESPI, Editorial Operations Manager; OMAR OTIEKU, Production Manager; STAN LEE, Chairman Emeritus. For information regarding advertising in Marvel
Comics or on Marvel.com, please contact Mitch Dane, Advertising Director, at mdane@marvel.com. For Marvel subscription inquiries, please call 800-217-9158.

10 9 8 7 6 5 4 3 2 1

CAPTAIN AMERICA
THE CHOSEN

WRITER: DAVID MORRELL

ARTIST: MITCH BREITWEISER

COLOR ARTIST: BRIAN REBER

LETTERER: VC'S CORY PETIT

COVERS: MITCH BREITWEISER

VARIANT COVERS: TRAVIS CHAREST & JUSTIN PONSOR

EDITORS: ANDY SCHMIDT & ALEJANDRO ARBONA

CAPTAIN AMERICA CREATED BY JOE SIMON & JACK KIRBY

COLLECTION EDITOR: JENNIFER GRÜNWALD

ASSISTANT EDITORS: CORY LEVINE & JOHN DENNING

EDITOR, SPECIAL PROJECTS: MARK D. BEAZLEY

SENIOR EDITOR, SPECIAL PROJECTS: JEFF YOUNGQUIST

SENIOR VICE PRESIDENT OF SALES: DAVID GABRIEL

PRODUCTION: JERRY KALINOWSKI

BOOK DESIGNER: RODOLFO MURAGUCHI

EDITOR IN CHIEF: JOE QUESADA

PUBLISHER: DAN BUCKLEY

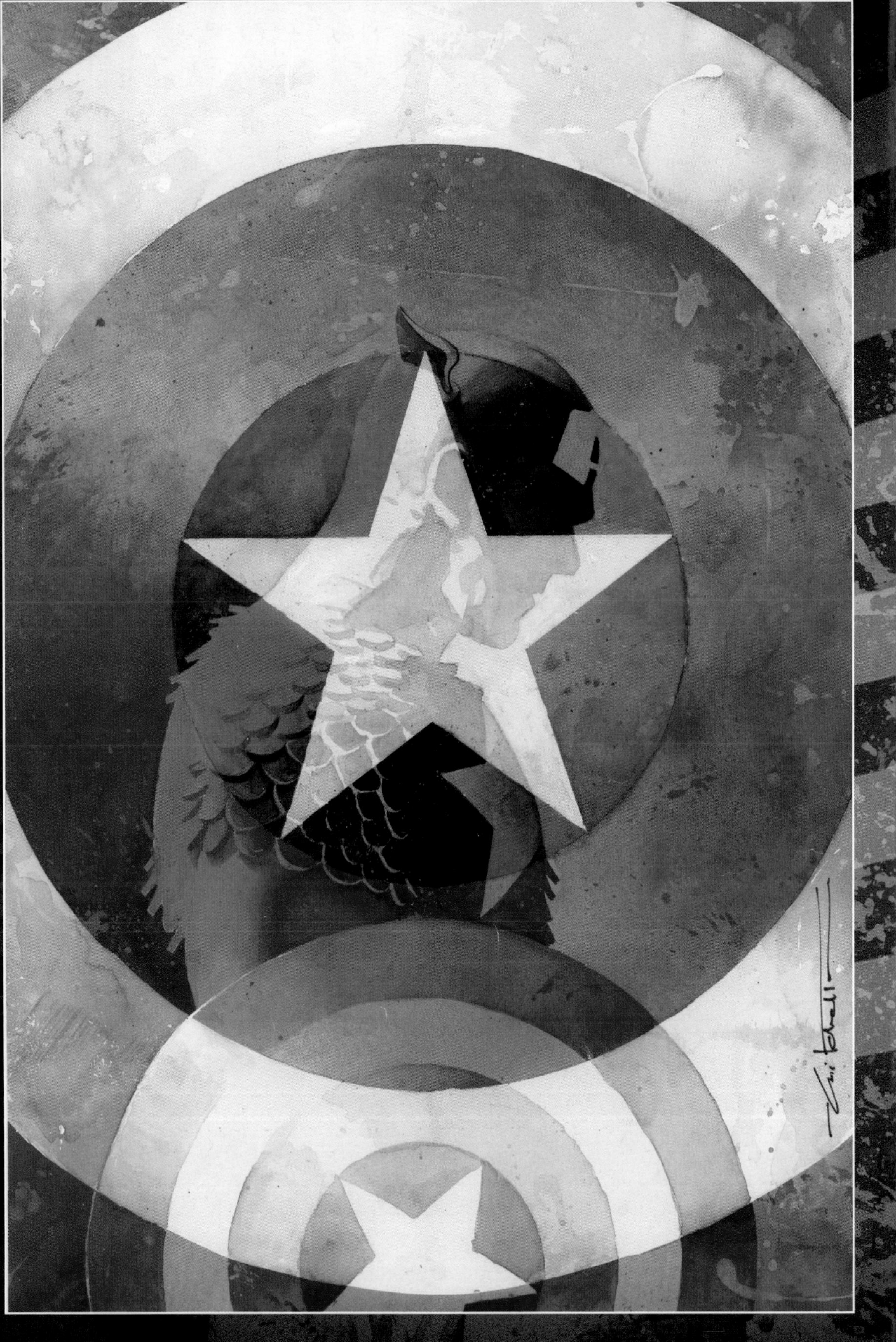

ONE

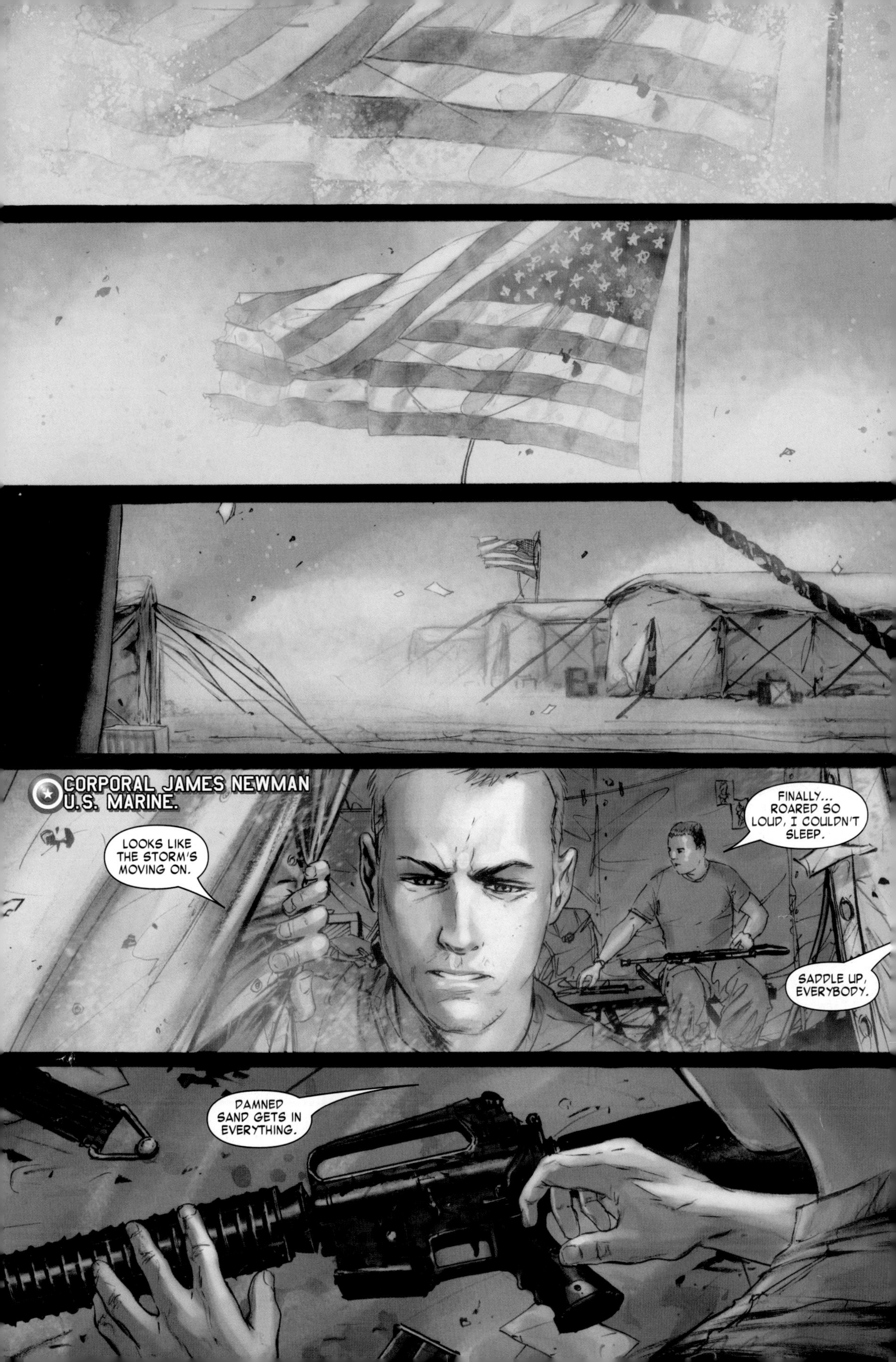
CORPORAL JAMES NEWMAN
U.S. MARINE.
LOOKS LIKE THE STORM'S MOVING ON.
FINALLY... ROARED SO LOUD, I COULDN'T SLEEP.
SADDLE UP, EVERYBODY.
DAMNED SAND GETS IN EVERYTHING.

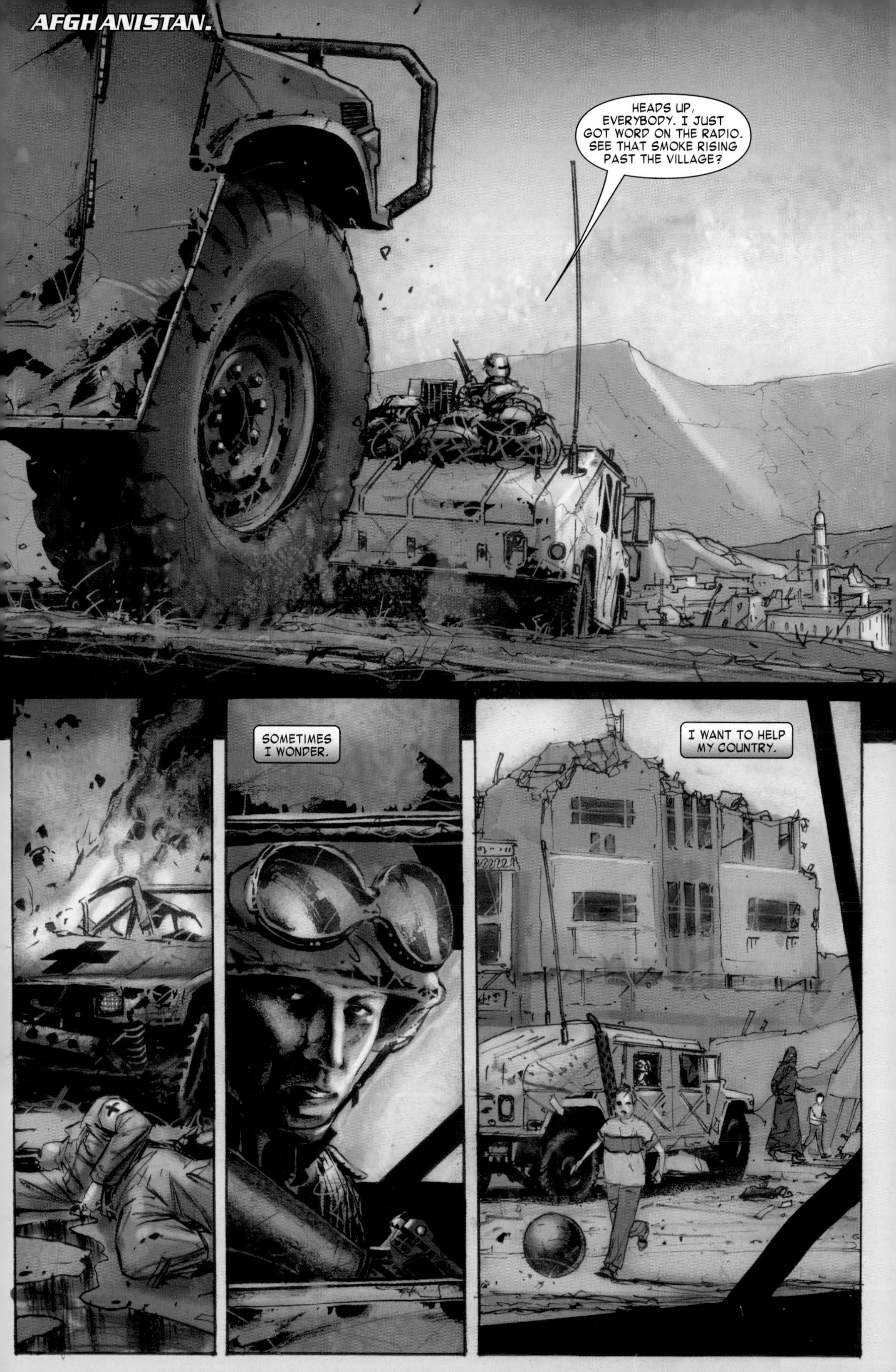
AFGHANISTAN.
HEADS UP, EVERYBODY. I JUST GOT WORD ON THE RADIO. SEE THAT SMOKE RISING PAST THE VILLAGE?
SOMETIMES I WONDER.
I WANT TO HELP MY COUNTRY.

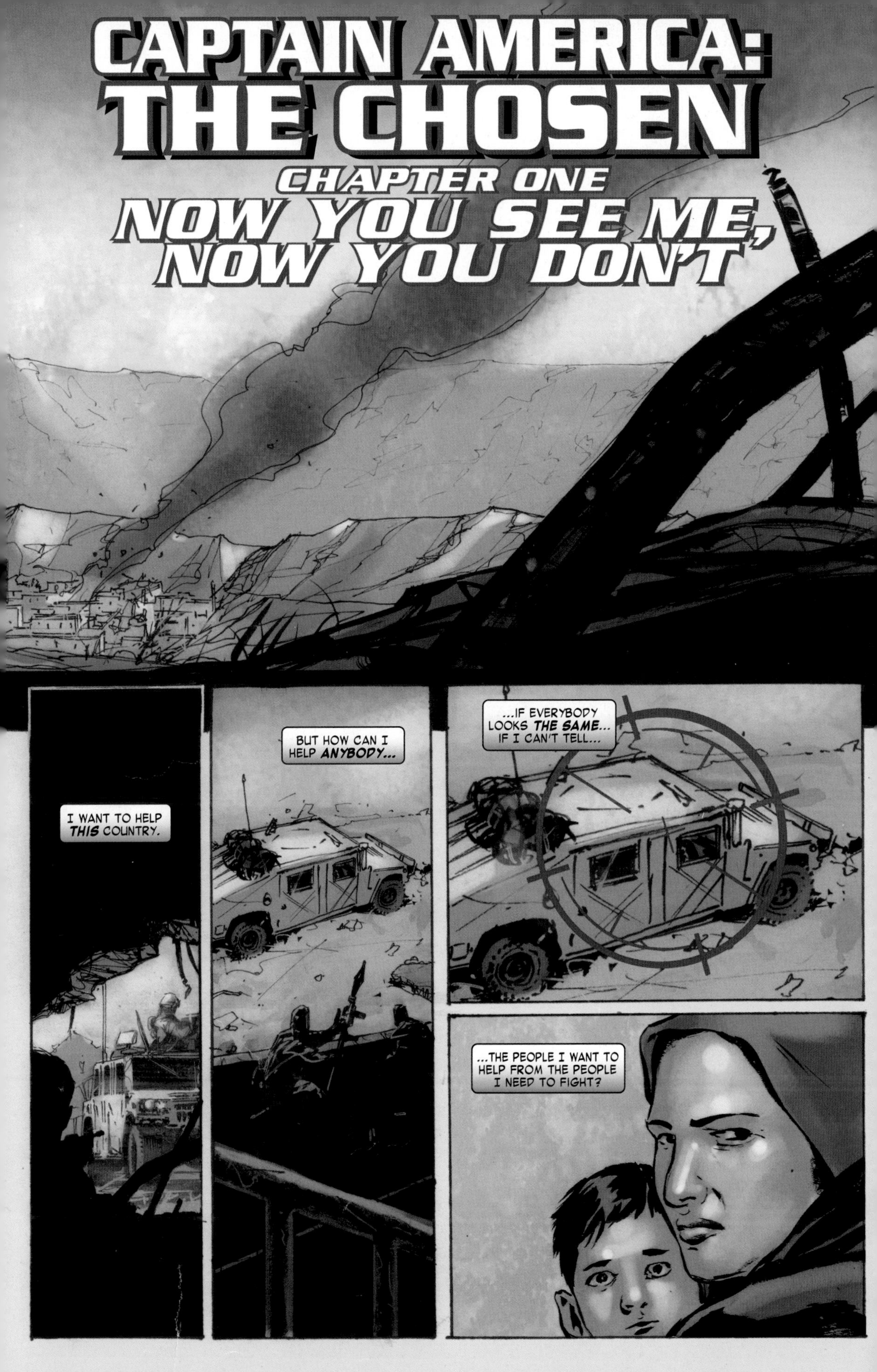

CAPTAIN AMERICA: THE CHOSEN
CHAPTER ONE
NOW YOU SEE ME, NOW YOU DON'T
I WANT TO HELP THIS COUNTRY.
BUT HOW CAN I HELP ANYBODY...
...IF EVERYBODY LOOKS THE SAME... IF I CAN'T TELL...
...THE PEOPLE I WANT TO HELP FROM THE PEOPLE I NEED TO FIGHT?

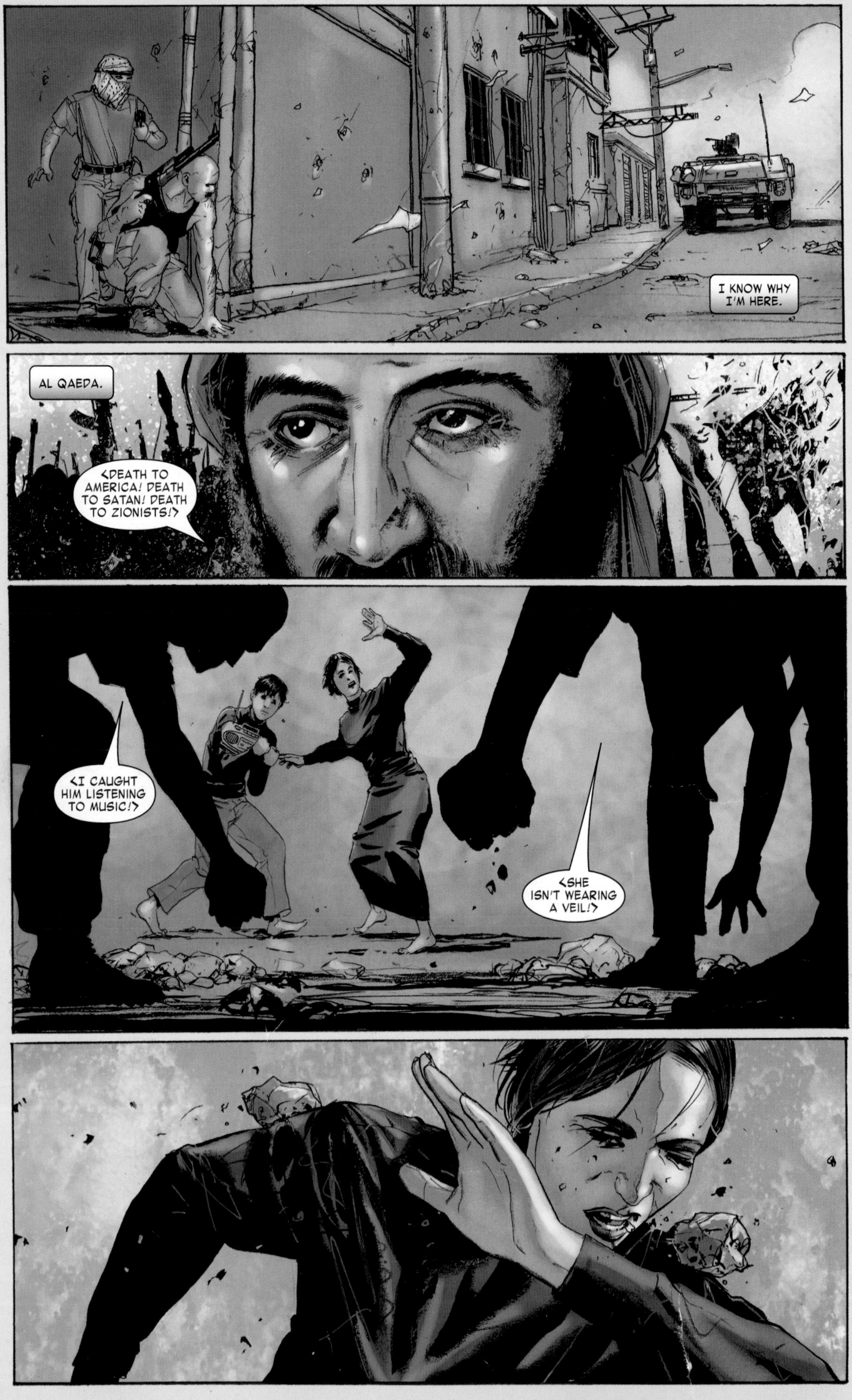
I KNOW WHY I'M HERE.
AL QAEDA.
<DEATH TO AMERICA! DEATH TO SATAN! DEATH TO ZIONISTS!>
<I CAUGHT HIM LISTENING TO MUSIC!>
<SHE ISN'T WEARING A VEIL!>

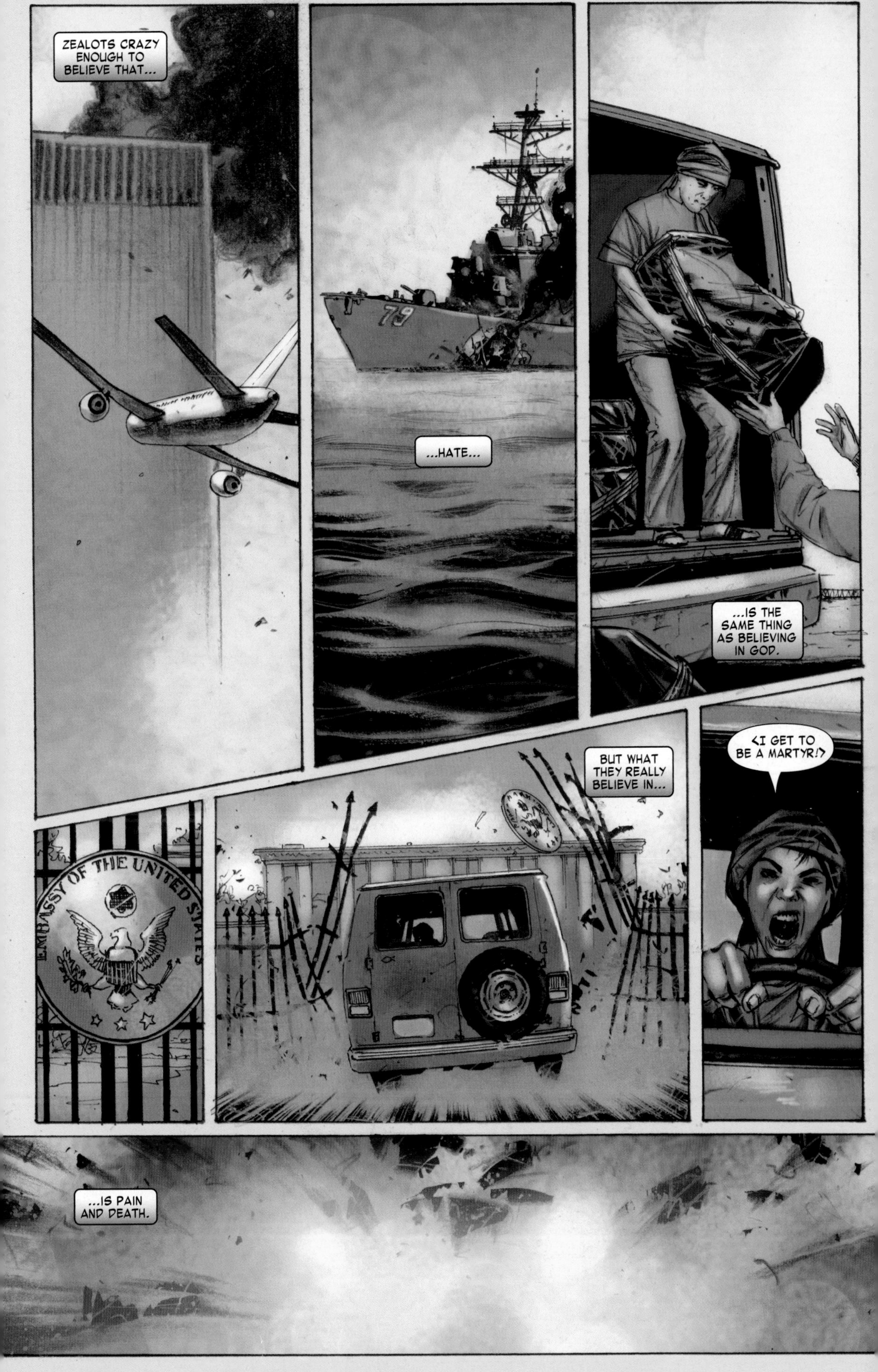
ZEALOTS CRAZY ENOUGH TO BELIEVE THAT...
...HATE...
...IS THE SAME THING AS BELIEVING IN GOD.
EMBASSY OF THE UNITED STATES
BUT WHAT THEY REALLY BELIEVE IN...
<I GET TO BE A MARTYR!>
...IS PAIN AND DEATH.

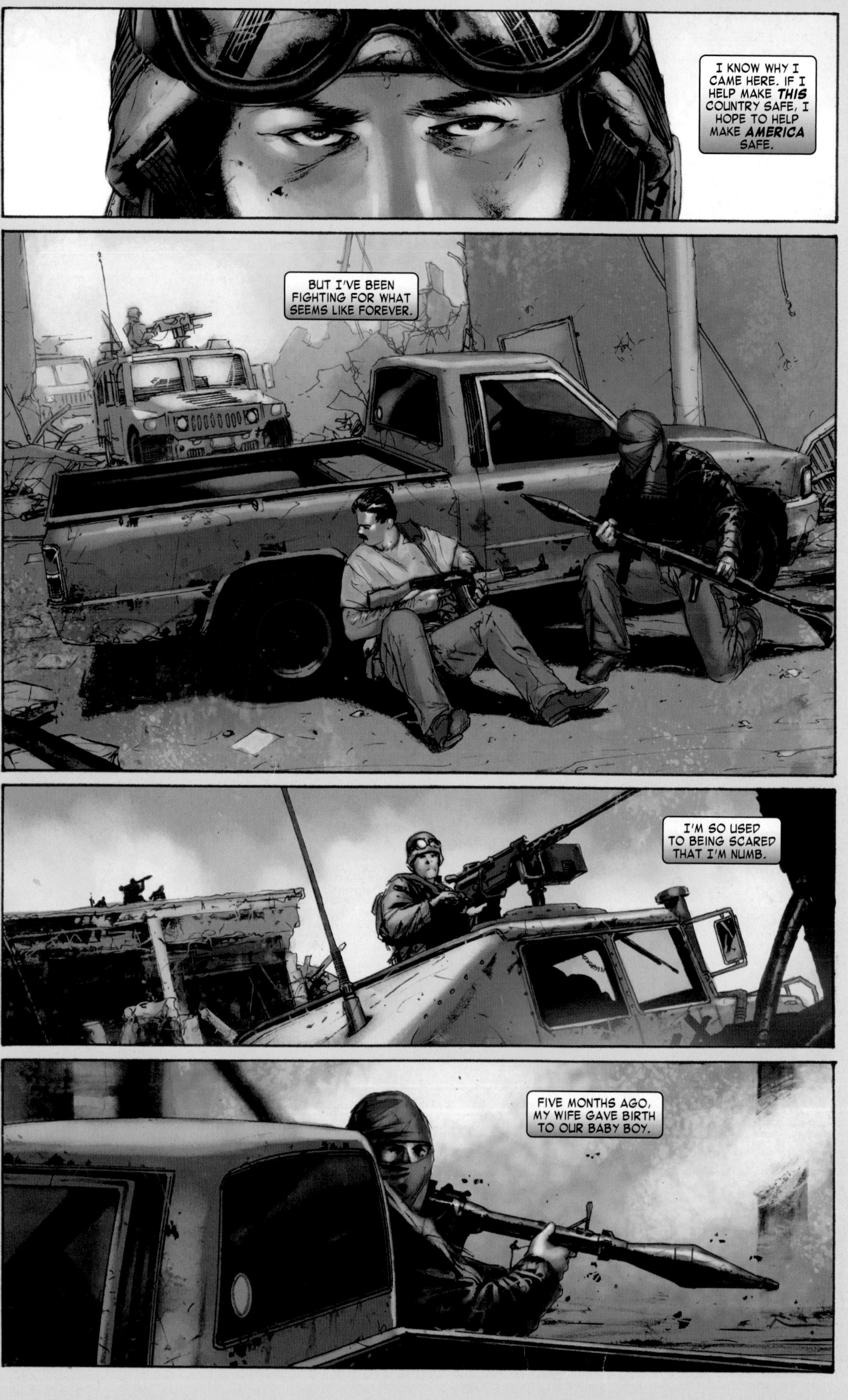
I KNOW WHY I CAME HERE. IF I HELP MAKE *THIS* COUNTRY SAFE, I HOPE TO HELP MAKE *AMERICA* SAFE.
BUT I'VE BEEN FIGHTING FOR WHAT SEEMS LIKE FOREVER.
I'M SO USED TO BEING SCARED THAT I'M NUMB.
FIVE MONTHS AGO, MY WIFE GAVE BIRTH TO OUR BABY BOY.

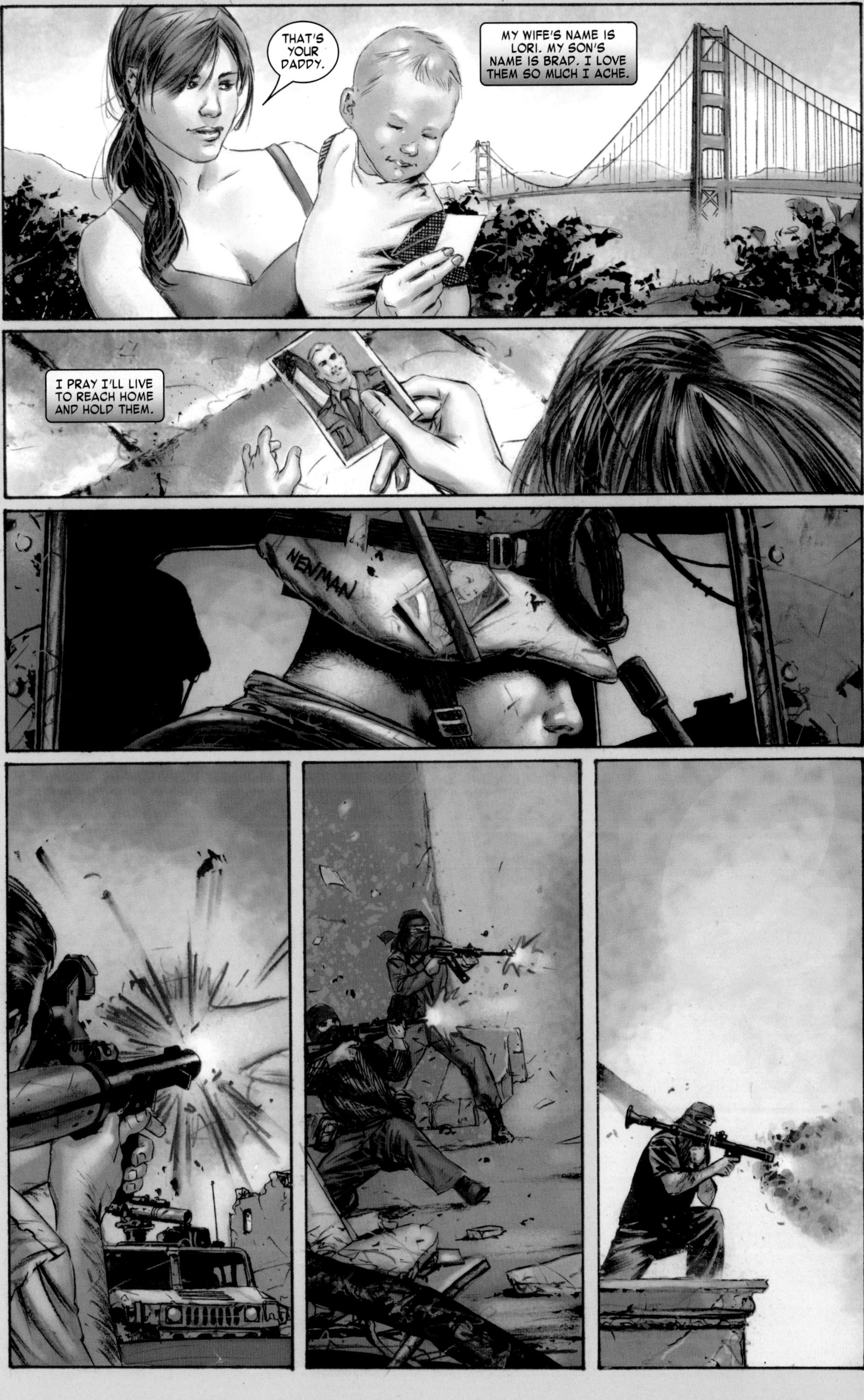
THAT'S YOUR DADDY.
MY WIFE'S NAME IS LORI. MY SON'S NAME IS BRAD. I LOVE THEM SO MUCH I ACHE.
I PRAY I'LL LIVE TO REACH HOME AND HOLD THEM.
NEWMAN

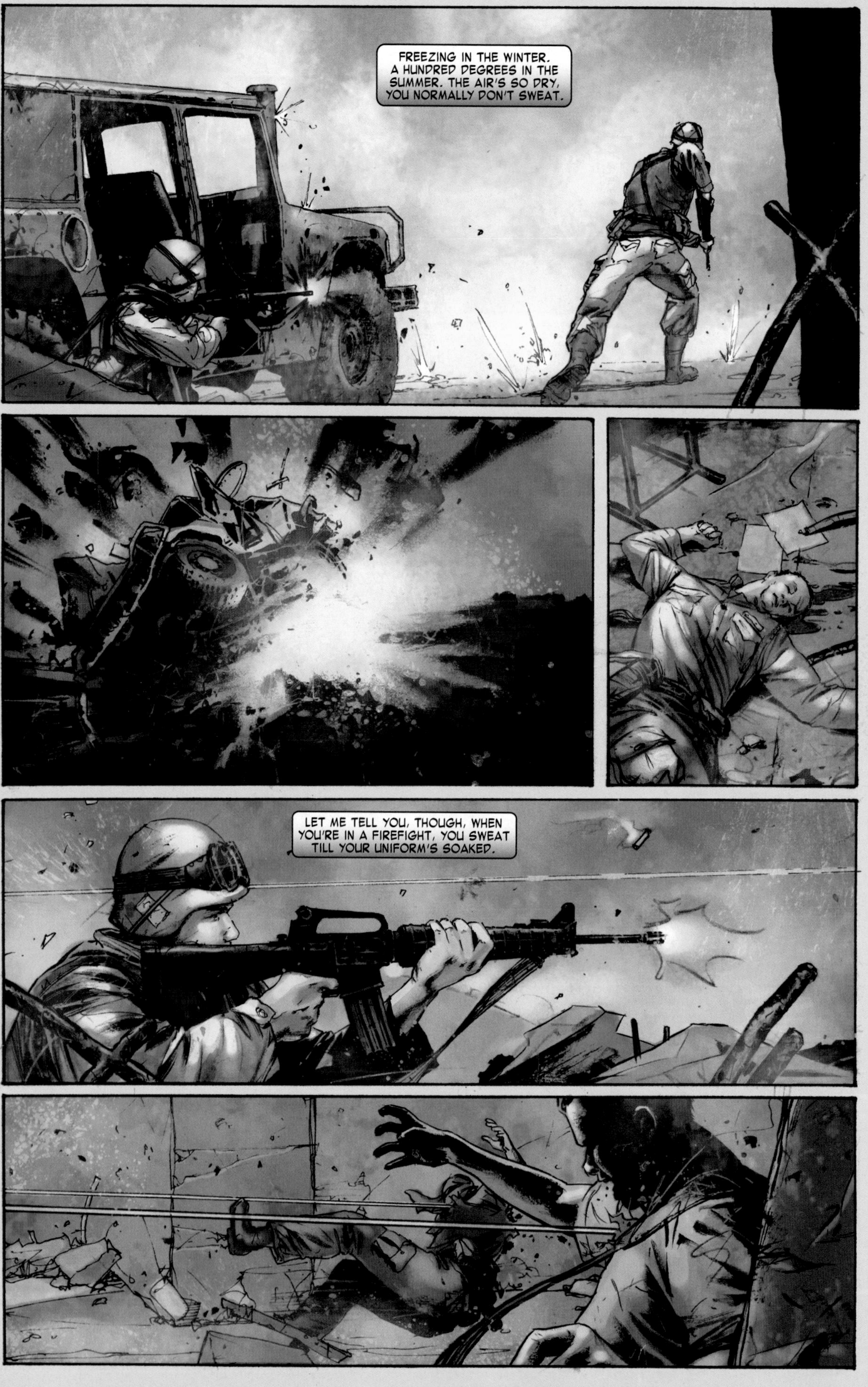
FREEZING IN THE WINTER. A HUNDRED DEGREES IN THE SUMMER. THE AIR'S SO DRY, YOU NORMALLY DON'T SWEAT.
LET ME TELL YOU, THOUGH, WHEN YOU'RE IN A FIREFIGHT, YOU SWEAT TILL YOUR UNIFORM'S SOAKED.

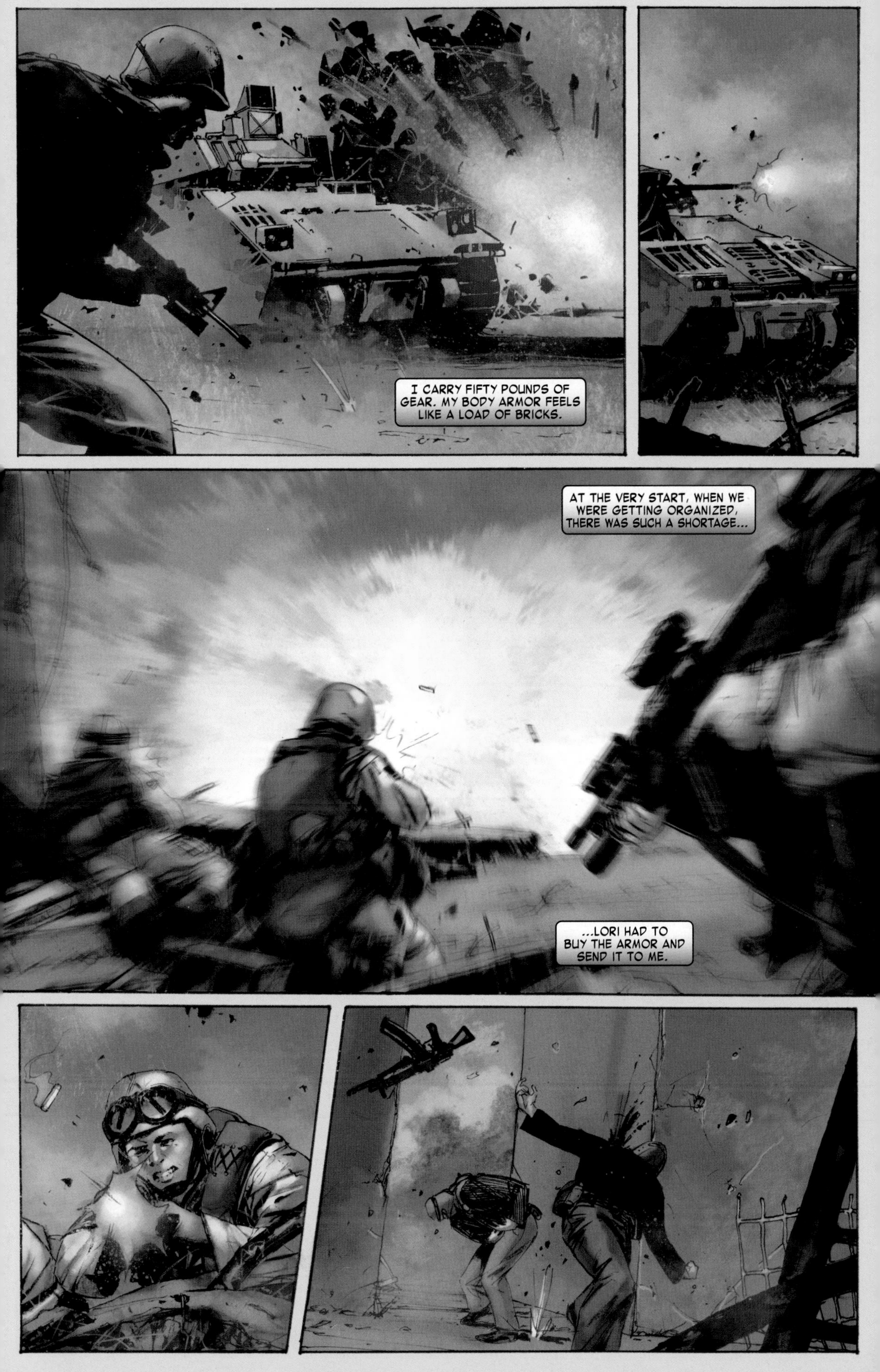
I CARRY FIFTY POUNDS OF GEAR. MY BODY ARMOR FEELS LIKE A LOAD OF BRICKS.
AT THE VERY START, WHEN WE WERE GETTING ORGANIZED, THERE WAS SUCH A SHORTAGE...
...LORI HAD TO BUY THE ARMOR AND SEND IT TO ME.

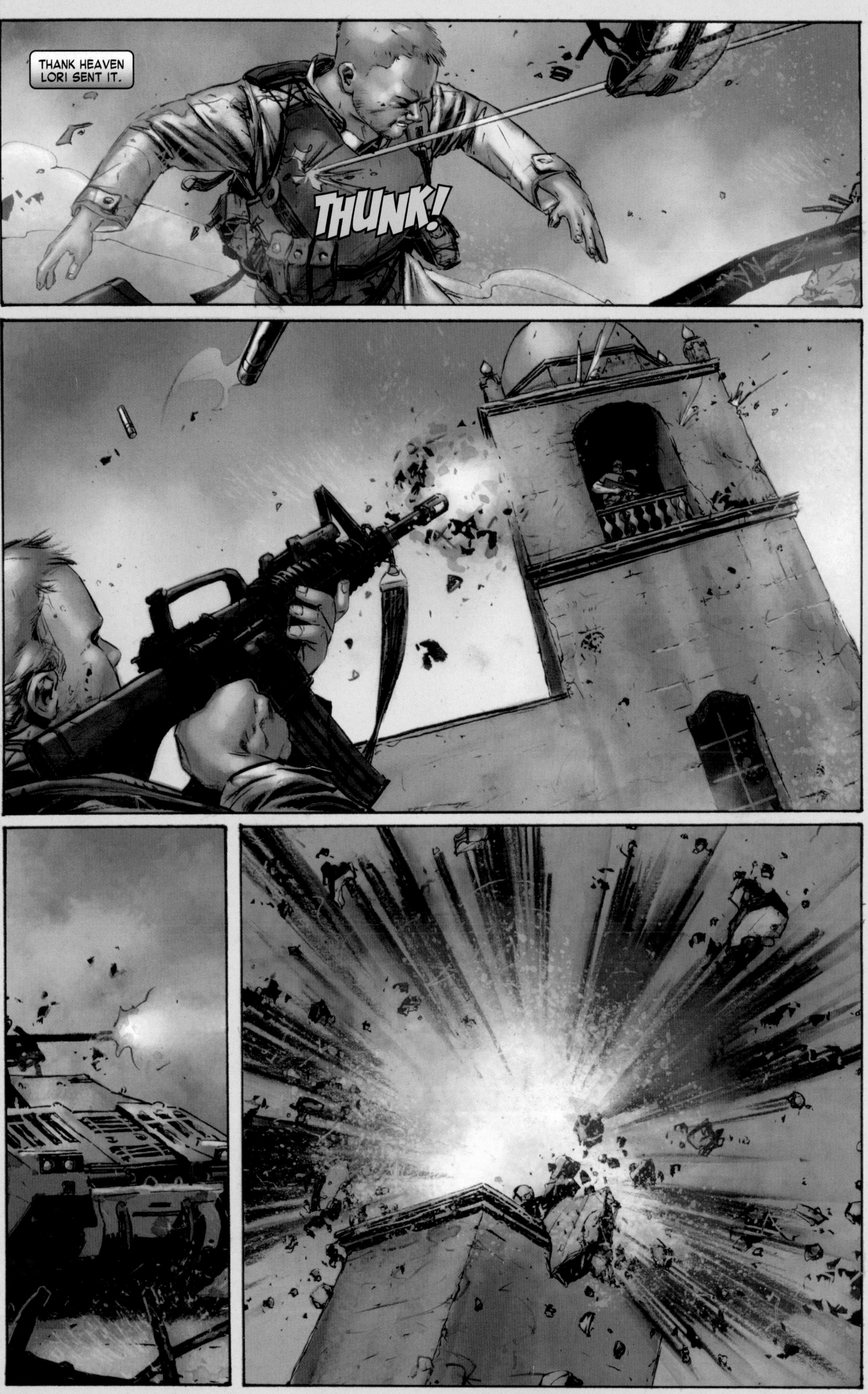
THANK HEAVEN LORI SENT IT.
THUNK!

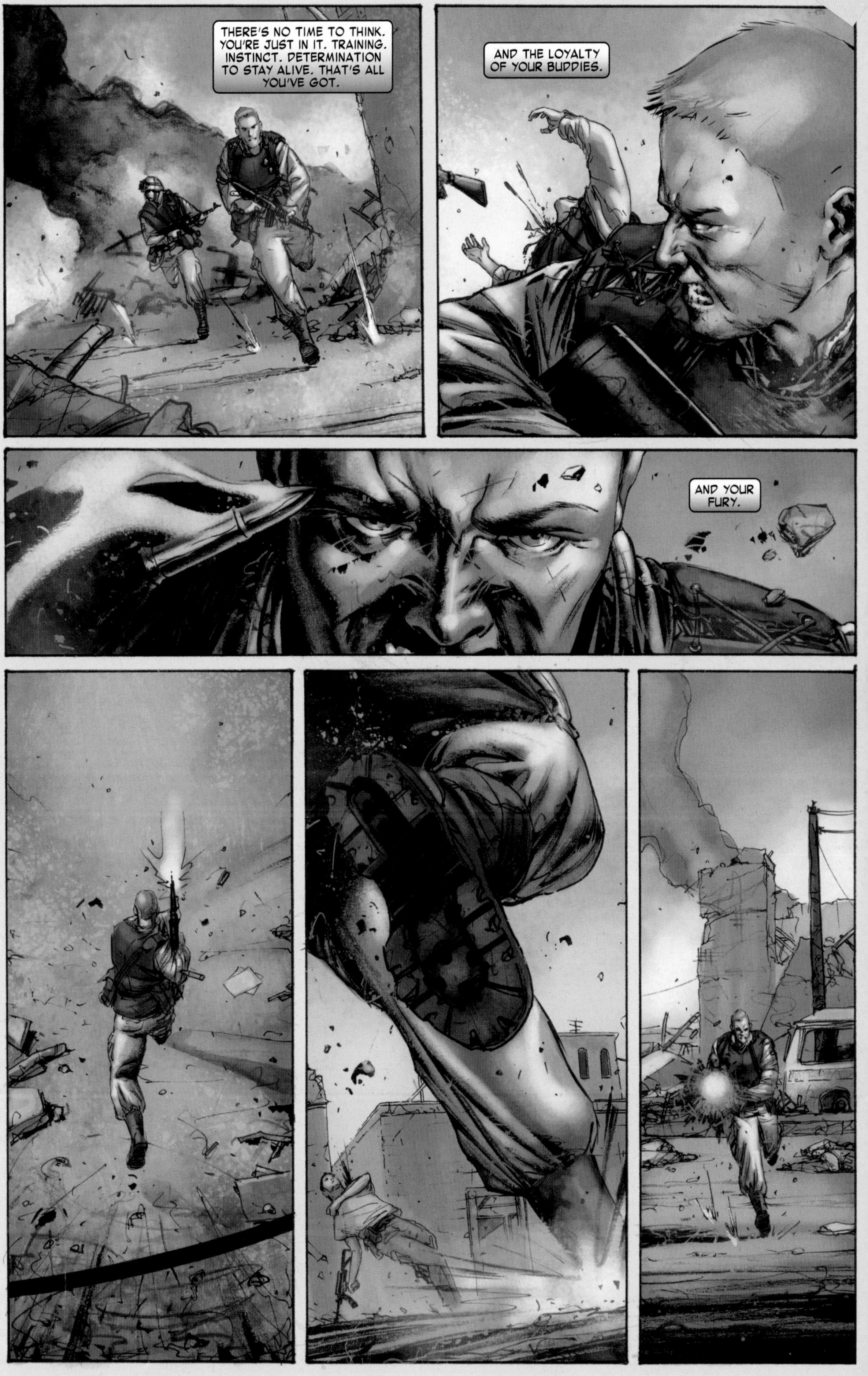
THERE'S NO TIME TO THINK. YOU'RE JUST IN IT. TRAINING. INSTINCT. DETERMINATION TO STAY ALIVE. THAT'S ALL YOU'VE GOT.
AND THE LOYALTY OF YOUR BUDDIES.
AND YOUR FURY.

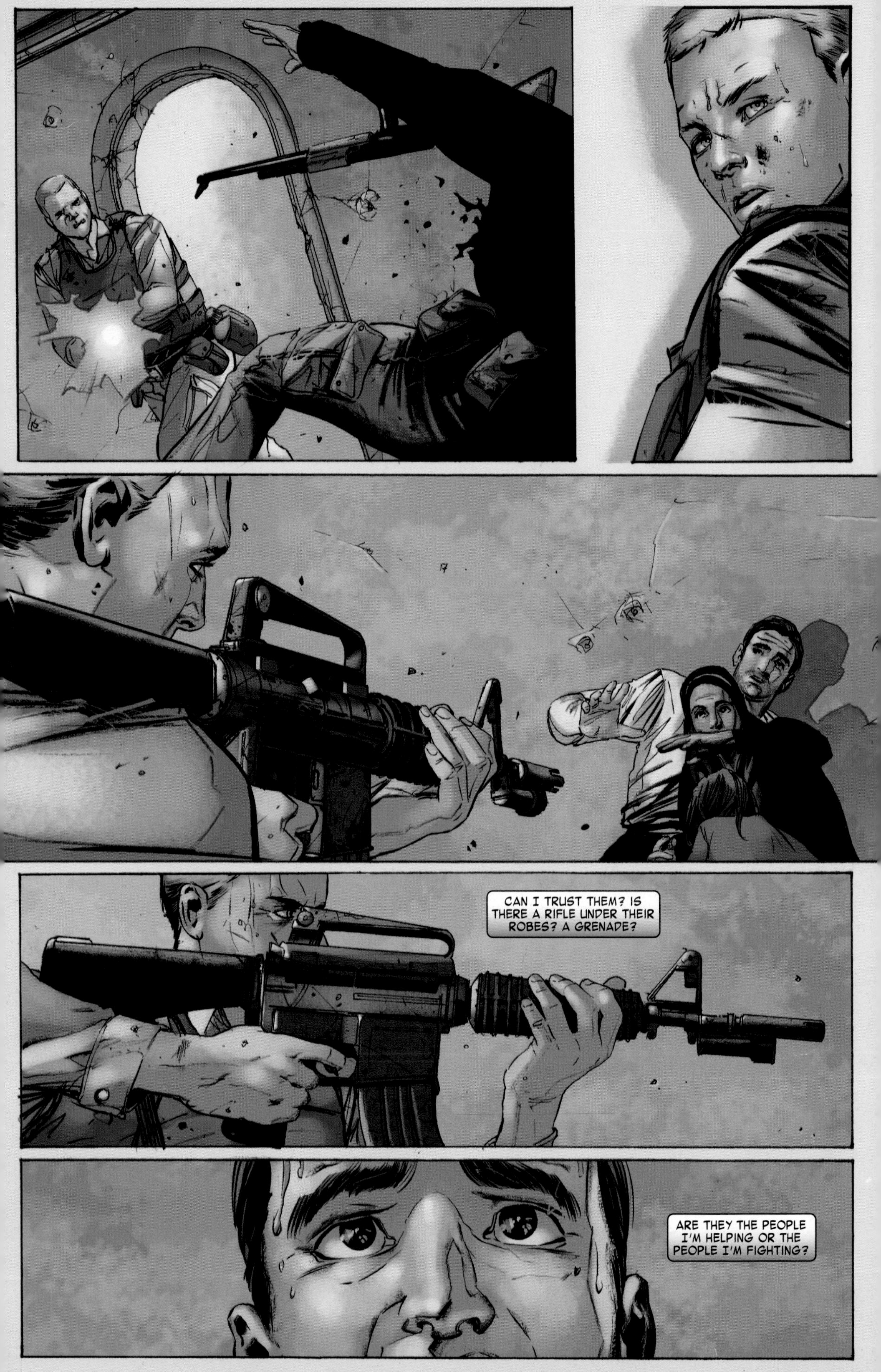
CAN I TRUST THEM? IS THERE A RIFLE UNDER THEIR ROBES? A GRENADE?
ARE THEY THE PEOPLE I'M HELPING OR THE PEOPLE I'M FIGHTING?

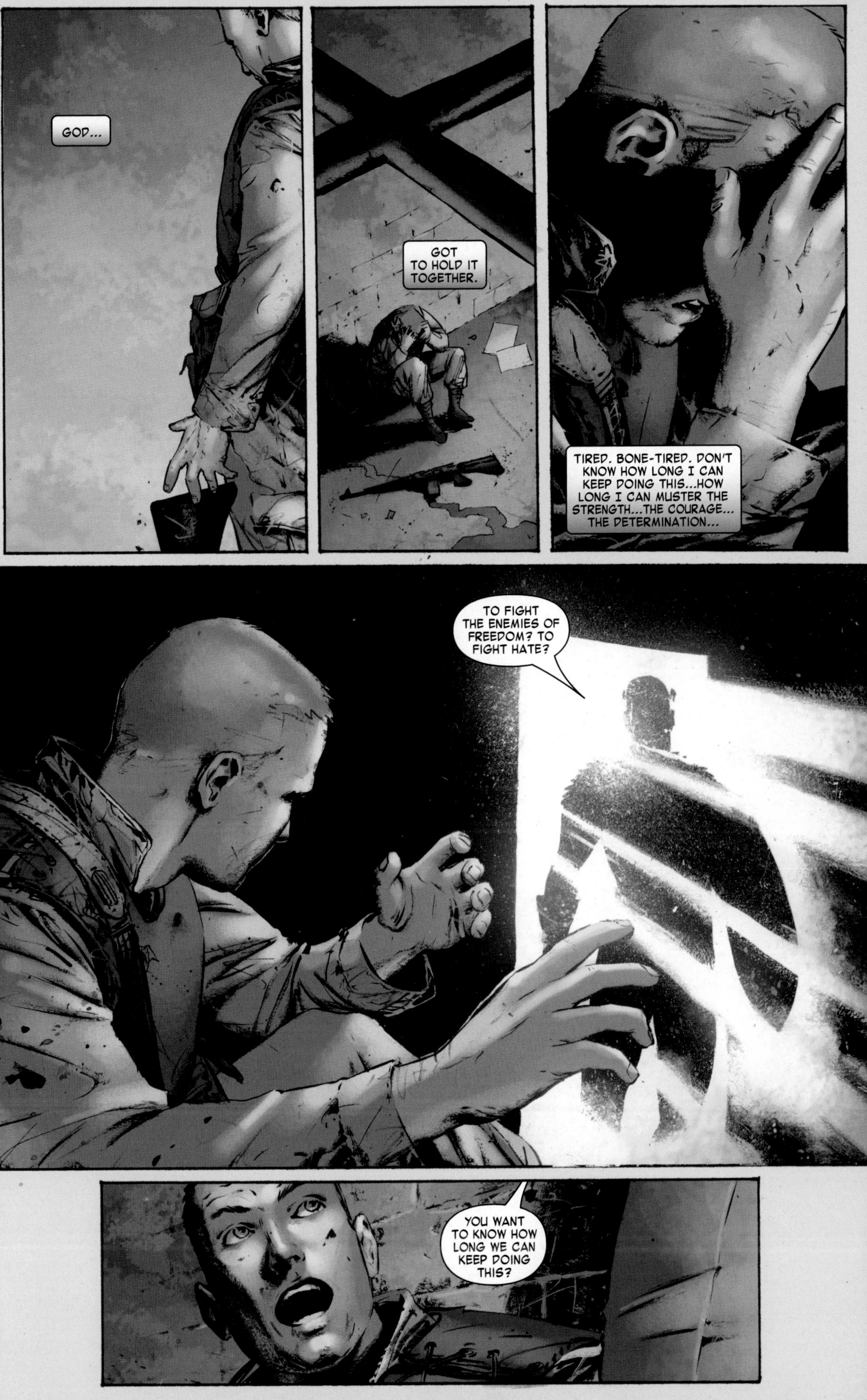

GOD...
GOT TO HOLD IT TOGETHER.
TIRED. BONE-TIRED. DON'T KNOW HOW LONG I CAN KEEP DOING THIS...HOW LONG I CAN MUSTER THE STRENGTH...THE COURAGE... THE DETERMINATION...
TO FIGHT THE ENEMIES OF FREEDOM? TO FIGHT HATE?
YOU WANT TO KNOW HOW LONG WE CAN KEEP DOING THIS?

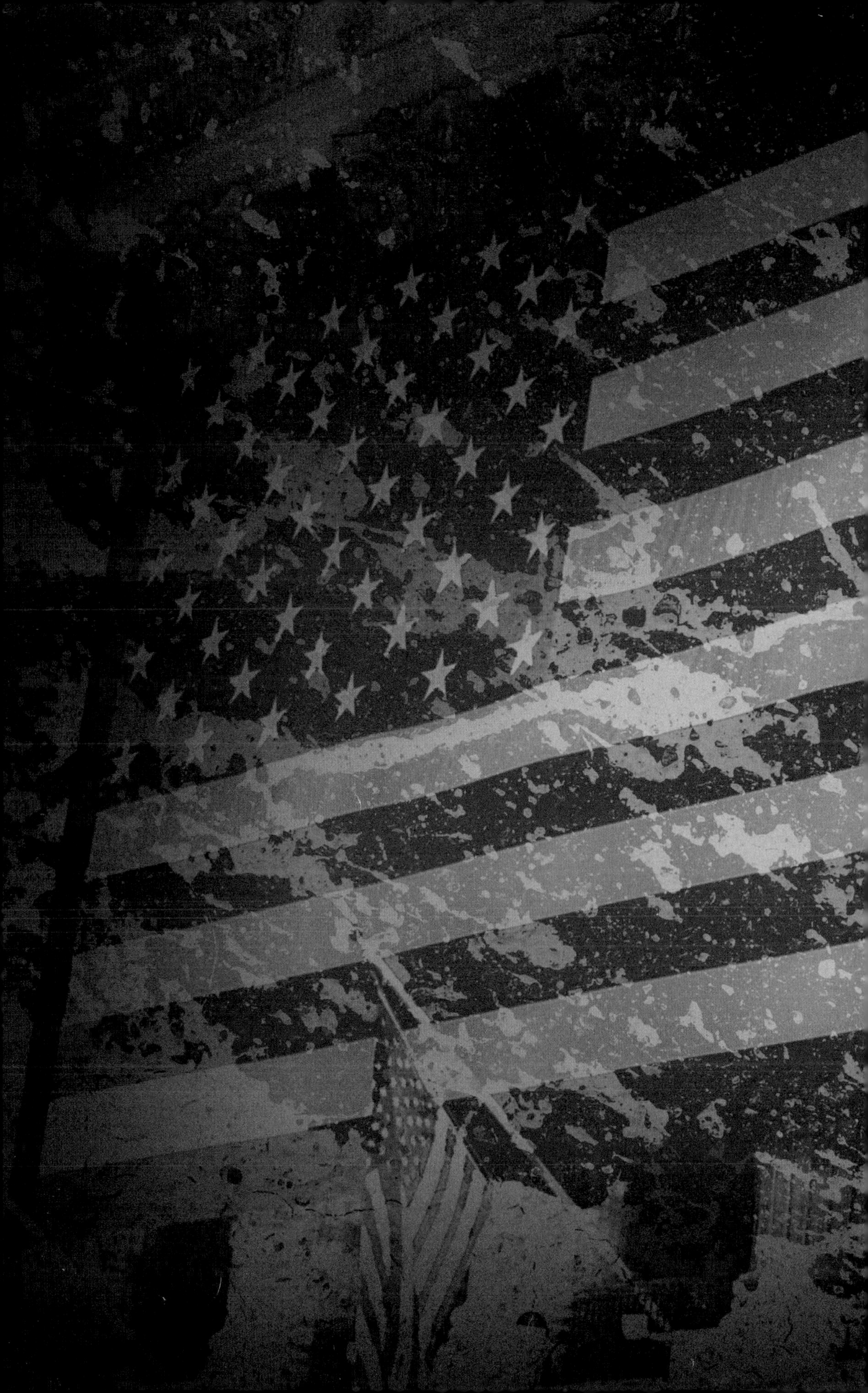

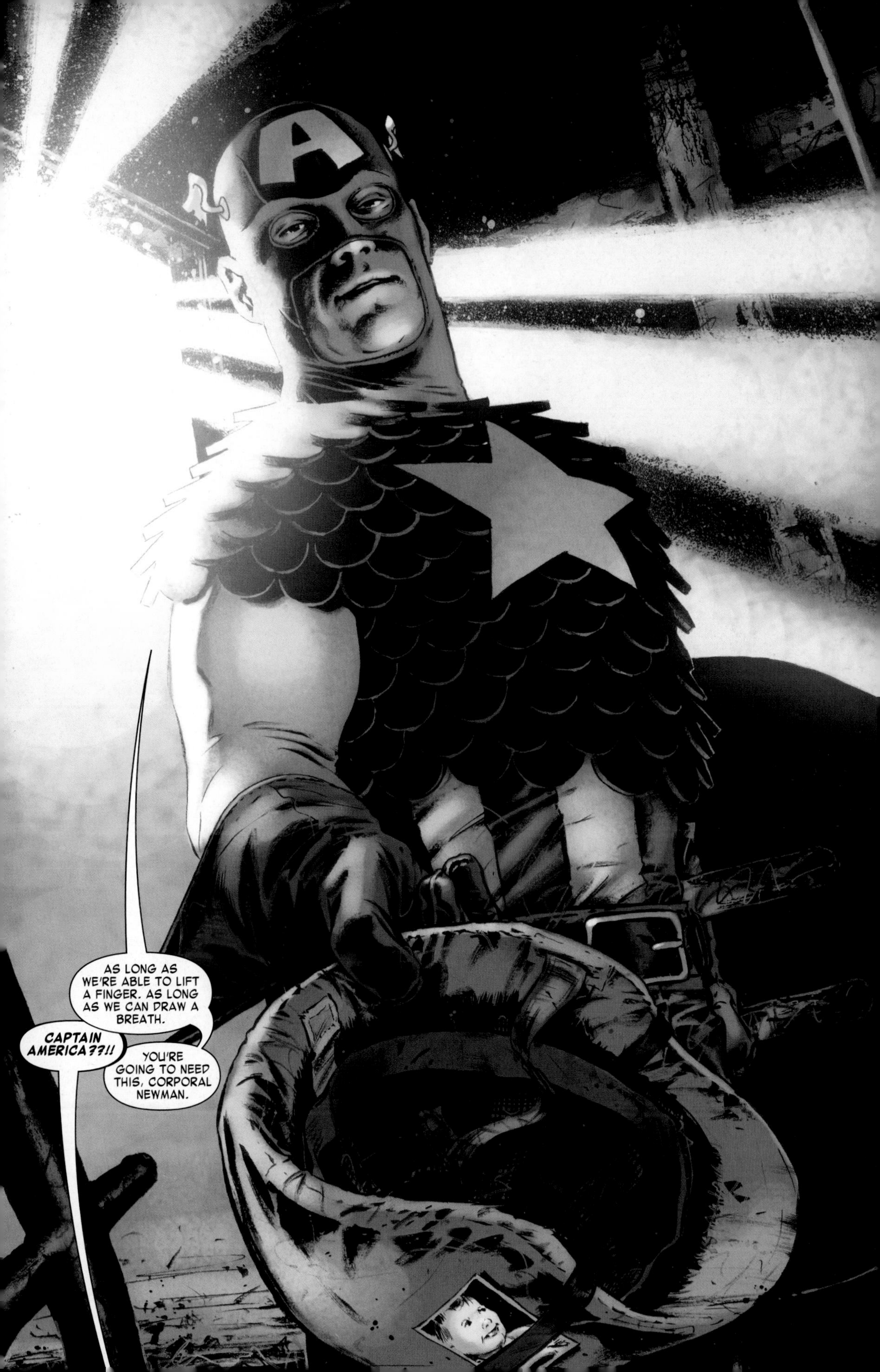
AS LONG AS WE'RE ABLE TO LIFT A FINGER. AS LONG AS WE CAN DRAW A BREATH.
CAPTAIN AMERICA??!!
YOU'RE GOING TO NEED THIS, CORPORAL NEWMAN.

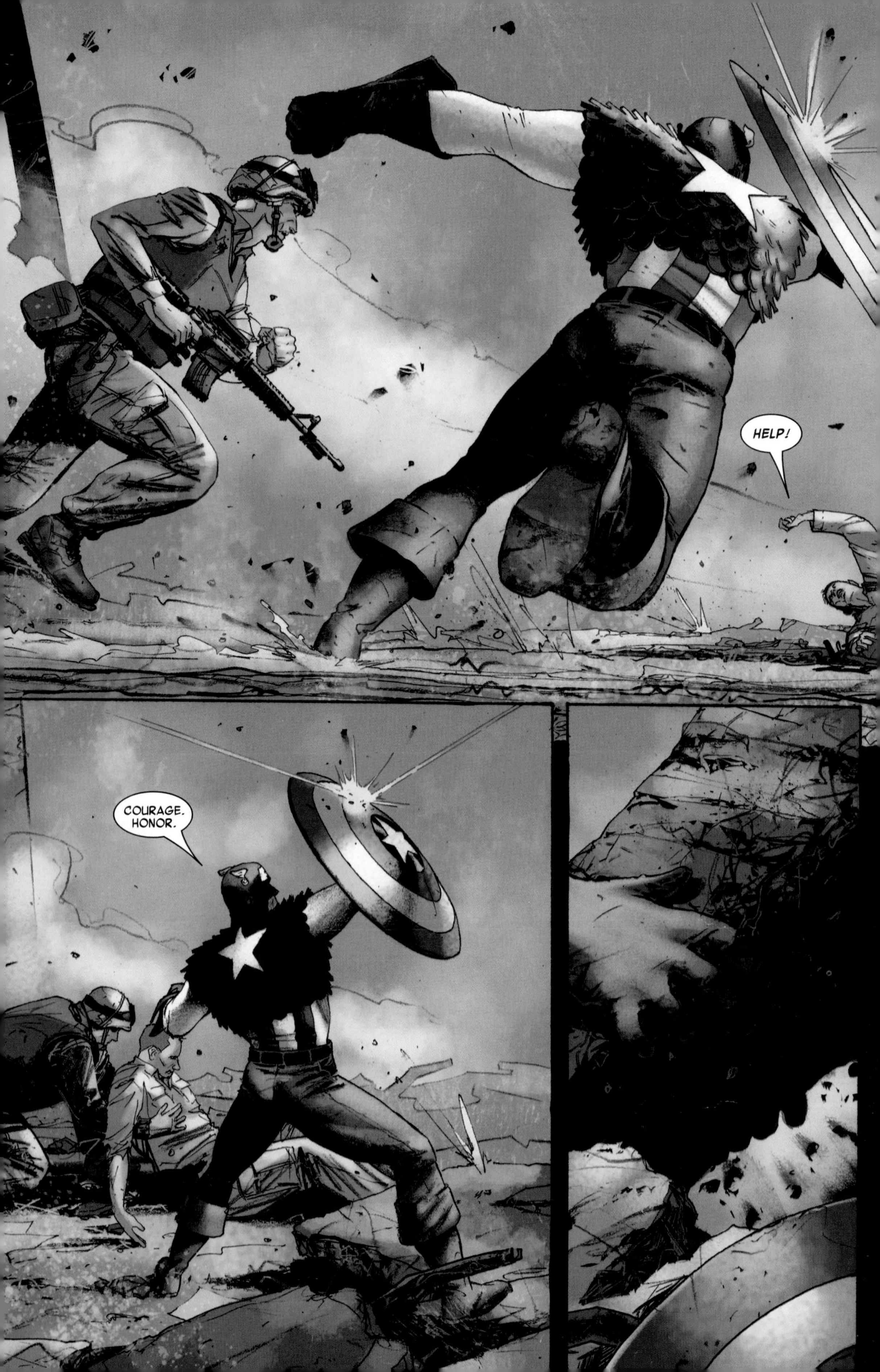
HELP!
COURAGE. HONOR.

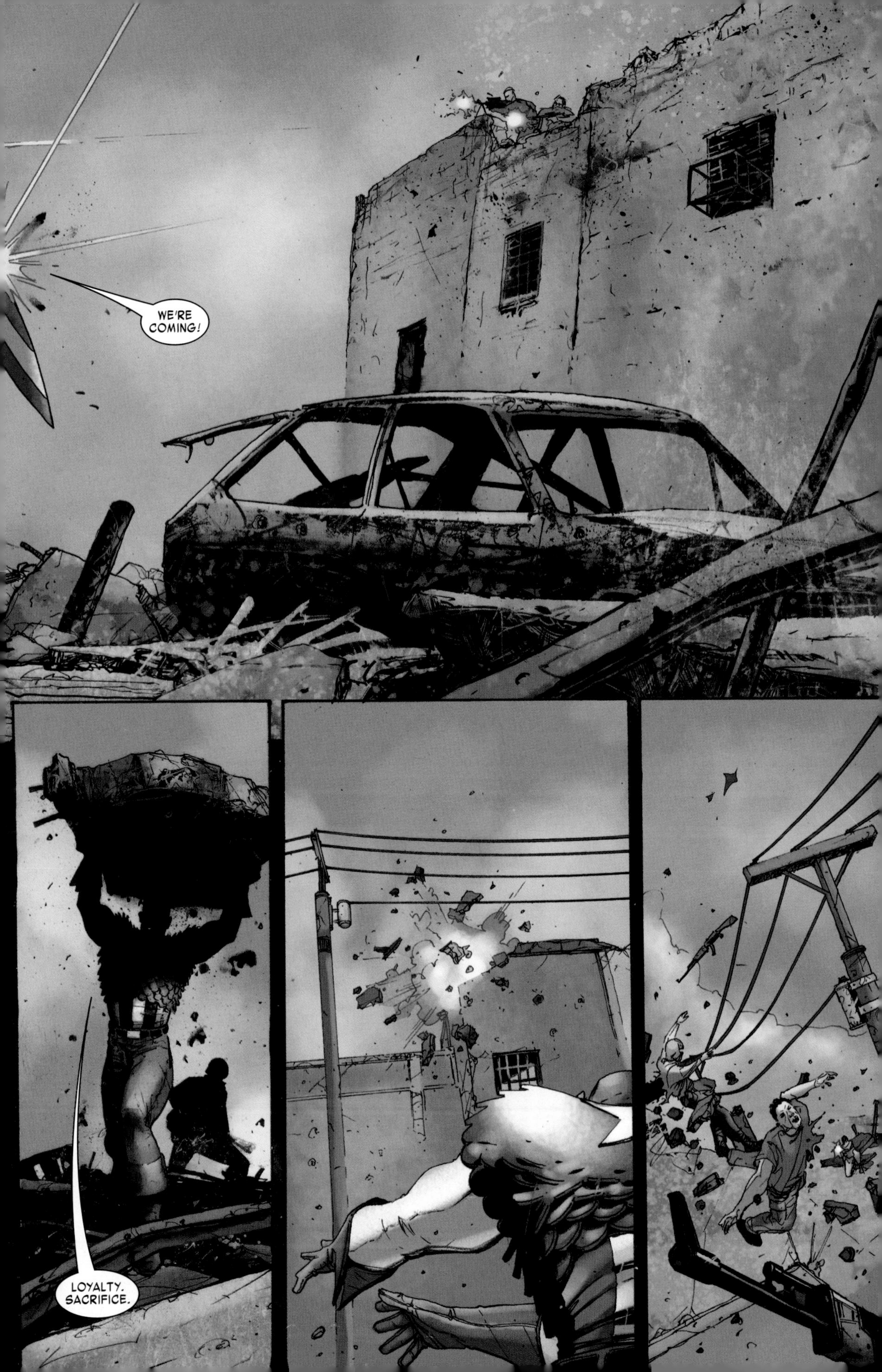
WE'RE COMING!
LOYALTY. SACRIFICE.

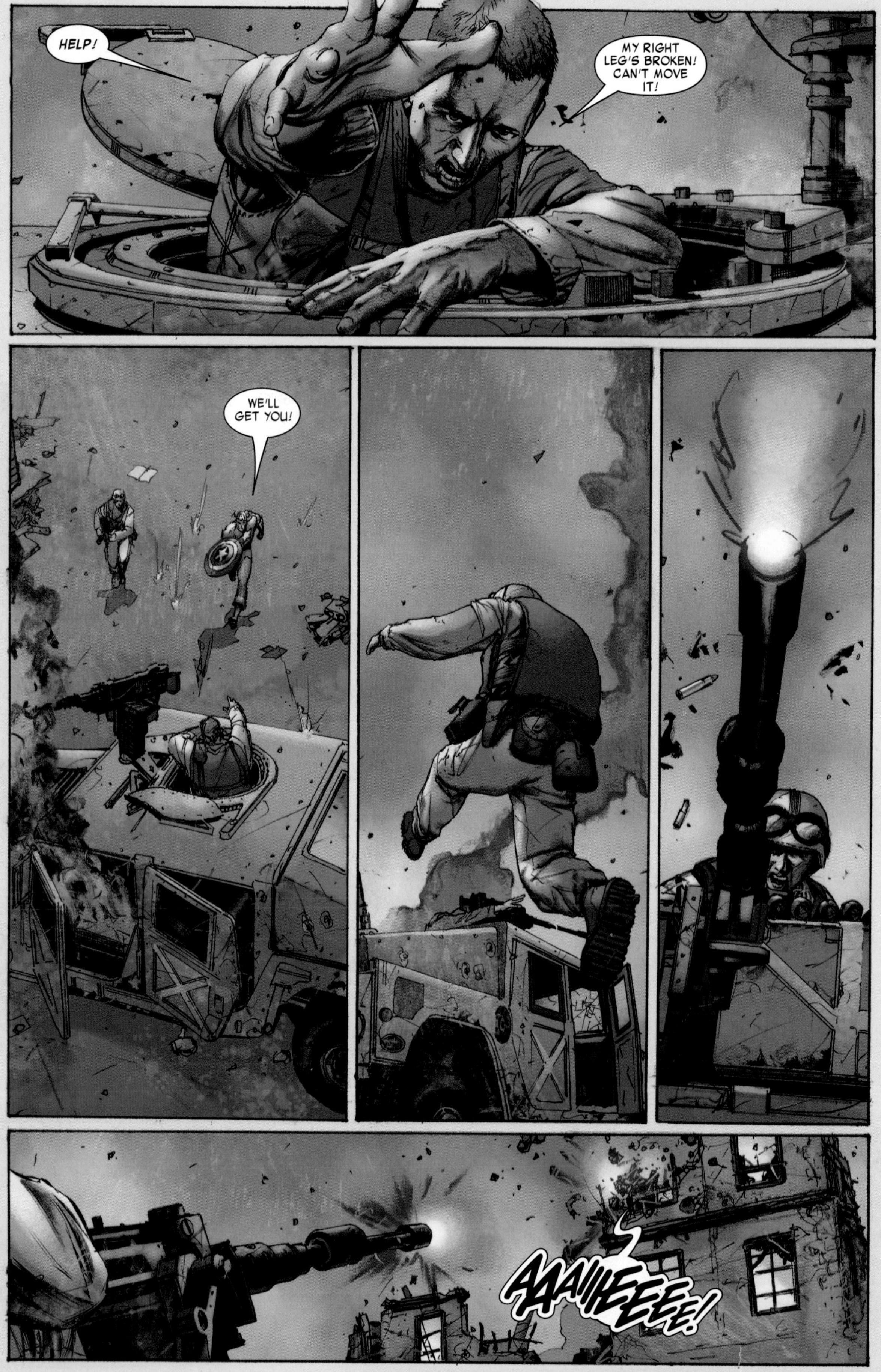
HELP!
MY RIGHT LEG'S BROKEN! CAN'T MOVE IT!
WE'LL GET YOU!
AAAIIIEEEE!

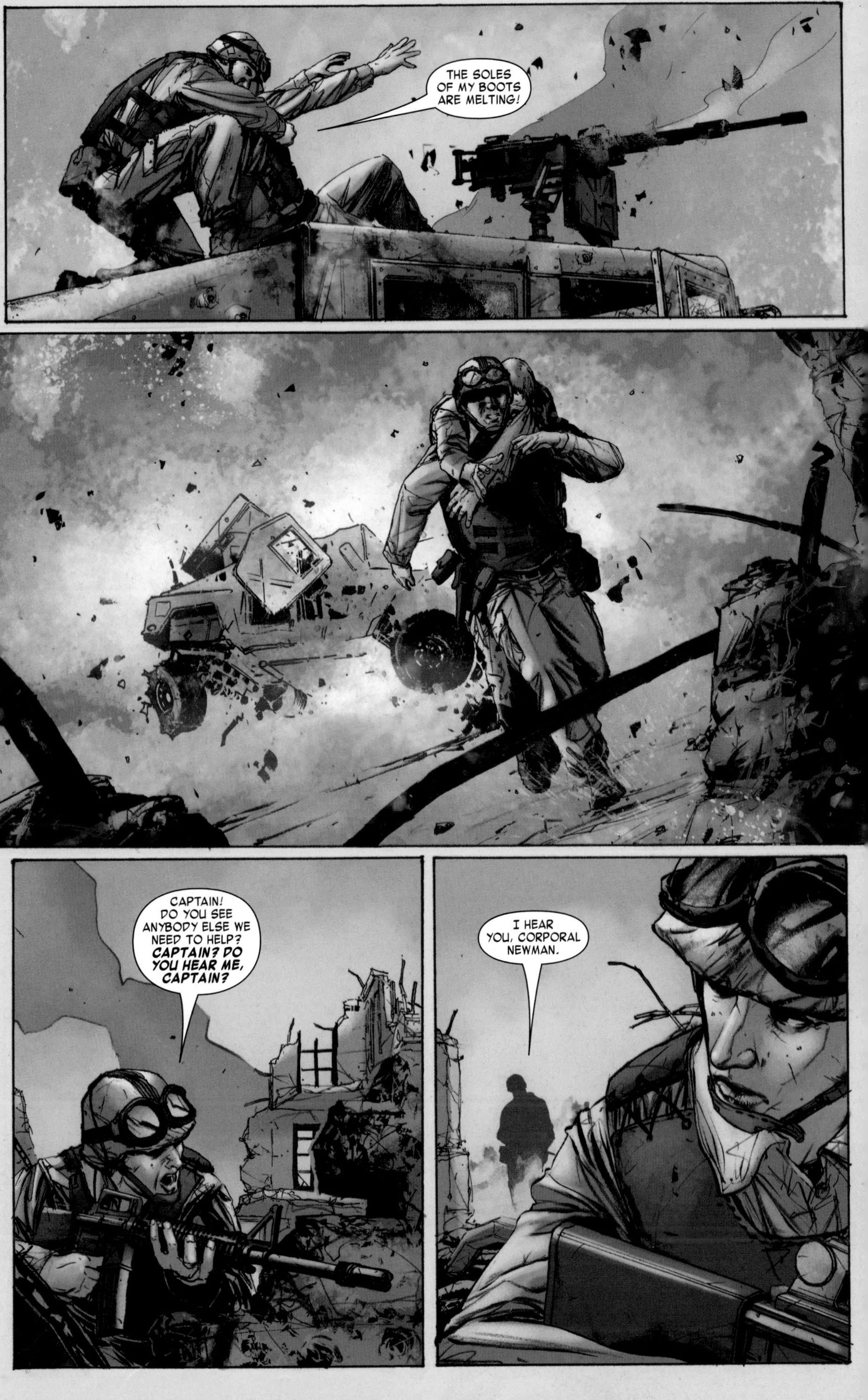
THE SOLES OF MY BOOTS ARE MELTING!
CAPTAIN! DO YOU SEE ANYBODY ELSE WE NEED TO HELP? CAPTAIN? DO YOU HEAR ME, CAPTAIN?
I HEAR YOU, CORPORAL NEWMAN.

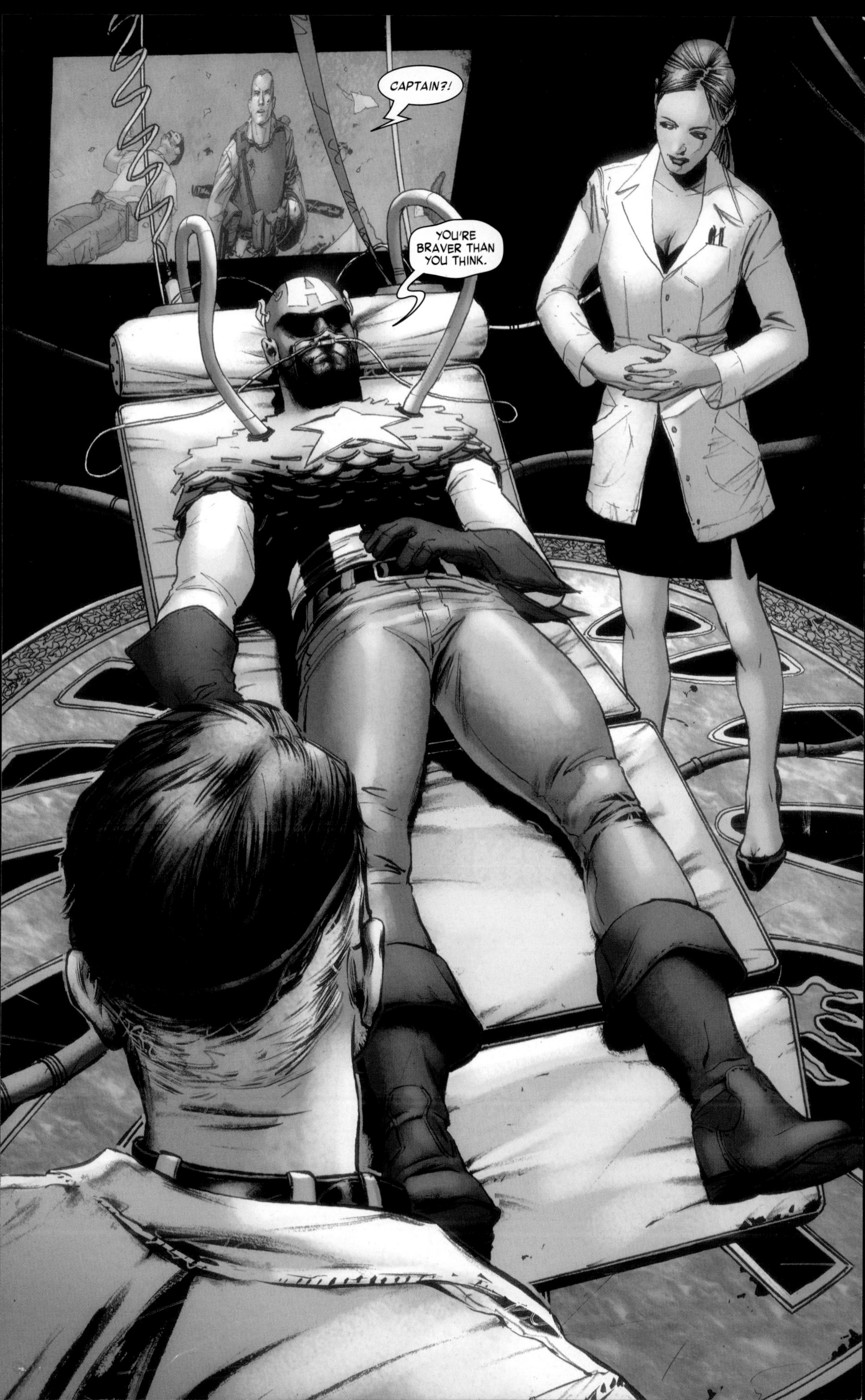
CAPTAIN?!
YOU'RE BRAVER THAN YOU THINK.

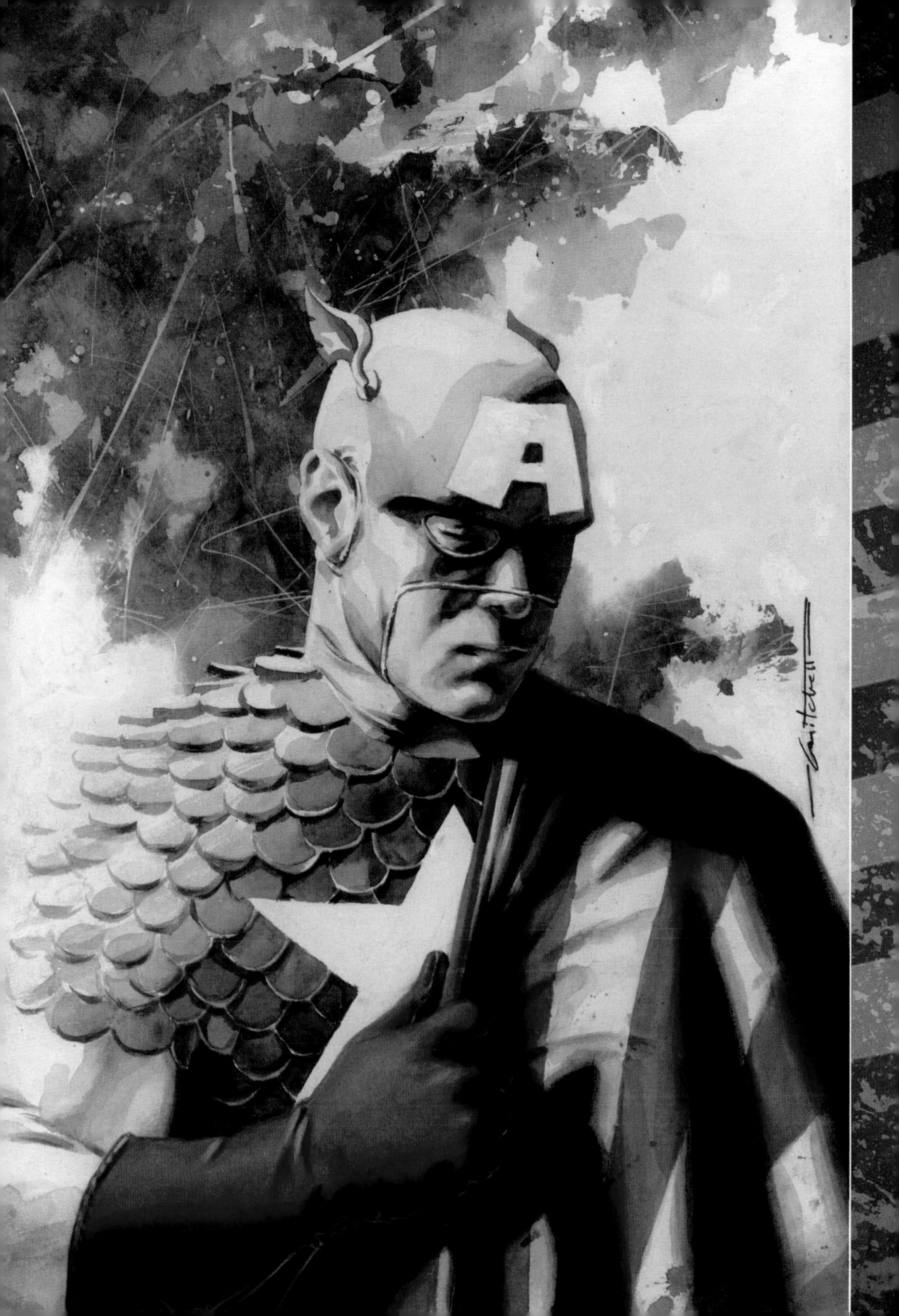

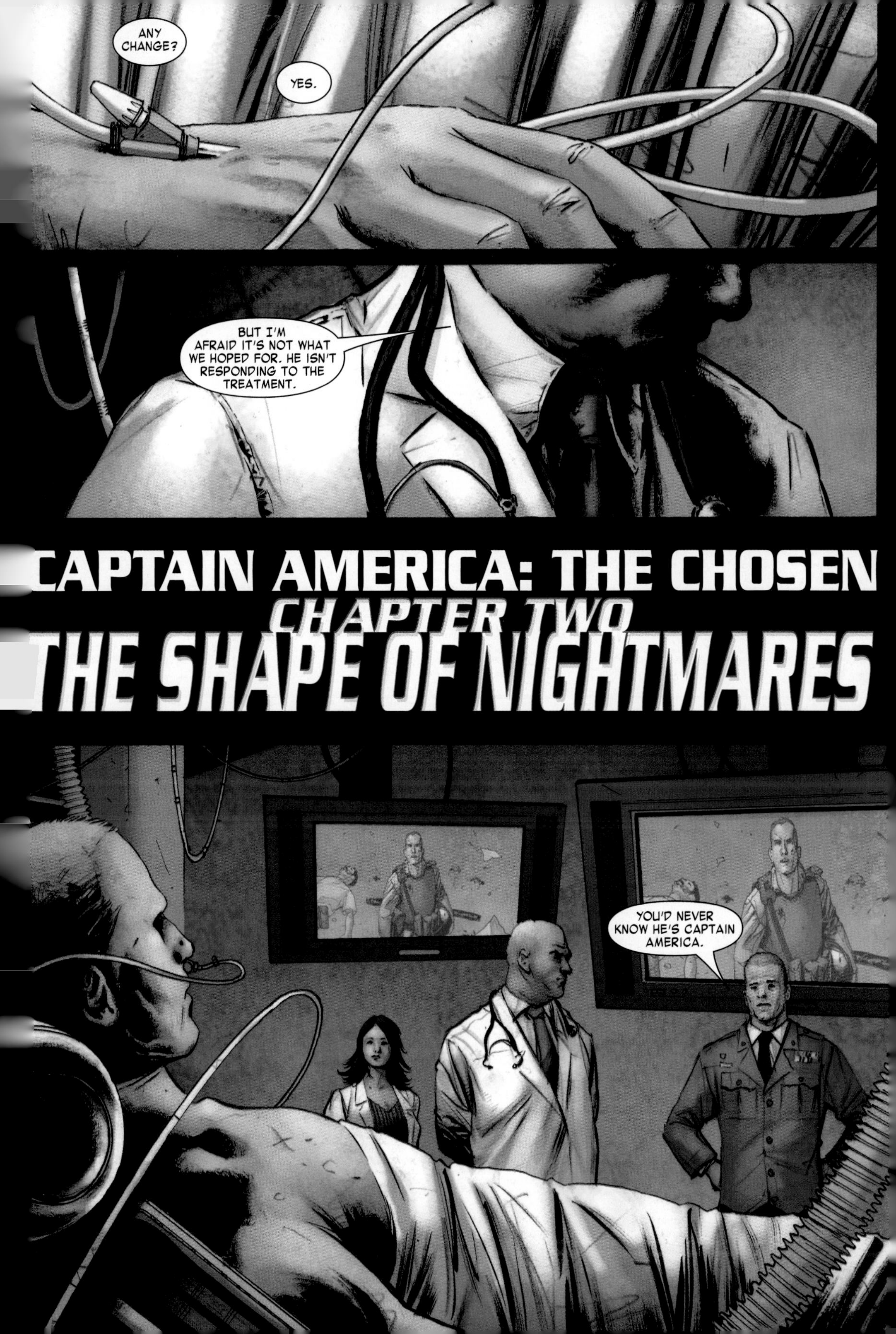
ANY CHANGE?
YES.
BUT I'M AFRAID IT'S NOT WHAT WE HOPED FOR. HE ISN'T RESPONDING TO THE TREATMENT.
CAPTAIN AMERICA: THE CHOSEN
CHAPTER TWO
THE SHAPE OF NIGHTMARES
YOU'D NEVER KNOW HE'S CAPTAIN AMERICA.

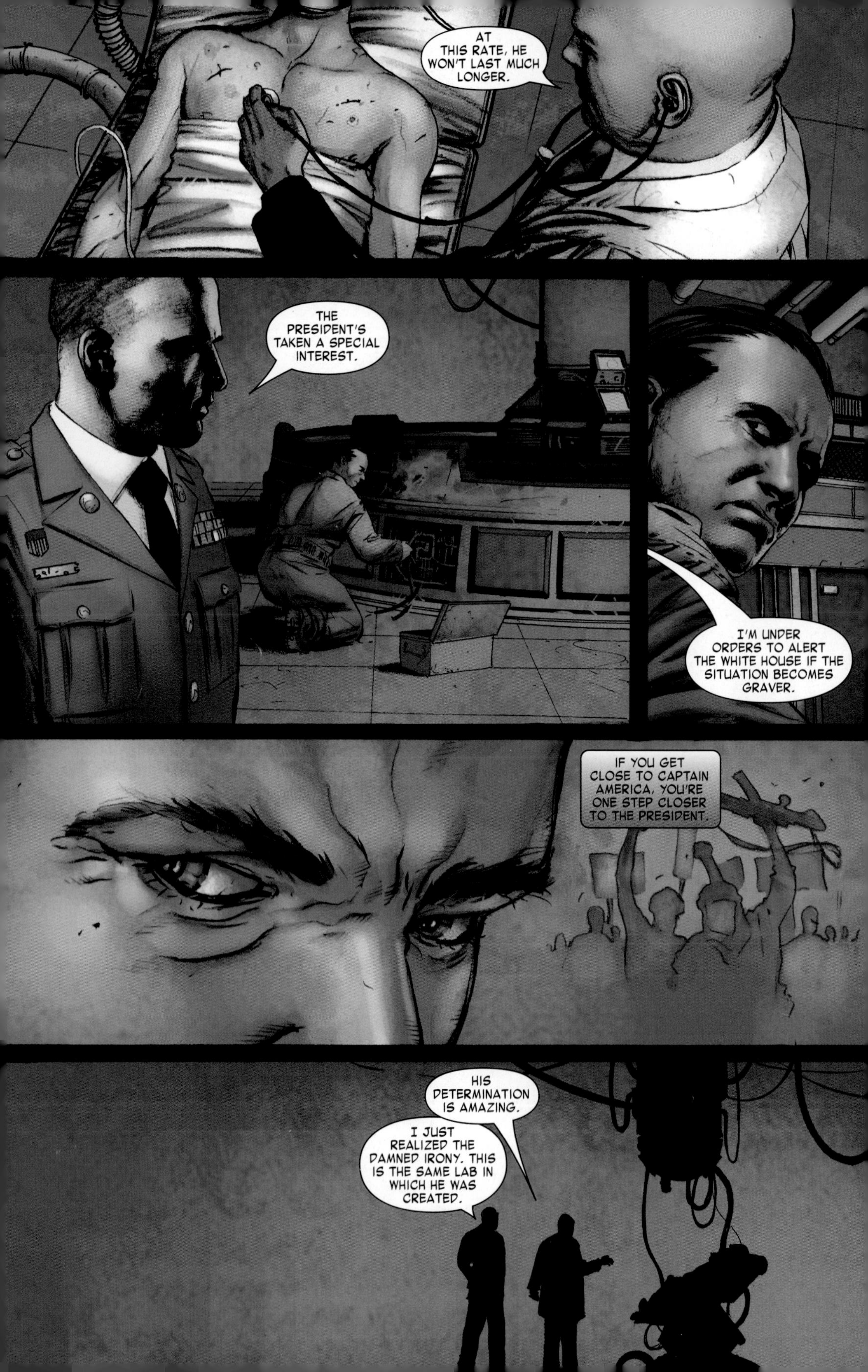
AT THIS RATE, HE WON'T LAST MUCH LONGER.
THE PRESIDENT'S TAKEN A SPECIAL INTEREST.
I'M UNDER ORDERS TO ALERT THE WHITE HOUSE IF THE SITUATION BECOMES GRAVER.
IF YOU GET CLOSE TO CAPTAIN AMERICA, YOU'RE ONE STEP CLOSER TO THE PRESIDENT.
HIS DETERMINATION IS AMAZING.
I JUST REALIZED THE DAMNED IRONY. THIS IS THE SAME LAB IN WHICH HE WAS CREATED.

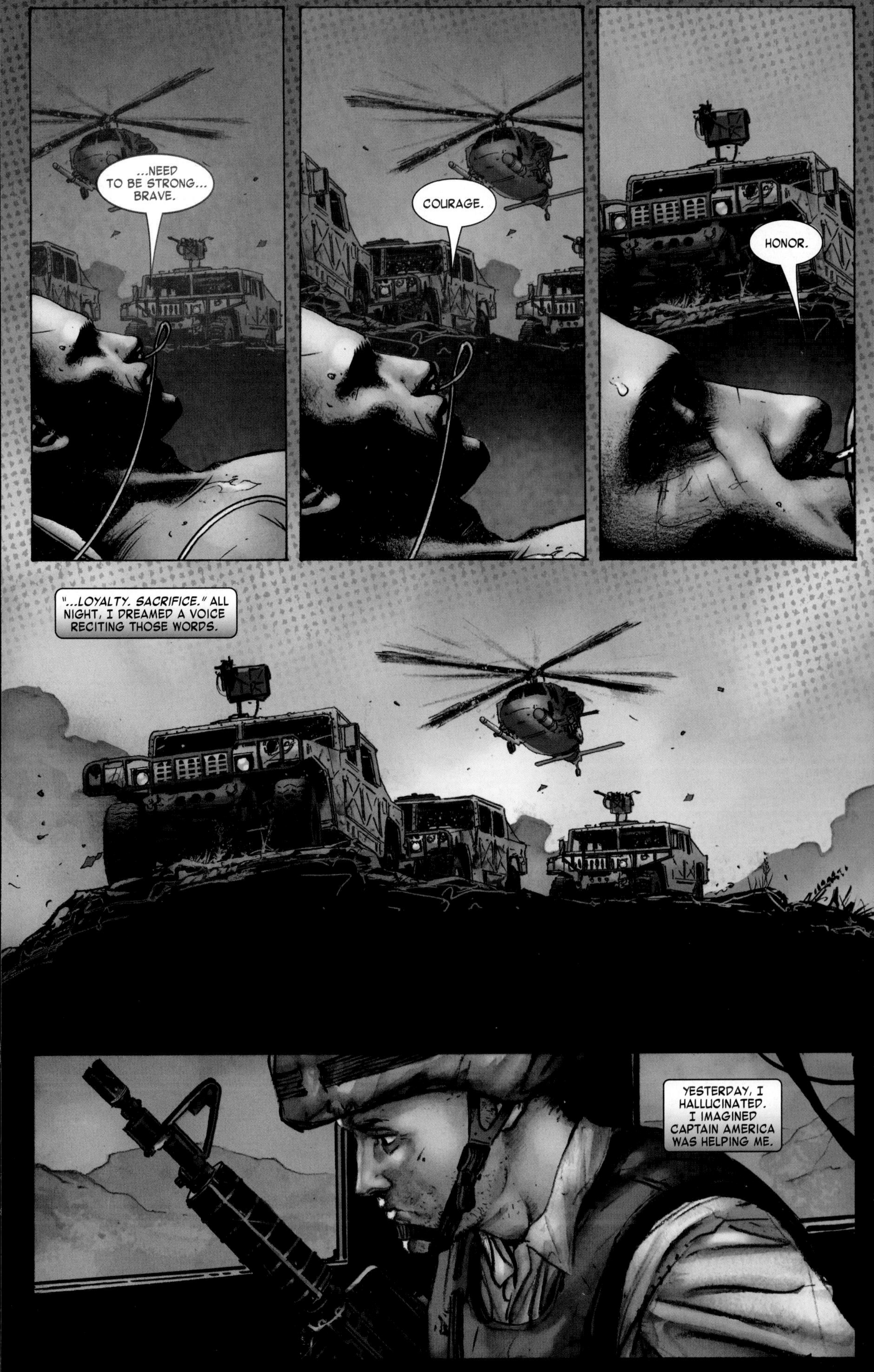
...NEED
TO BE STRONG...
BRAVE.
COURAGE.
HONOR.
"...LOYALTY. SACRIFICE." ALL NIGHT, I DREAMED A VOICE RECITING THOSE WORDS.
YESTERDAY, I HALLUCINATED. I IMAGINED CAPTAIN AMERICA WAS HELPING ME.

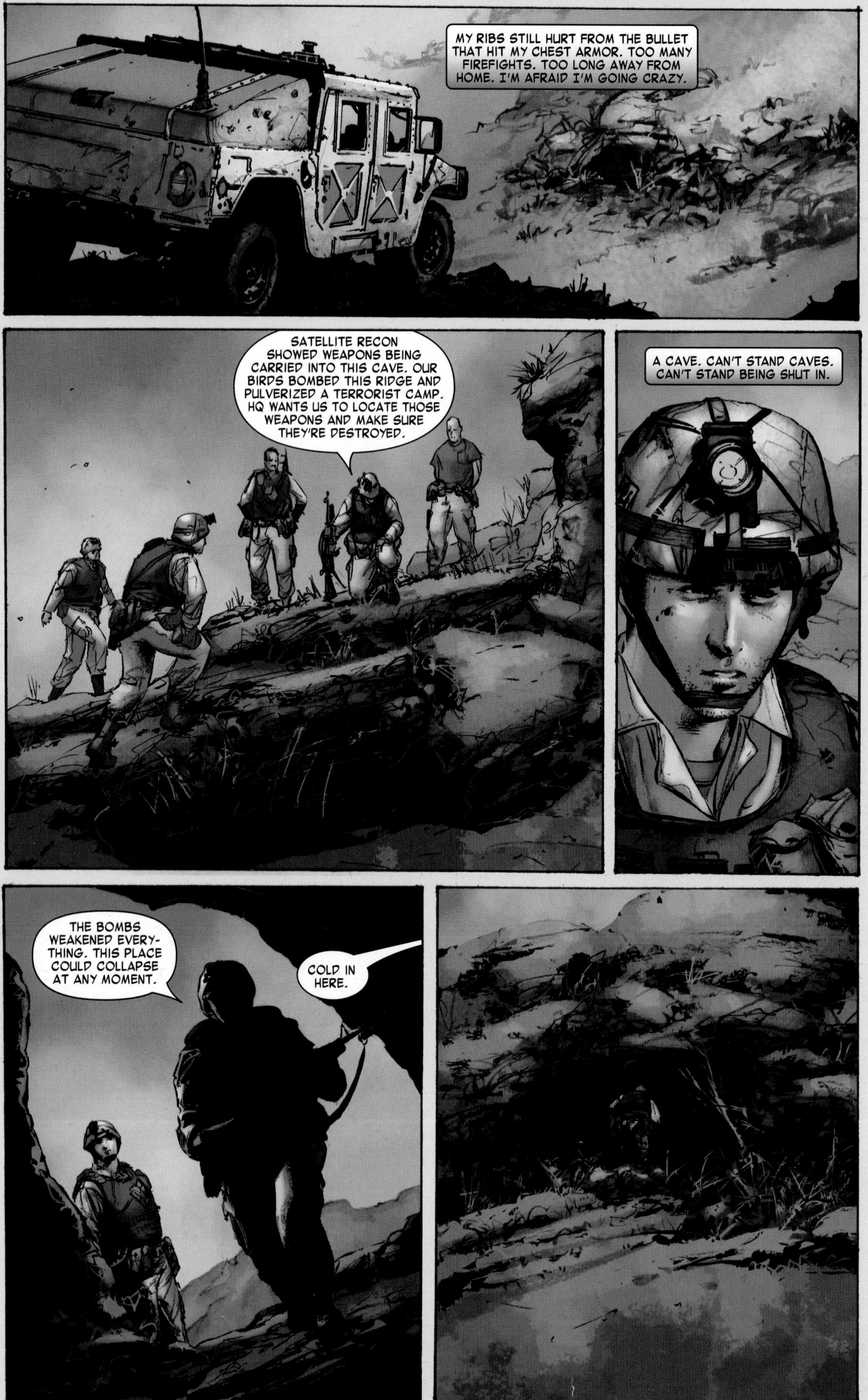
MY RIBS STILL HURT FROM THE BULLET THAT HIT MY CHEST ARMOR. TOO MANY FIREFIGHTS. TOO LONG AWAY FROM HOME. I'M AFRAID I'M GOING CRAZY.
SATELLITE RECON SHOWED WEAPONS BEING CARRIED INTO THIS CAVE. OUR BIRDS BOMBED THIS RIDGE AND PULVERIZED A TERRORIST CAMP. HQ WANTS US TO LOCATE THOSE WEAPONS AND MAKE SURE THEY'RE DESTROYED.
A CAVE. CAN'T STAND CAVES. CAN'T STAND BEING SHUT IN.
THE BOMBS WEAKENED EVERY-THING. THIS PLACE COULD COLLAPSE AT ANY MOMENT.
COLD IN HERE.

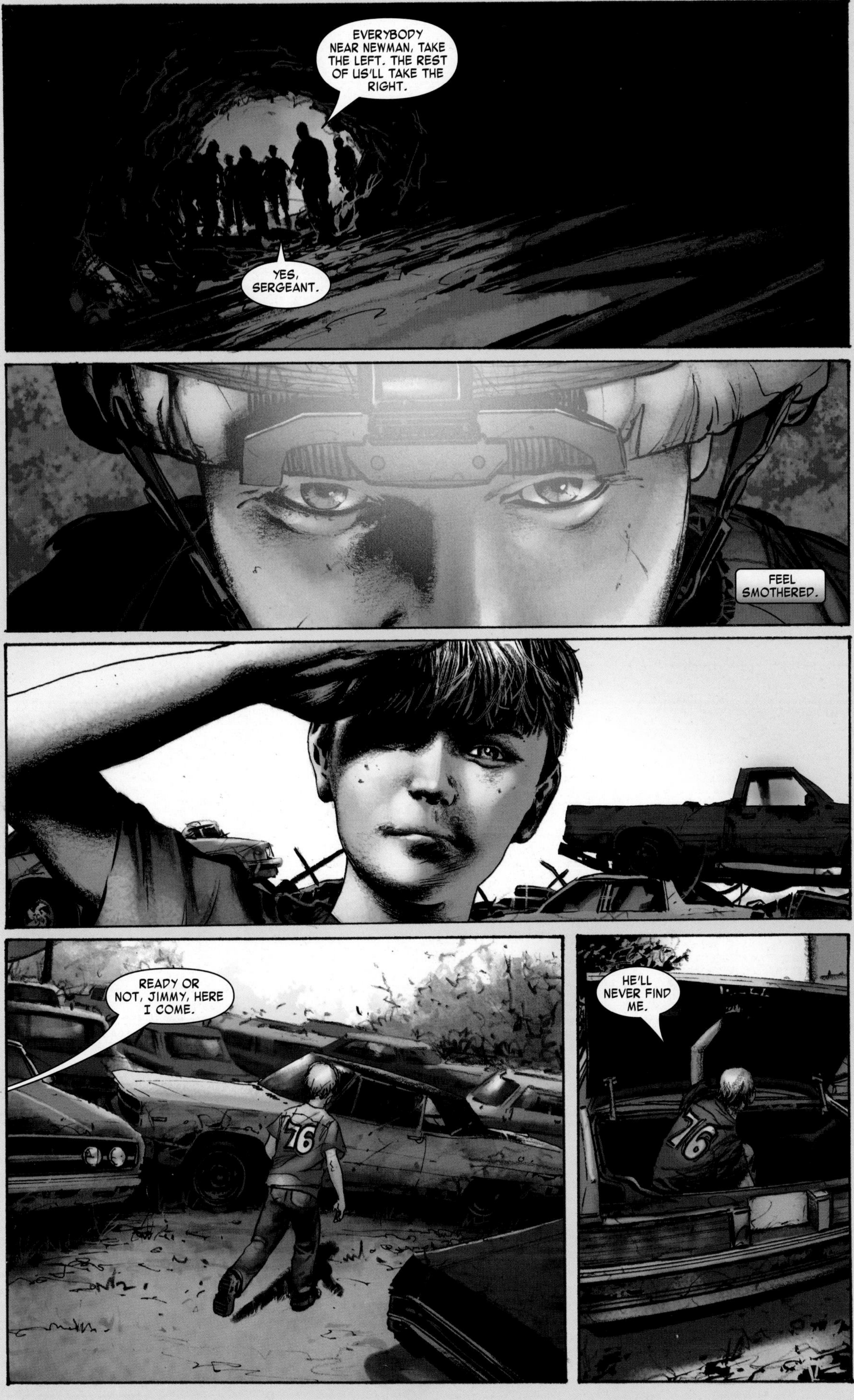
EVERYBODY NEAR NEWMAN, TAKE THE LEFT. THE REST OF US'LL TAKE THE RIGHT.
YES, SERGEANT.
FEEL SMOTHERED.
READY OR NOT, JIMMY, HERE I COME.
HE'LL NEVER FIND ME.

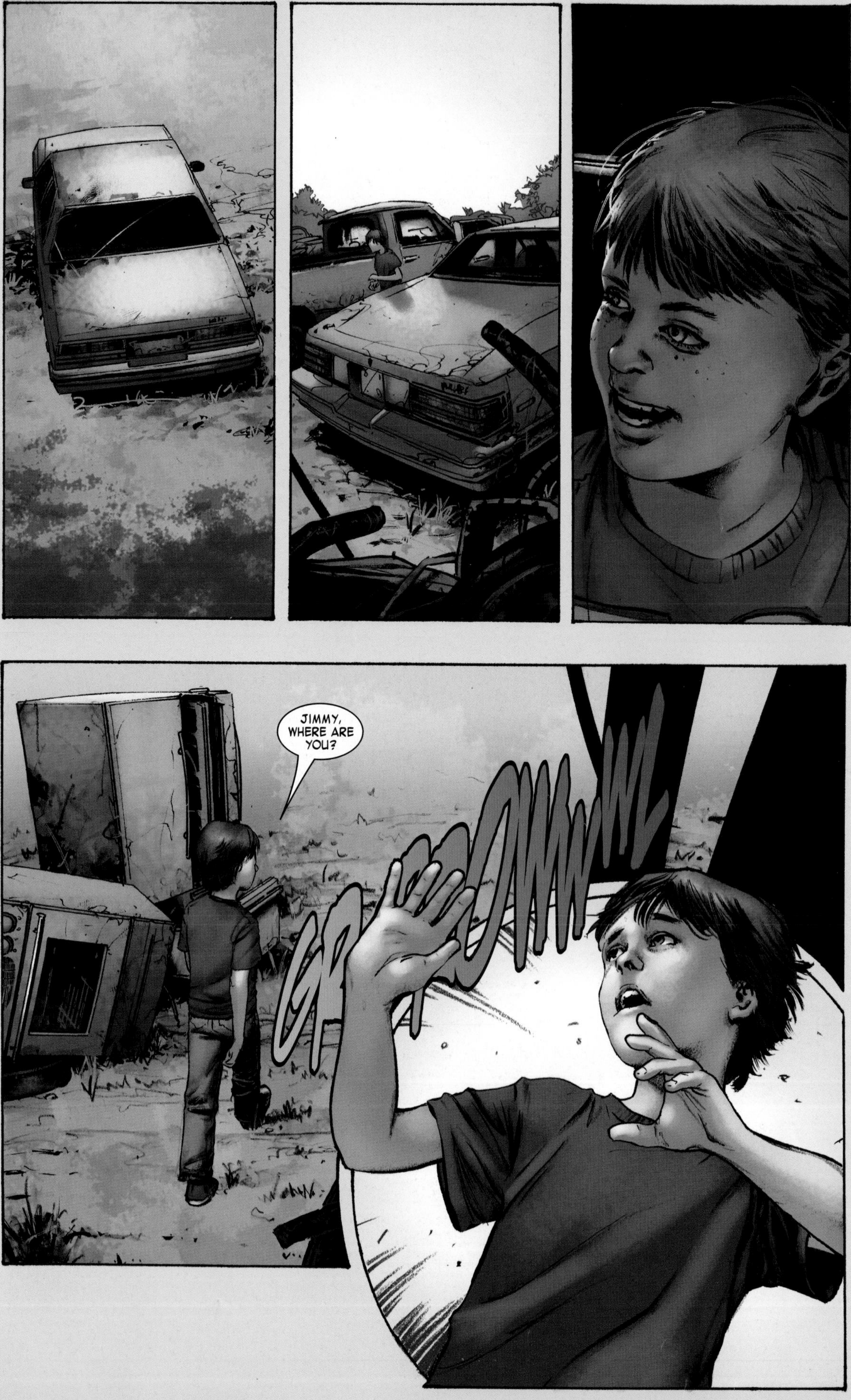
JIMMY, WHERE ARE YOU?

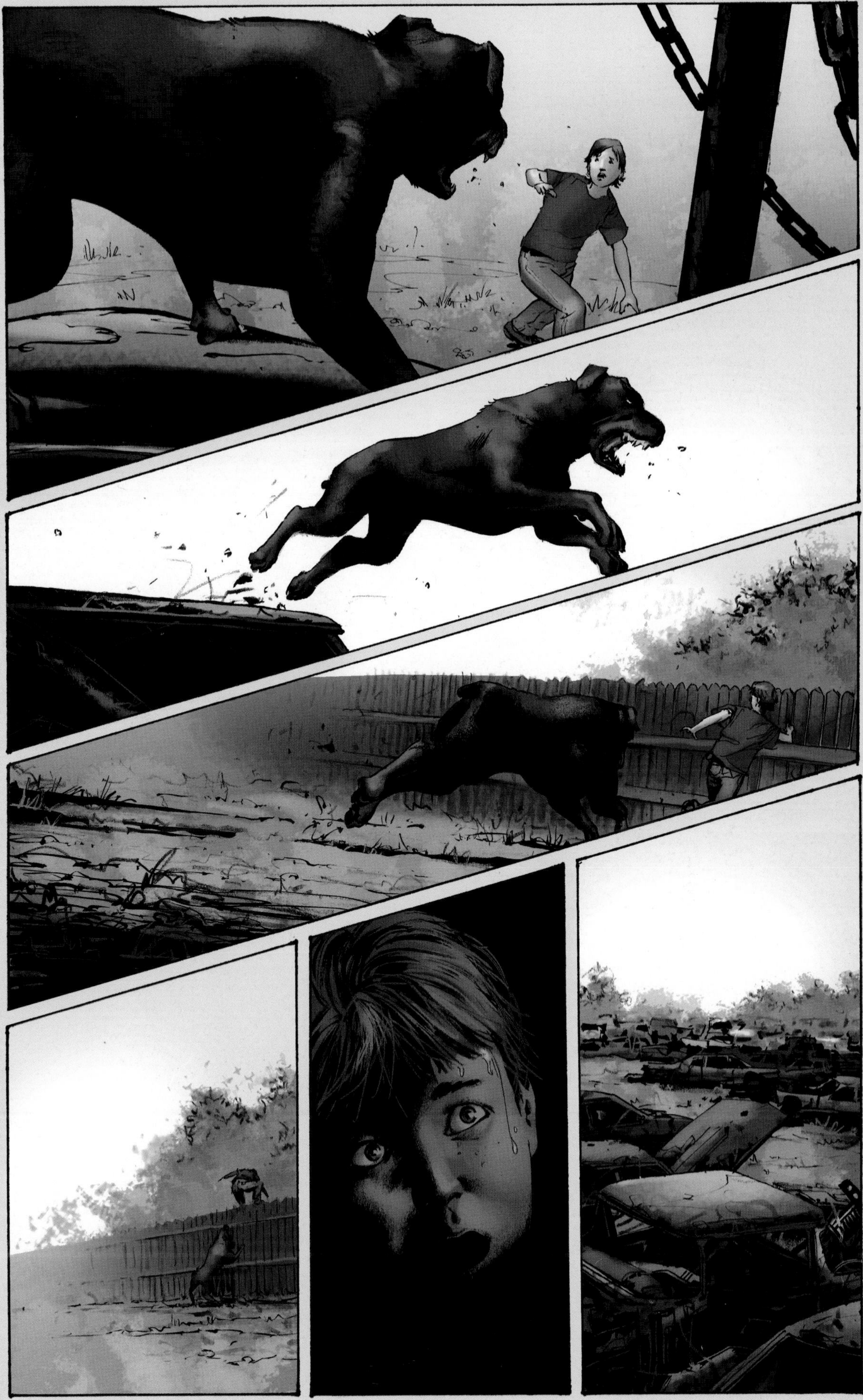

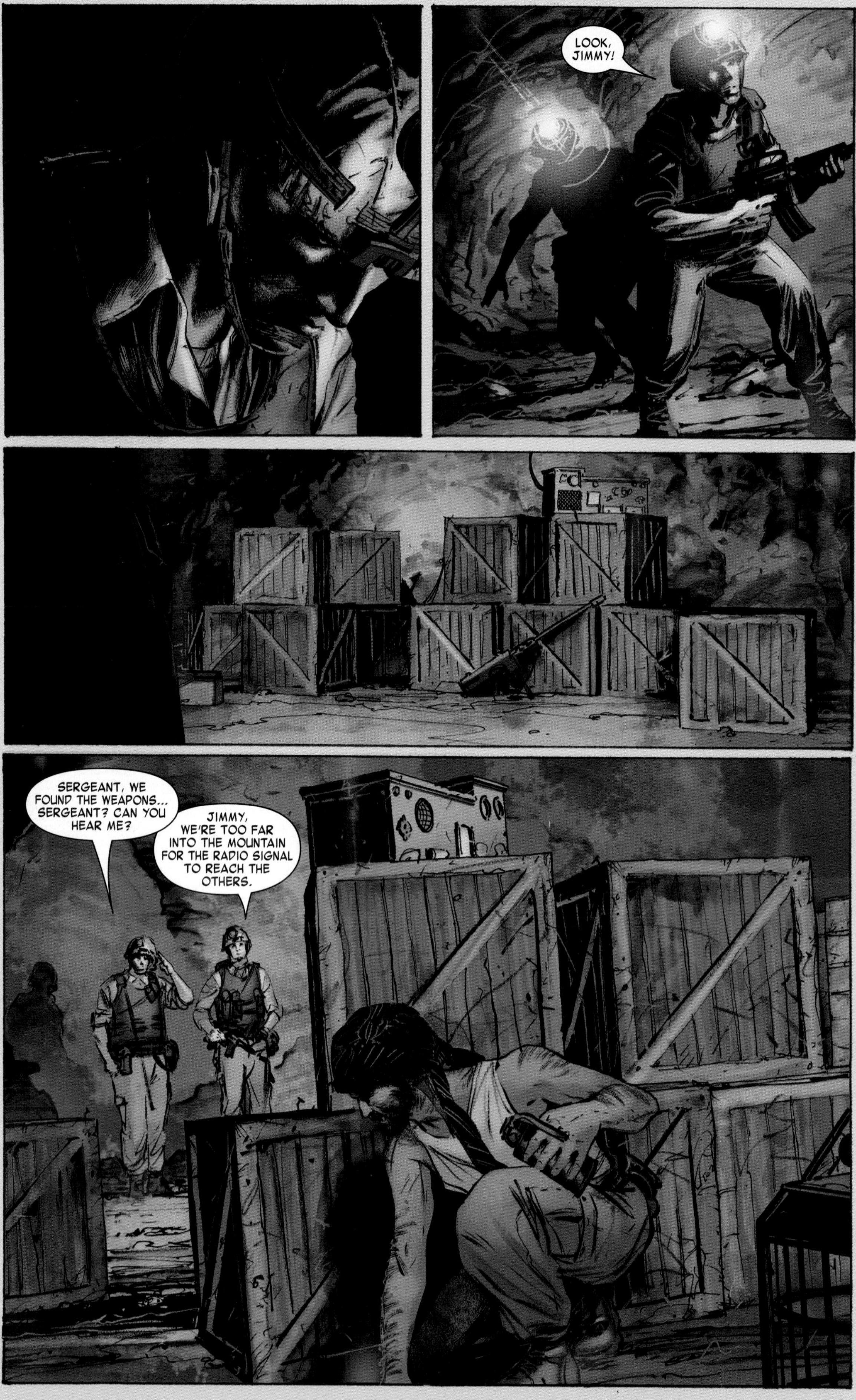
LOOK, JIMMY!
SERGEANT, WE FOUND THE WEAPONS... SERGEANT? CAN YOU HEAR ME?
JIMMY, WE'RE TOO FAR INTO THE MOUNTAIN FOR THE RADIO SIGNAL TO REACH THE OTHERS.

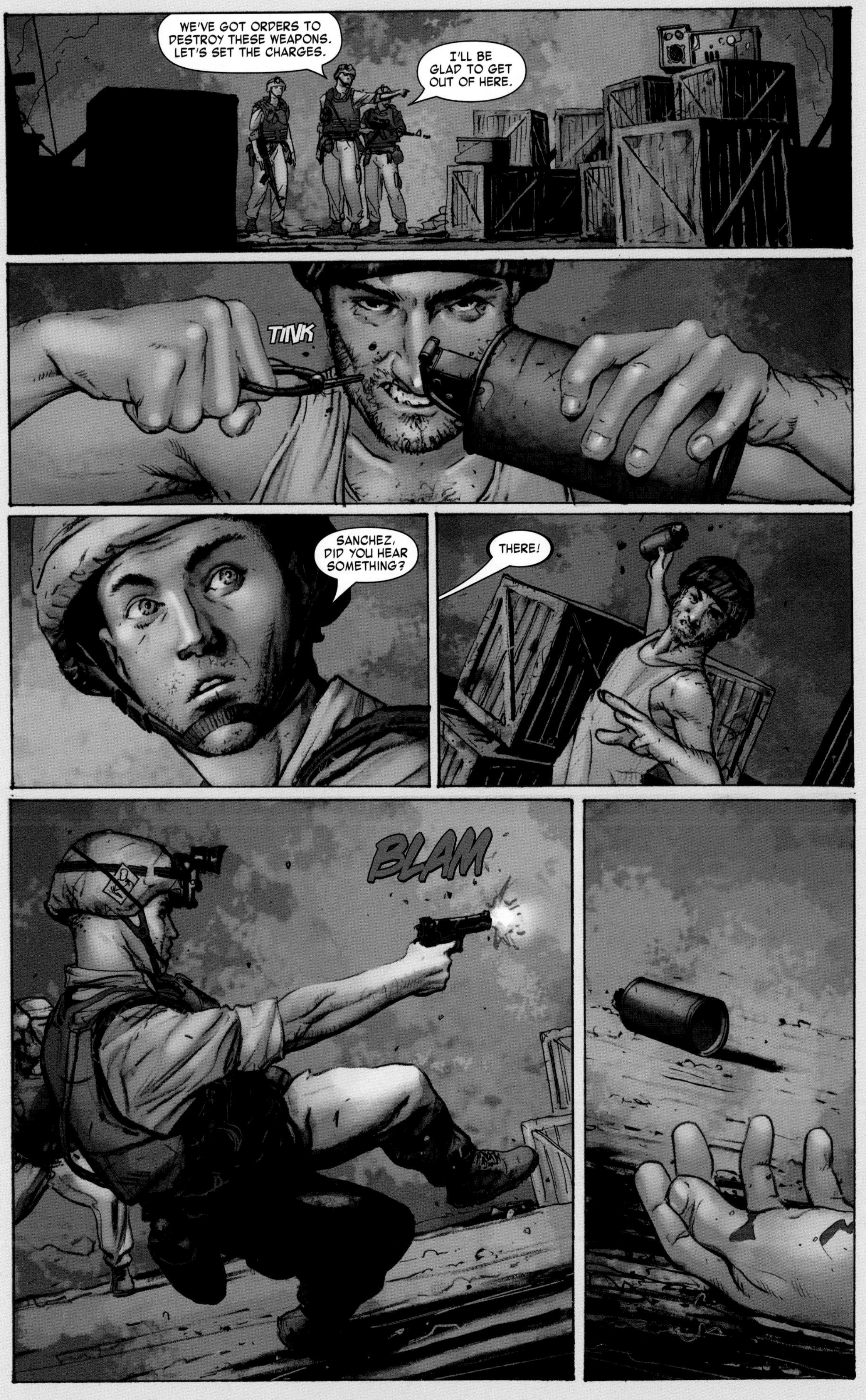
WE'VE GOT ORDERS TO DESTROY THESE WEAPONS. LET'S SET THE CHARGES.
I'LL BE GLAD TO GET OUT OF HERE.
TINK
SANCHEZ, DID YOU HEAR SOMETHING?
THERE!
BLAM

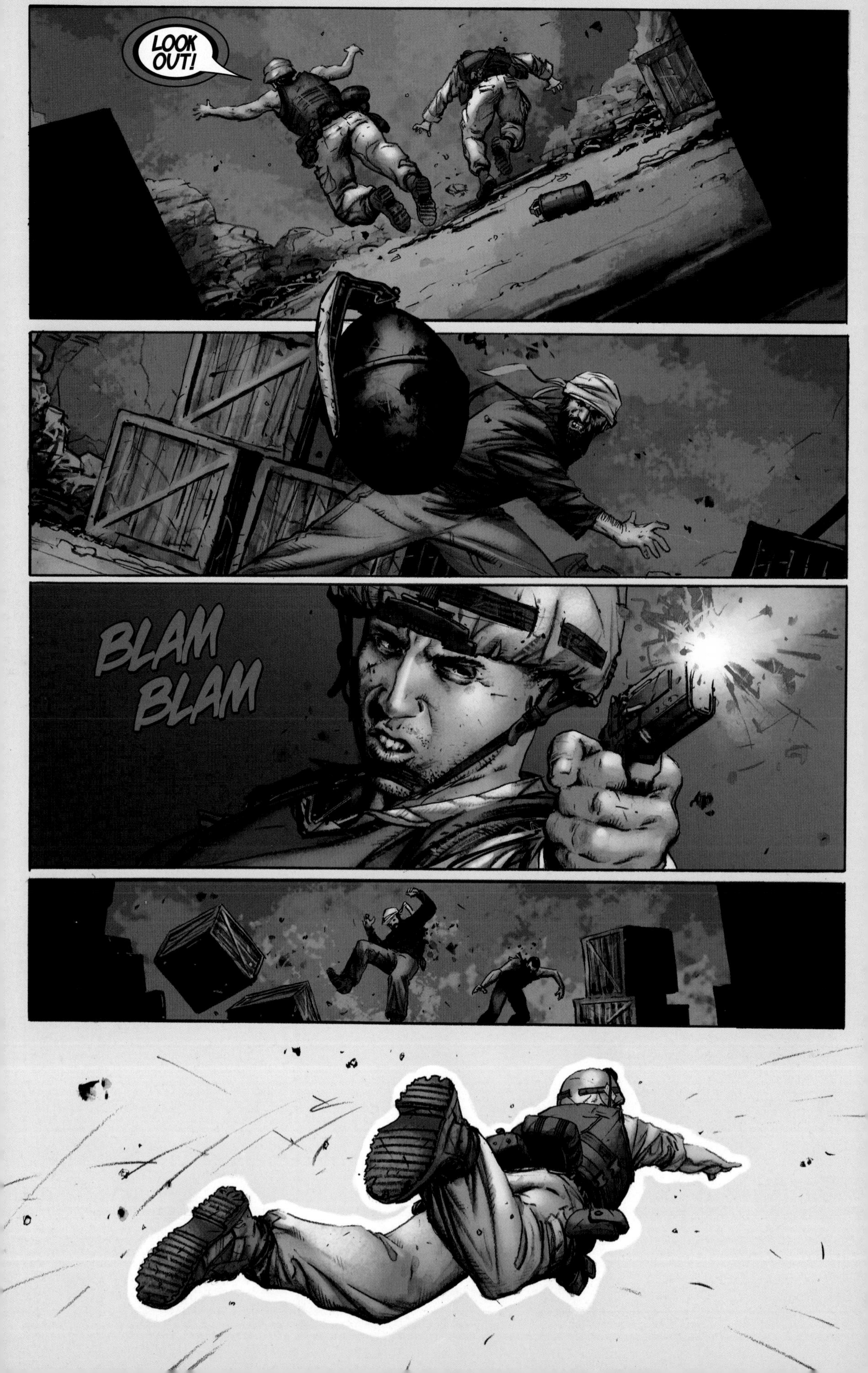
LOOK OUT!
BLAM BLAM

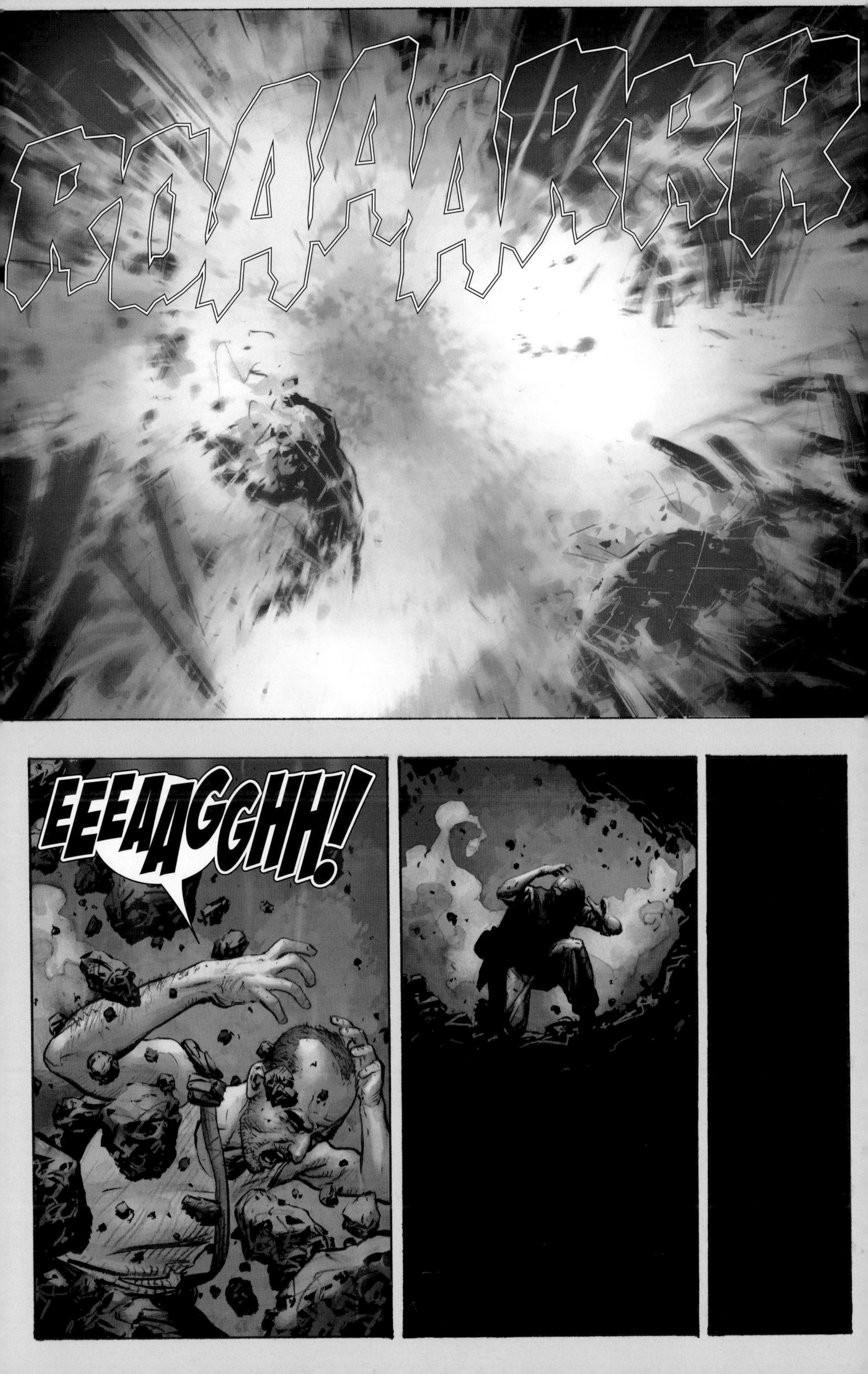
ROAARRR
EEEAAGGHH!

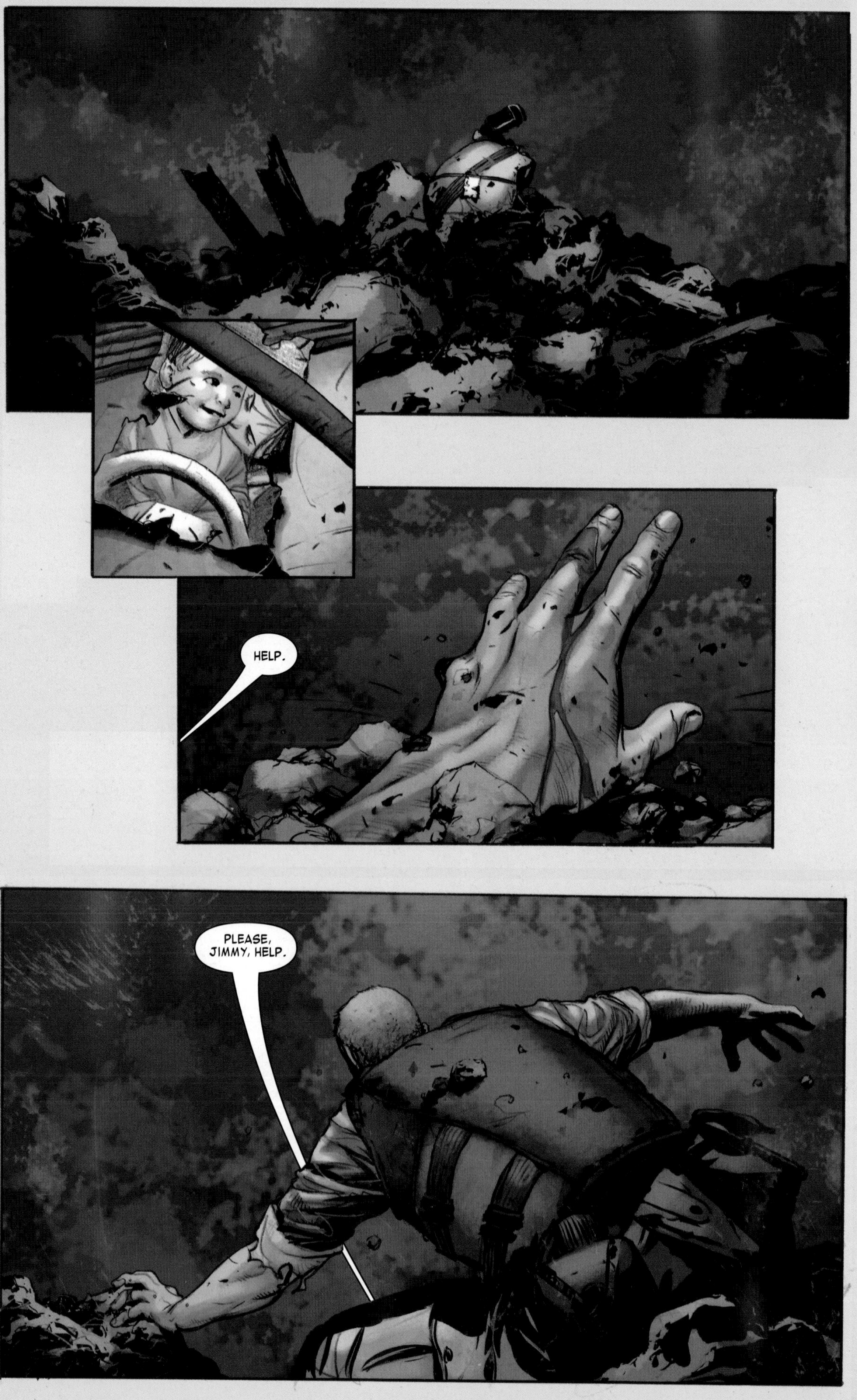
HELP.
PLEASE, JIMMY, HELP.

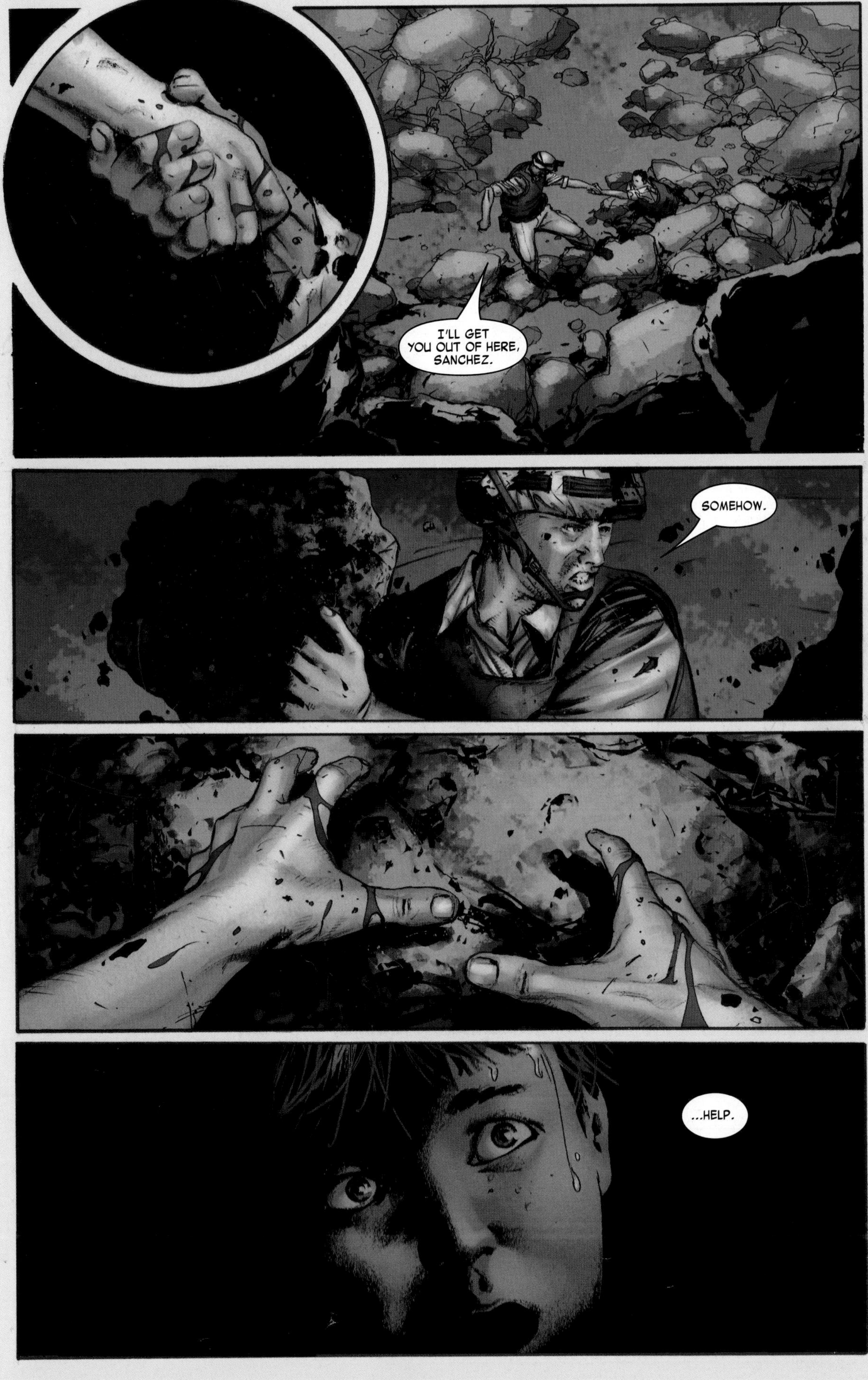
I'LL GET YOU OUT OF HERE, SANCHEZ.
SOMEHOW.
...HELP.

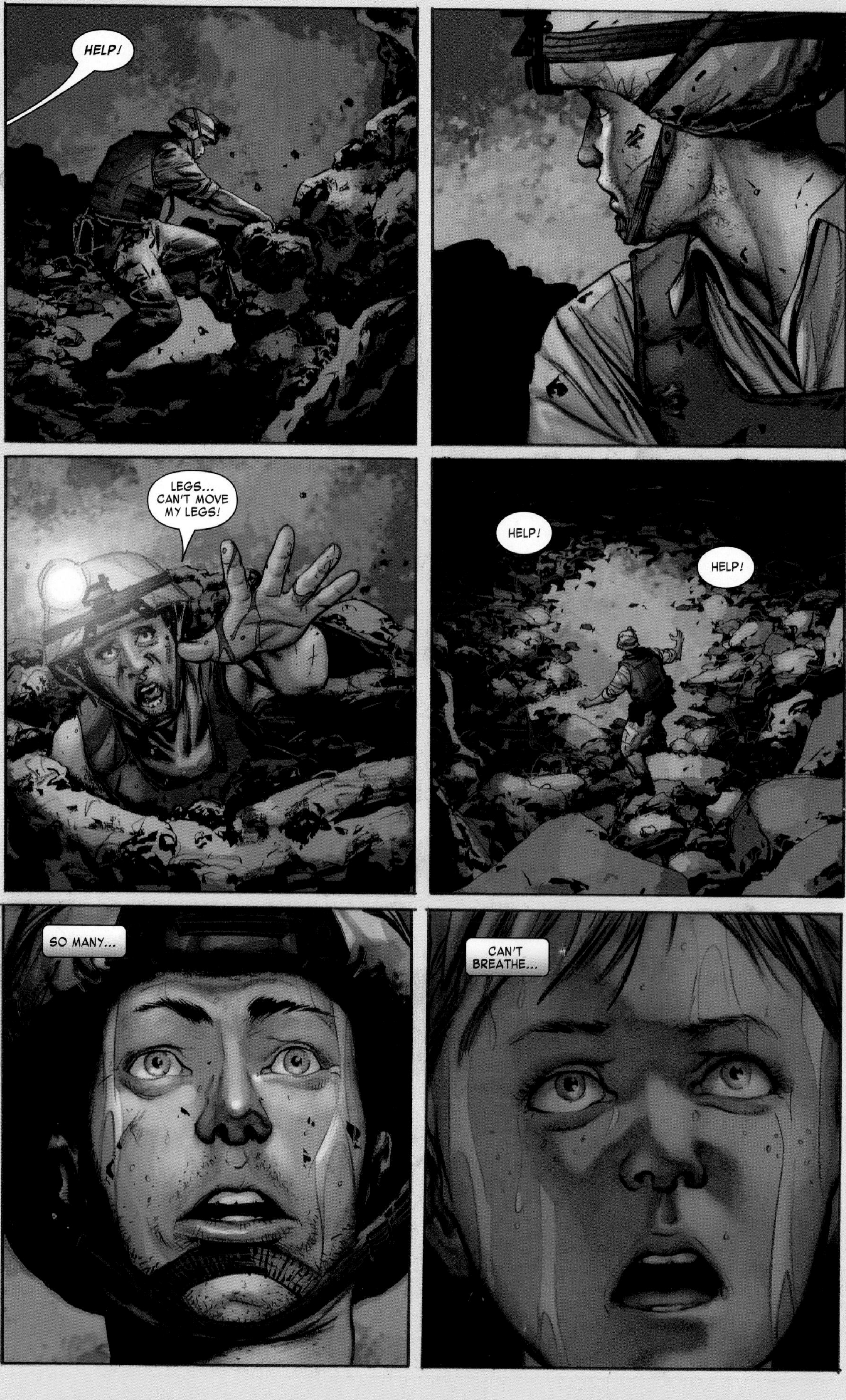
HELP!
LEGS... CAN'T MOVE MY LEGS!
HELP!
HELP!
SO MANY...
CAN'T BREATHE...

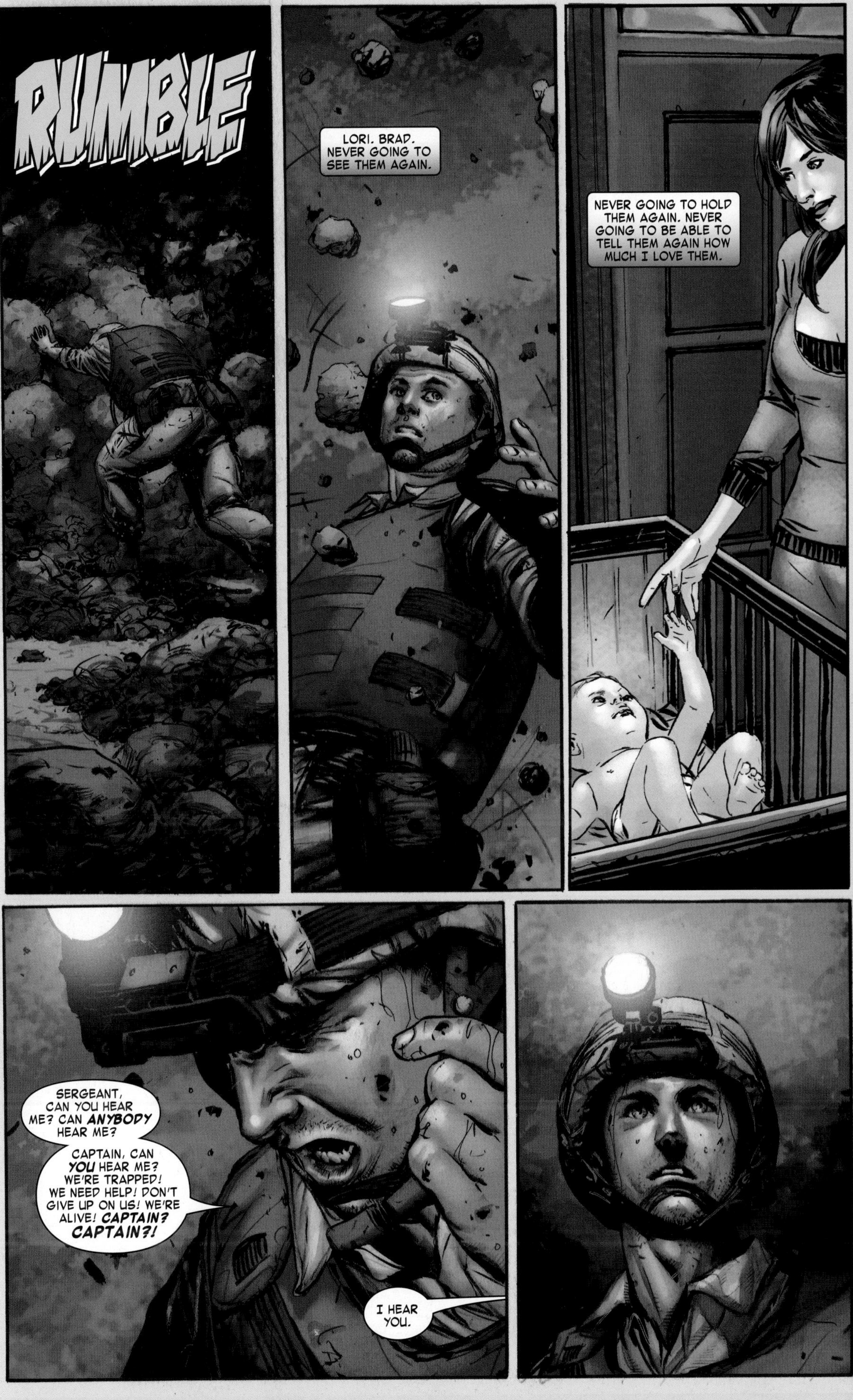
RUMBLE
LORI. BRAD. NEVER GOING TO SEE THEM AGAIN.
NEVER GOING TO HOLD THEM AGAIN. NEVER GOING TO BE ABLE TO TELL THEM AGAIN HOW MUCH I LOVE THEM.
SERGEANT, CAN YOU HEAR ME? CAN ANYBODY HEAR ME?
CAPTAIN, CAN YOU HEAR ME? WE'RE TRAPPED! WE NEED HELP! DON'T GIVE UP ON US! WE'RE ALIVE! CAPTAIN? CAPTAIN?!
I HEAR YOU.

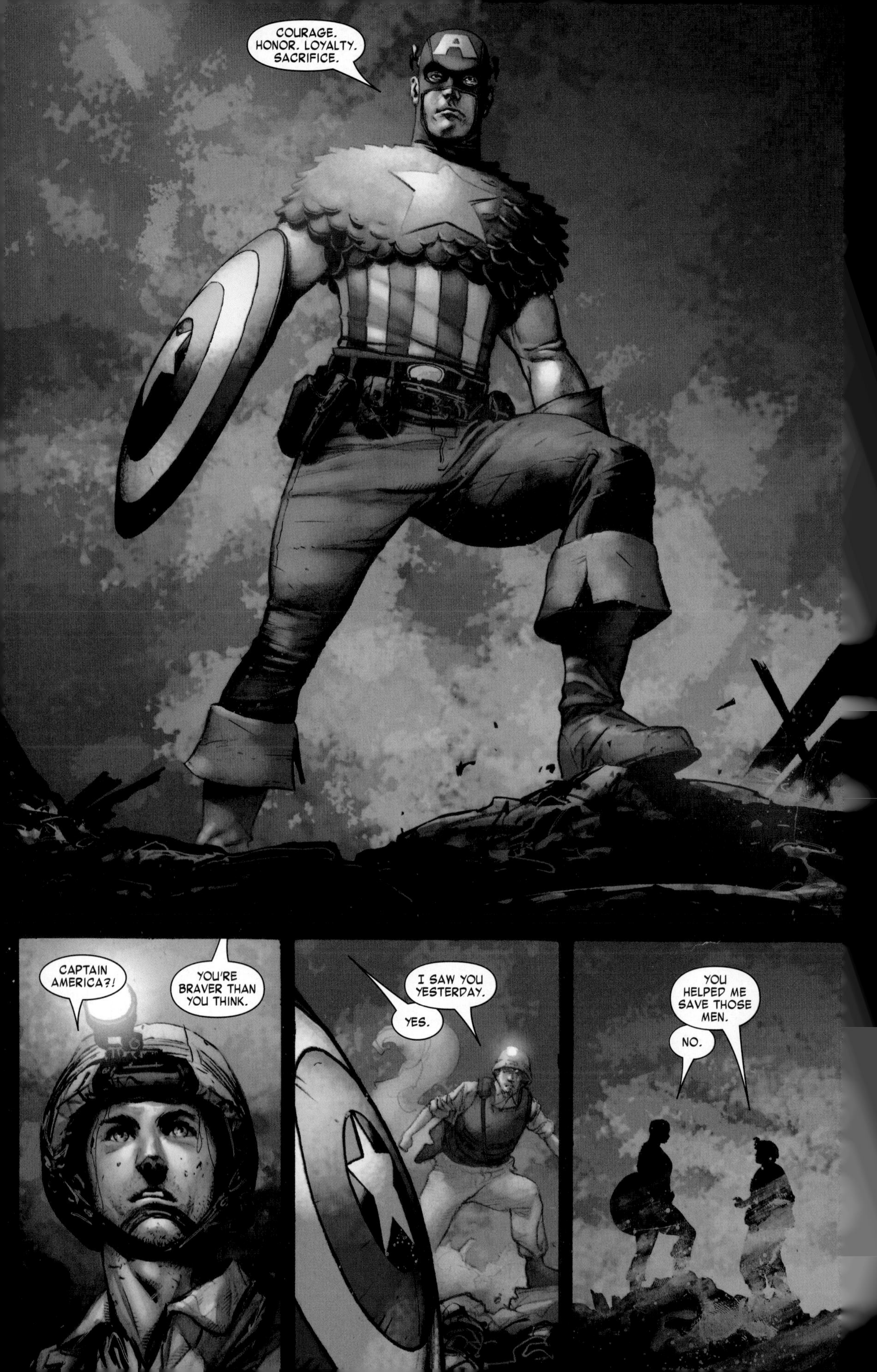
COURAGE. HONOR. LOYALTY. SACRIFICE.
CAPTAIN AMERICA?!
YOU'RE BRAVER THAN YOU THINK.
I SAW YOU YESTERDAY.
YES.
YOU HELPED ME SAVE THOSE MEN.
NO.

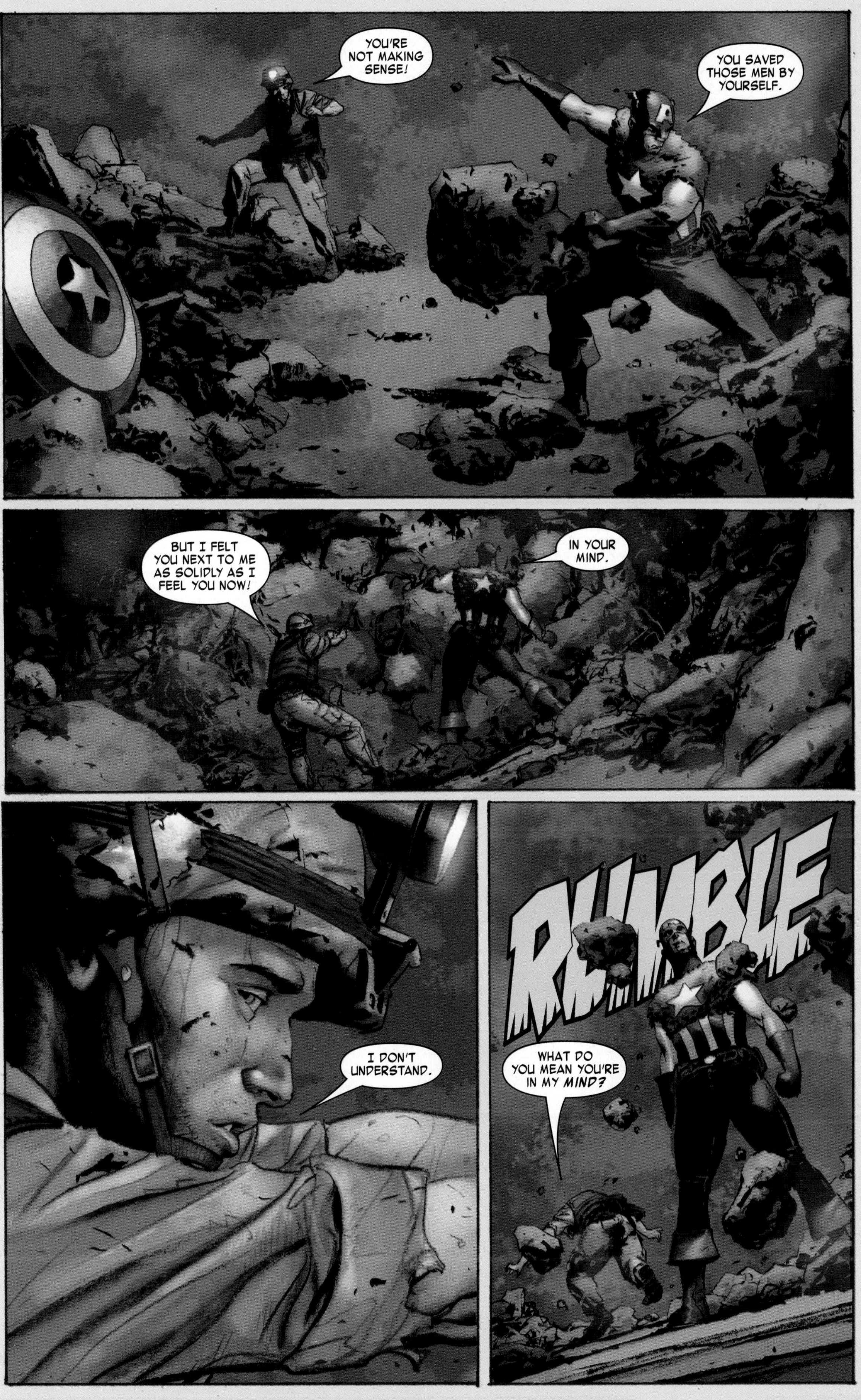
YOU'RE NOT MAKING SENSE!
YOU SAVED THOSE MEN BY YOURSELF.
BUT I FELT YOU NEXT TO ME AS SOLIDLY AS I FEEL YOU NOW!
IN YOUR MIND.
I DON'T UNDERSTAND.
RUMBLE
WHAT DO YOU MEAN YOU'RE IN MY *MIND?*

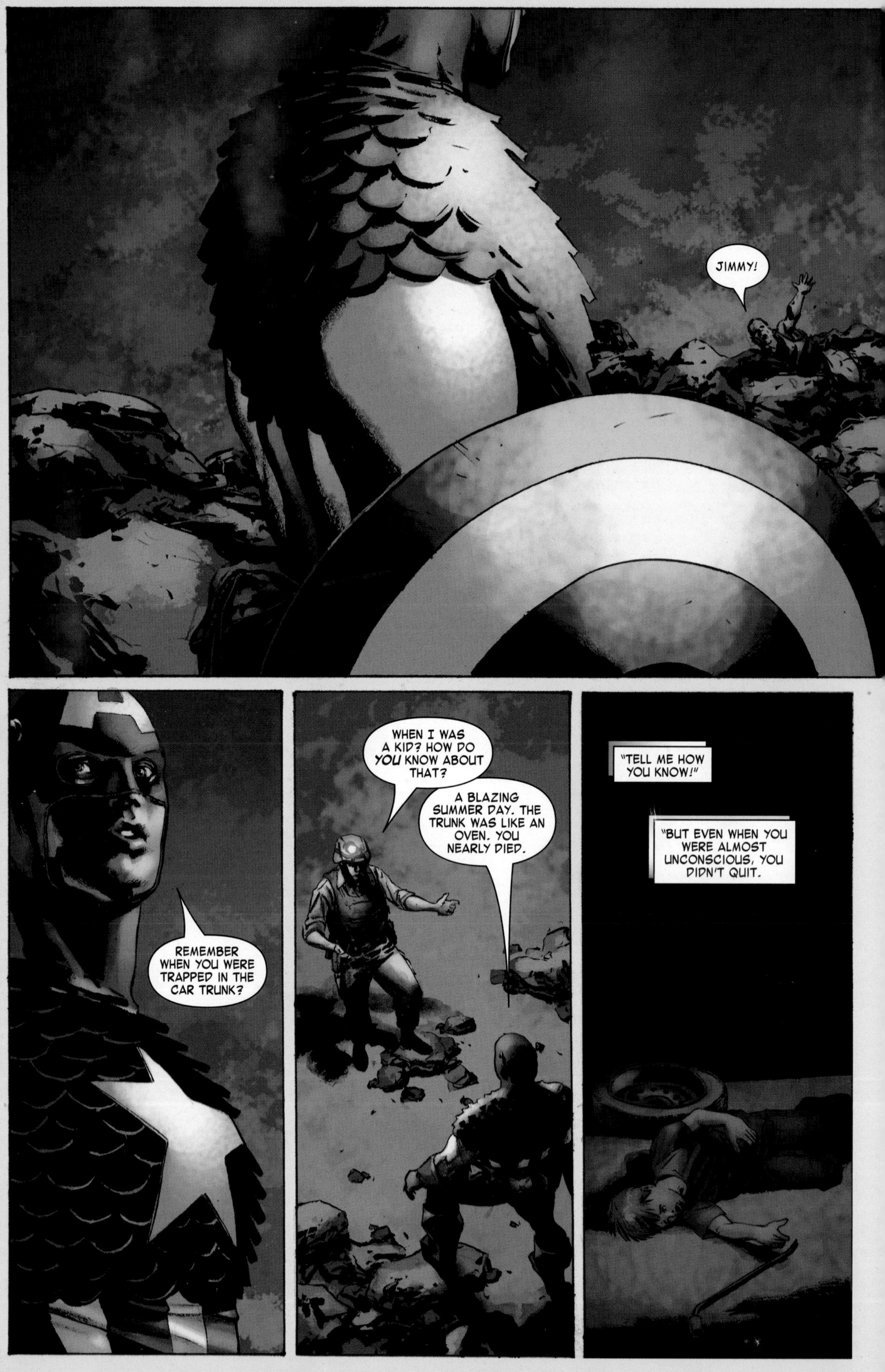
JIMMY!
REMEMBER WHEN YOU WERE TRAPPED IN THE CAR TRUNK?
WHEN I WAS A KID? HOW DO *YOU* KNOW ABOUT THAT?
A BLAZING SUMMER DAY. THE TRUNK WAS LIKE AN OVEN. YOU NEARLY DIED.
"TELL ME HOW YOU KNOW!"
"BUT EVEN WHEN YOU WERE ALMOST UNCONSCIOUS, YOU DIDN'T QUIT.

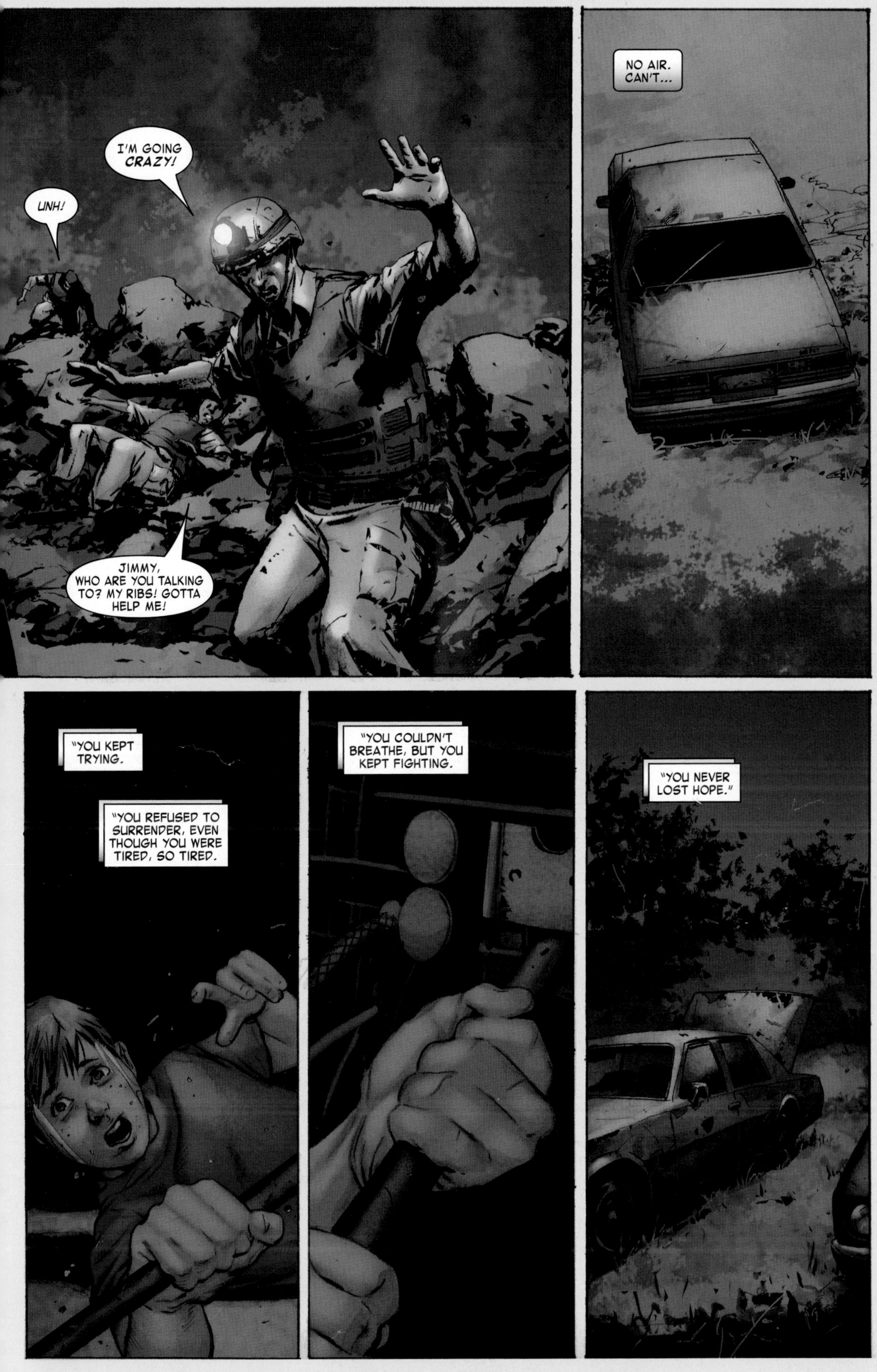
UNH!
I'M GOING CRAZY!
JIMMY, WHO ARE YOU TALKING TO? MY RIBS! GOTTA HELP ME!
NO AIR. CAN'T...
"YOU KEPT TRYING.
"YOU REFUSED TO SURRENDER, EVEN THOUGH YOU WERE TIRED, SO TIRED.
"YOU COULDN'T BREATHE, BUT YOU KEPT FIGHTING.
"YOU NEVER LOST HOPE."

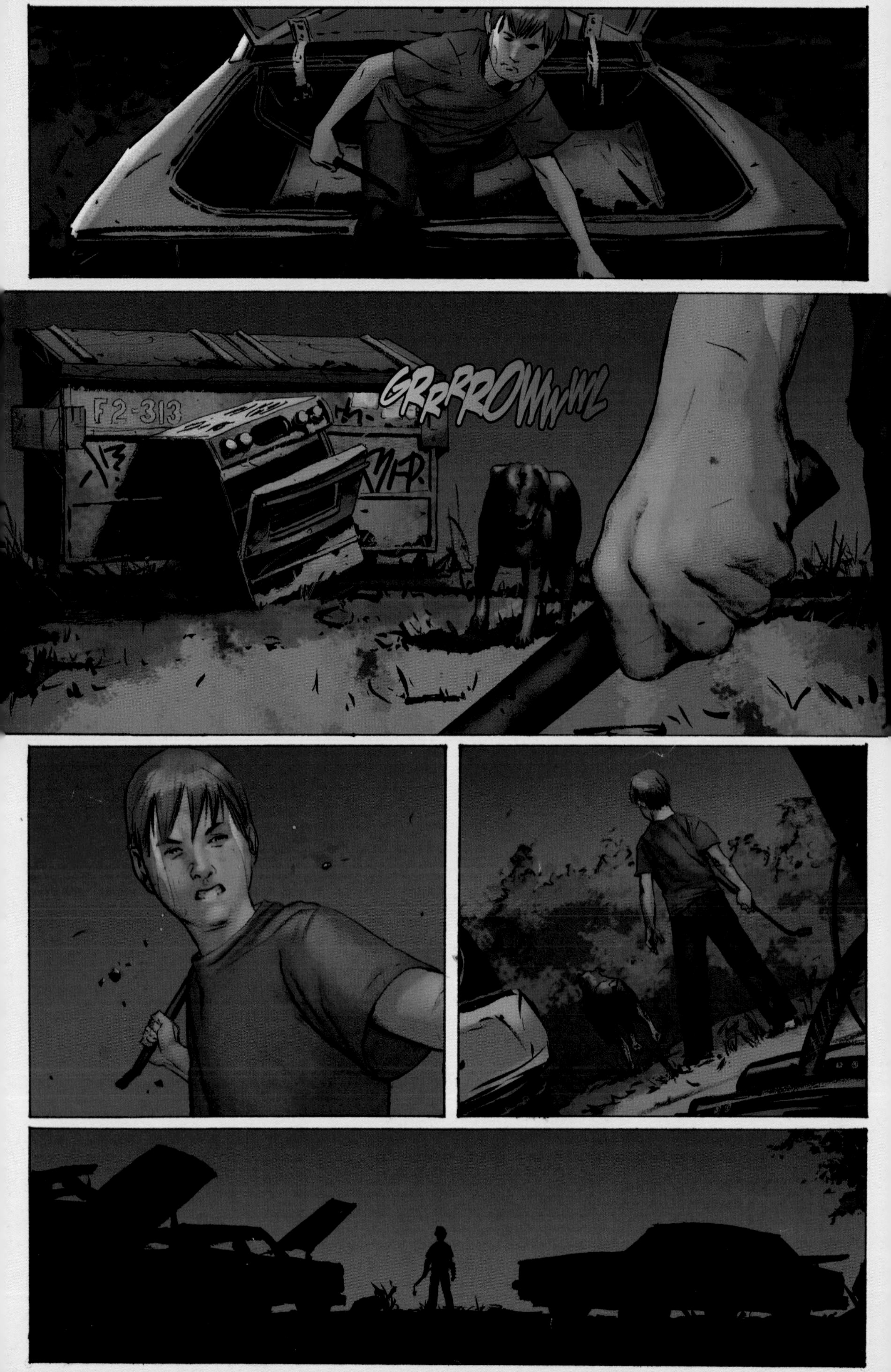
F2-313
GRRRROWWWL

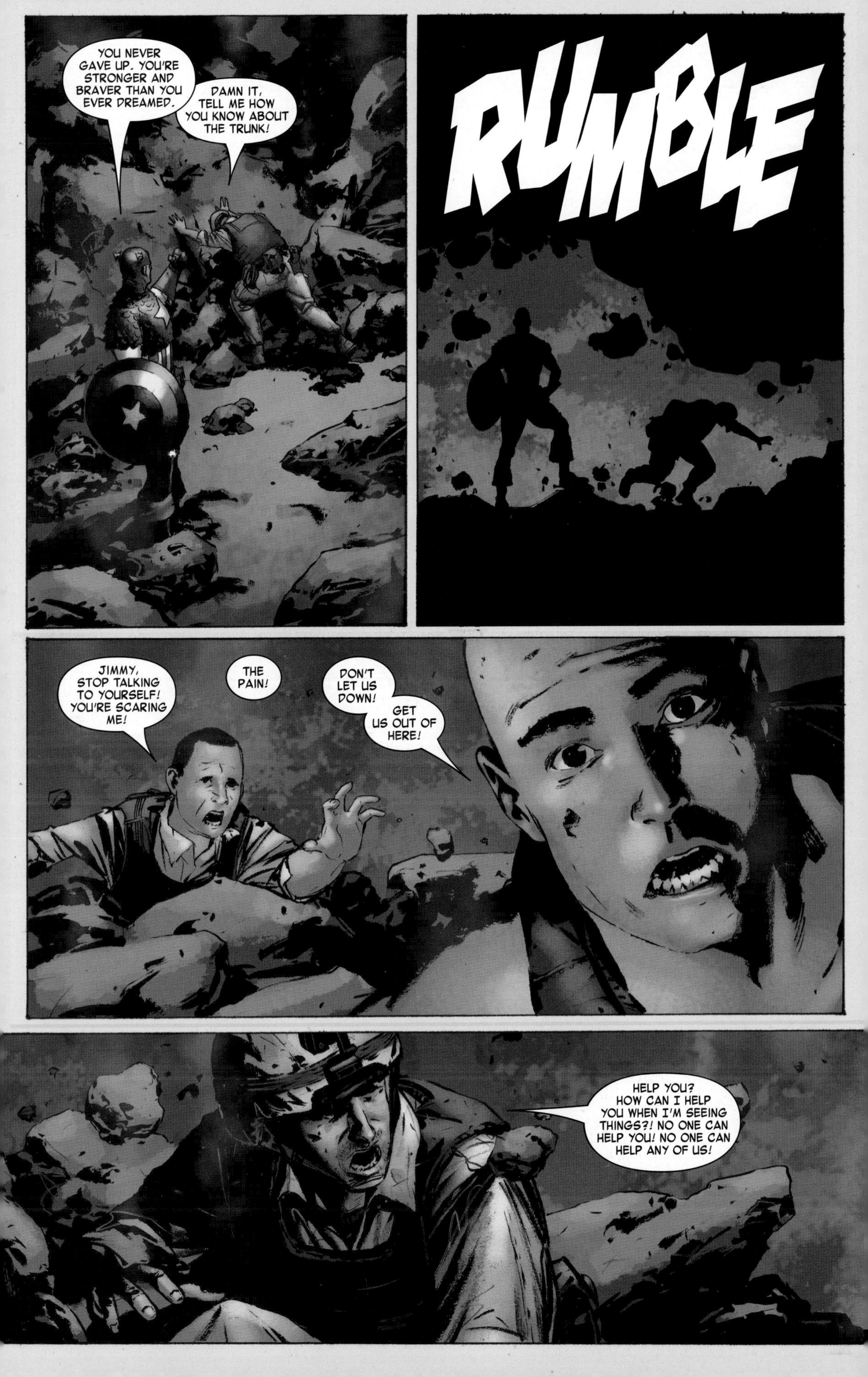
YOU NEVER GAVE UP. YOU'RE STRONGER AND BRAVER THAN YOU EVER DREAMED.
DAMN IT, TELL ME HOW YOU KNOW ABOUT THE TRUNK!
RUMBLE
JIMMY, STOP TALKING TO YOURSELF! YOU'RE SCARING ME!
THE PAIN!
DON'T LET US DOWN!
GET US OUT OF HERE!
HELP YOU? HOW CAN I HELP YOU WHEN I'M SEEING THINGS?! NO ONE CAN HELP YOU! NO ONE CAN HELP ANY OF US!

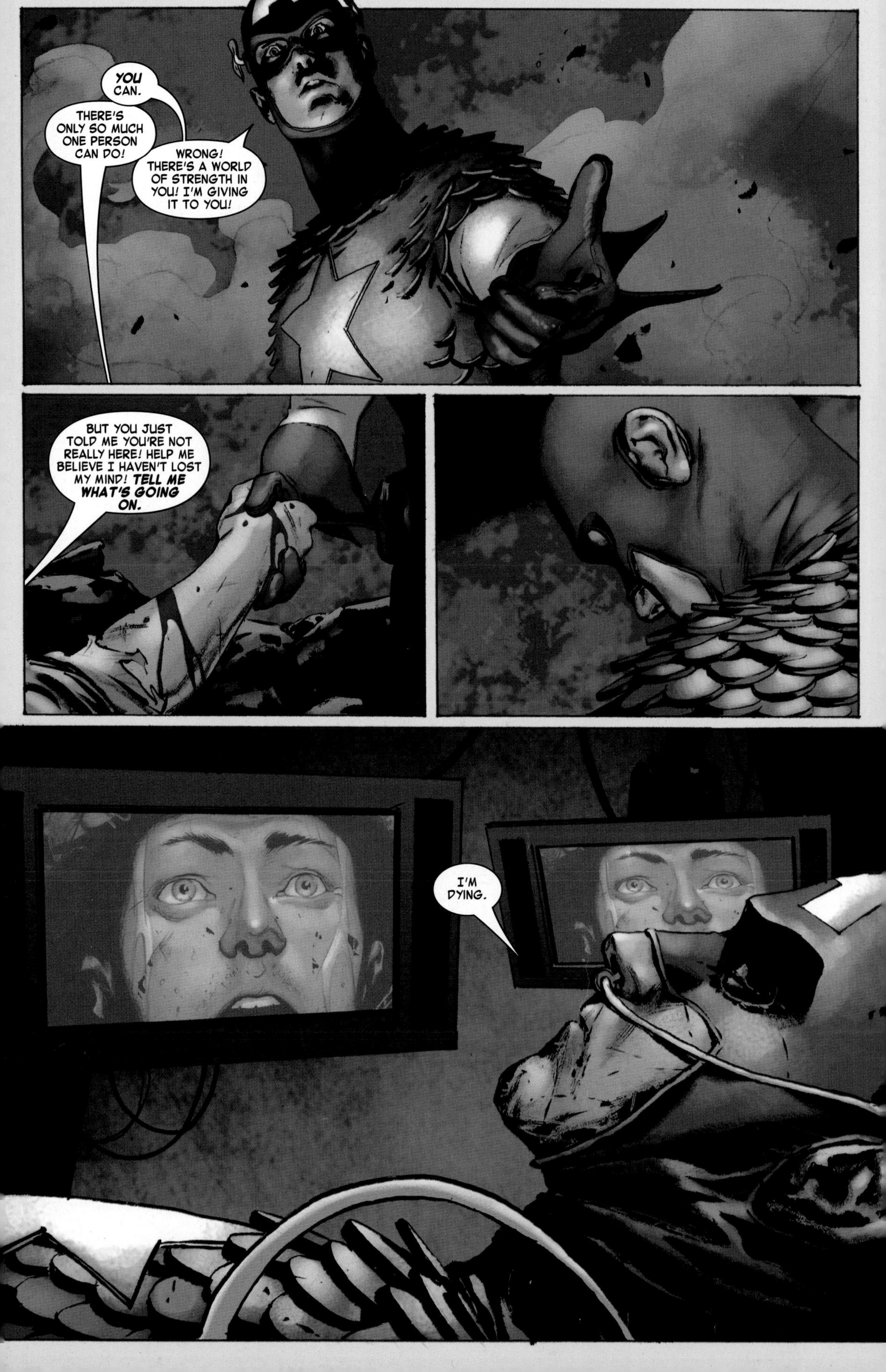

THERE'S ONLY SO MUCH ONE PERSON CAN DO!
YOU CAN.
WRONG! THERE'S A WORLD OF STRENGTH IN YOU! I'M GIVING IT TO YOU!
BUT YOU JUST TOLD ME YOU'RE NOT REALLY HERE! HELP ME BELIEVE I HAVEN'T LOST MY MIND! TELL ME WHAT'S GOING ON.
I'M DYING.

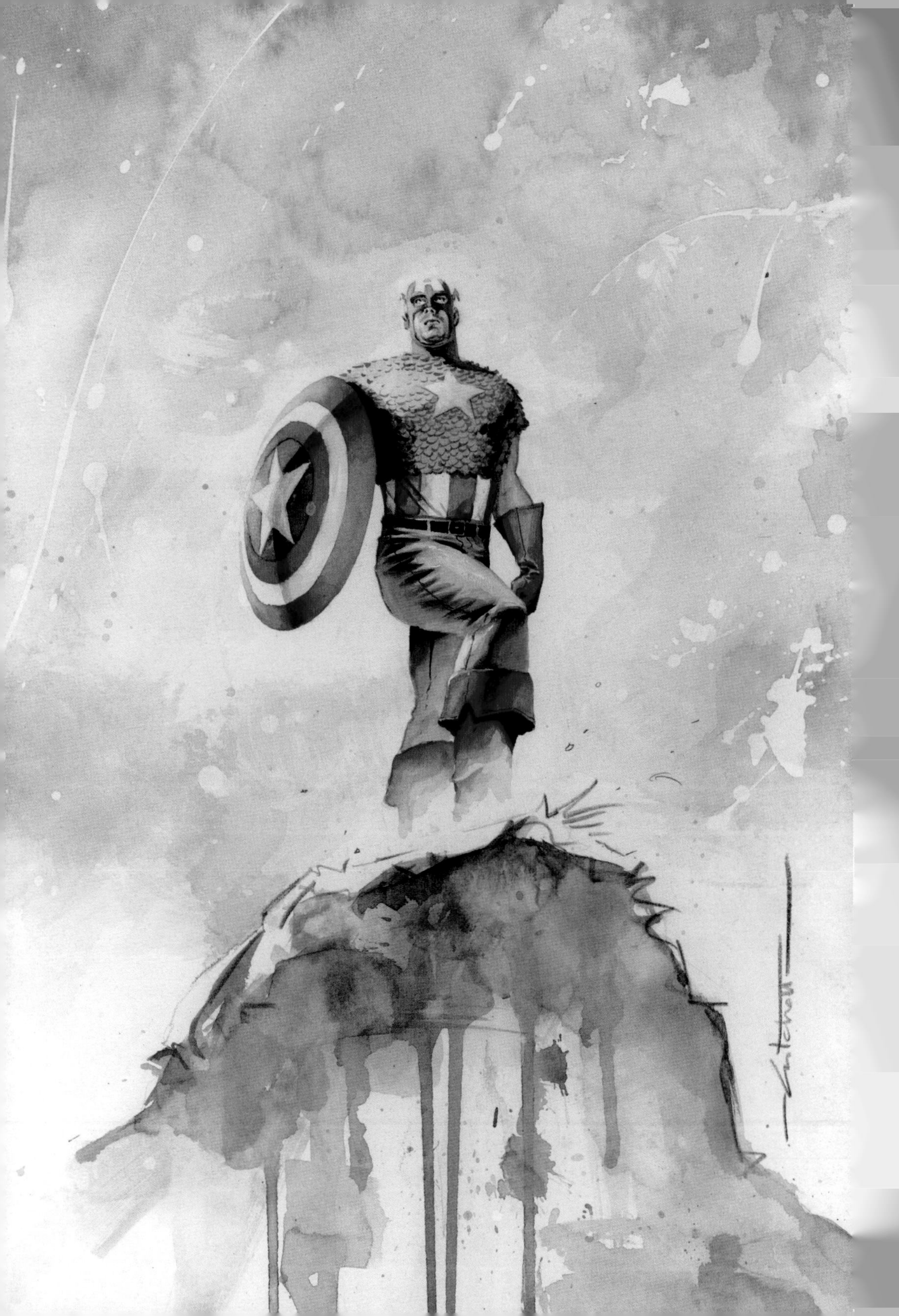

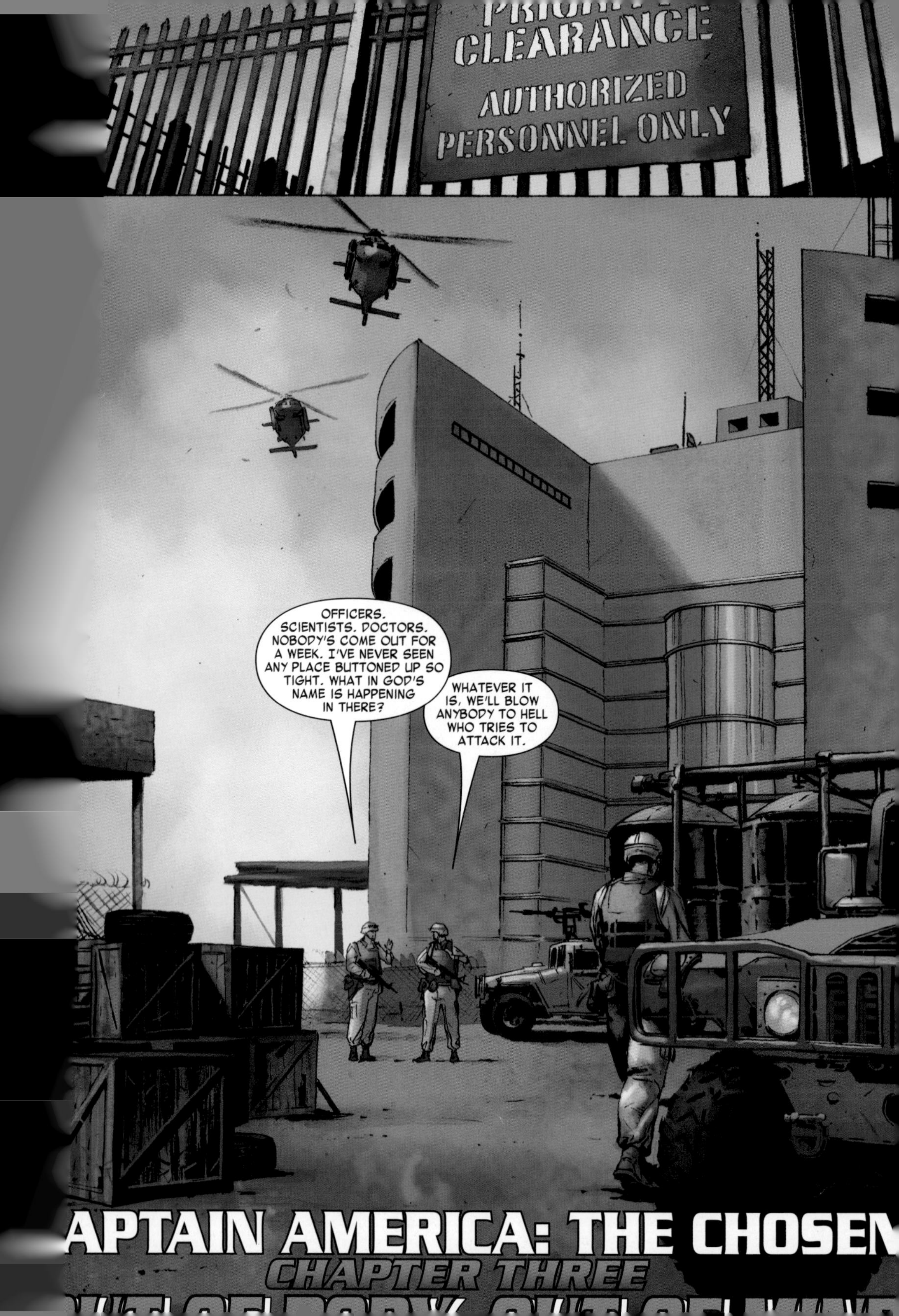
CLEARANCE
AUTHORIZED PERSONNEL ONLY
OFFICERS. SCIENTISTS. DOCTORS. NOBODY'S COME OUT FOR A WEEK. I'VE NEVER SEEN ANY PLACE BUTTONED UP SO TIGHT. WHAT IN GOD'S NAME IS HAPPENING IN THERE?
WHATEVER IT IS, WE'LL BLOW ANYBODY TO HELL WHO TRIES TO ATTACK IT.
APTAIN AMERICA: THE CHOSEN
CHAPTER THREE

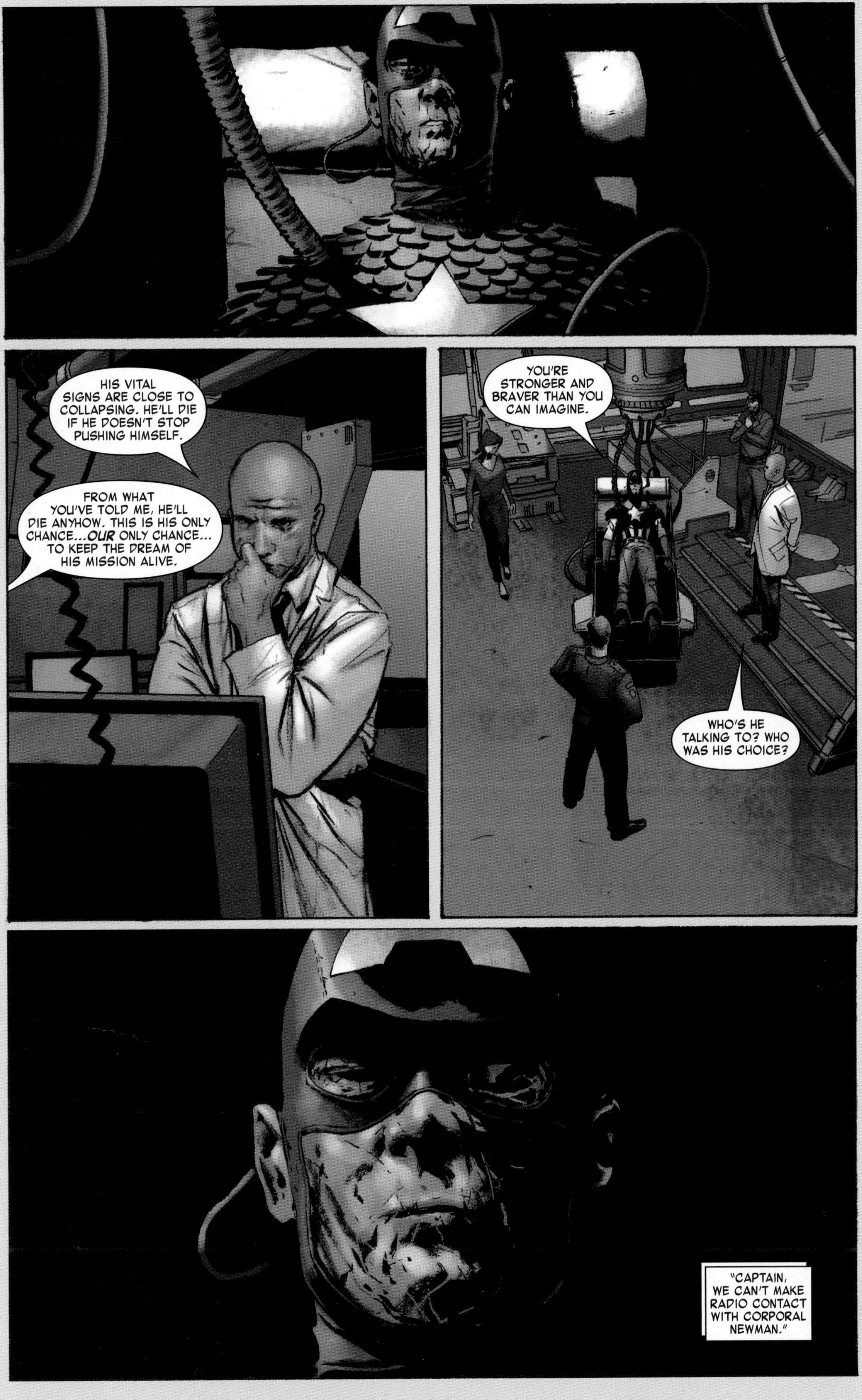
HIS VITAL SIGNS ARE CLOSE TO COLLAPSING. HE'LL DIE IF HE DOESN'T STOP PUSHING HIMSELF.
FROM WHAT YOU'VE TOLD ME, HE'LL DIE ANYHOW. THIS IS HIS ONLY CHANCE...OUR ONLY CHANCE... TO KEEP THE DREAM OF HIS MISSION ALIVE.
YOU'RE STRONGER AND BRAVER THAN YOU CAN IMAGINE.
WHO'S HE TALKING TO? WHO WAS HIS CHOICE?
"CAPTAIN, WE CAN'T MAKE RADIO CONTACT WITH CORPORAL NEWMAN."

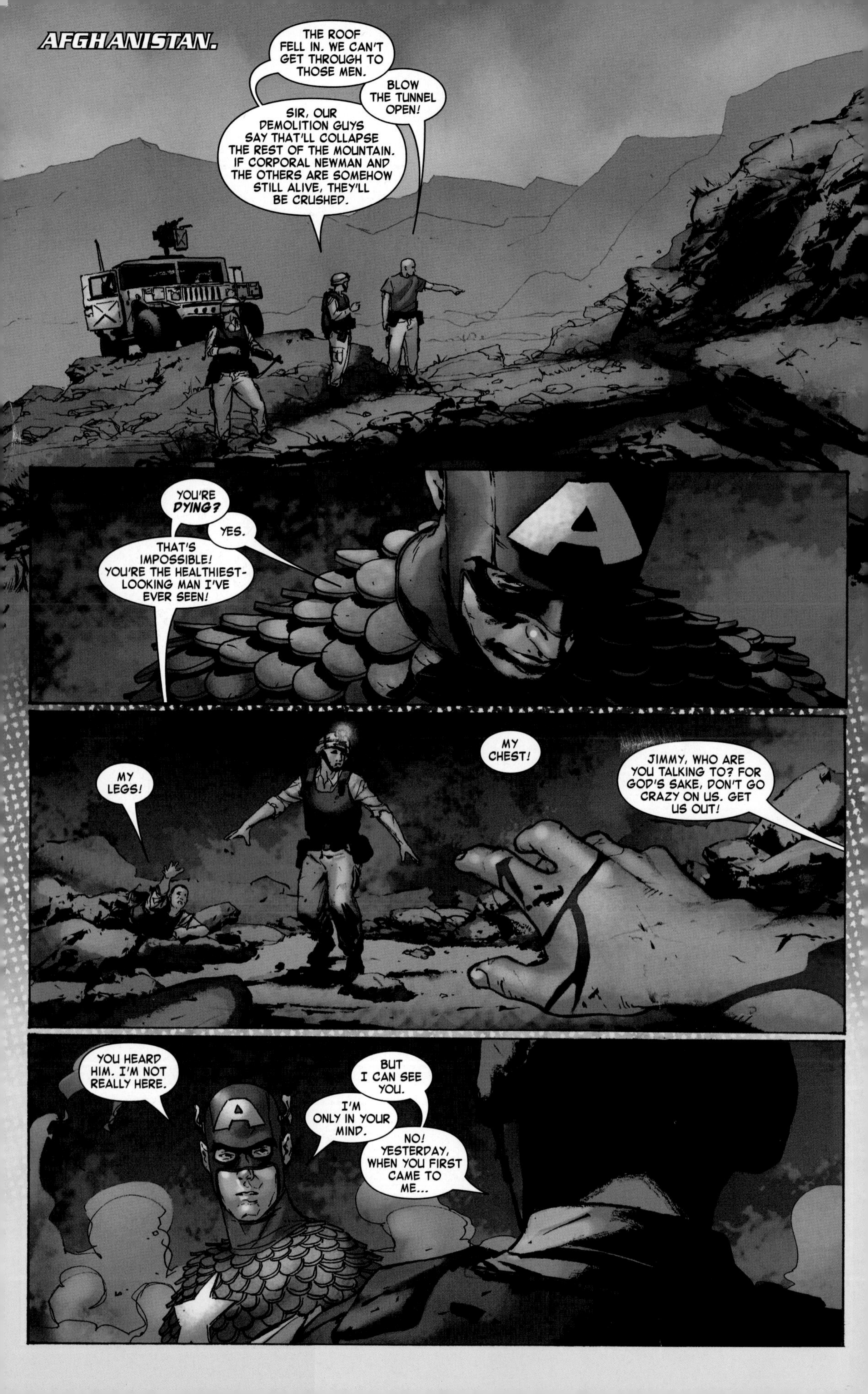
AFGHANISTAN.
THE ROOF FELL IN. WE CAN'T GET THROUGH TO THOSE MEN.
BLOW THE TUNNEL OPEN!
SIR, OUR DEMOLITION GUYS SAY THAT'LL COLLAPSE THE REST OF THE MOUNTAIN. IF CORPORAL NEWMAN AND THE OTHERS ARE SOMEHOW STILL ALIVE, THEY'LL BE CRUSHED.
YOU'RE DYING?
YES.
THAT'S IMPOSSIBLE! YOU'RE THE HEALTHIEST-LOOKING MAN I'VE EVER SEEN!
MY LEGS!
MY CHEST!
JIMMY, WHO ARE YOU TALKING TO? FOR GOD'S SAKE, DON'T GO CRAZY ON US. GET US OUT!
YOU HEARD HIM. I'M NOT REALLY HERE.
BUT I CAN SEE YOU.
I'M ONLY IN YOUR MIND.
NO! YESTERDAY, WHEN YOU FIRST CAME TO ME...

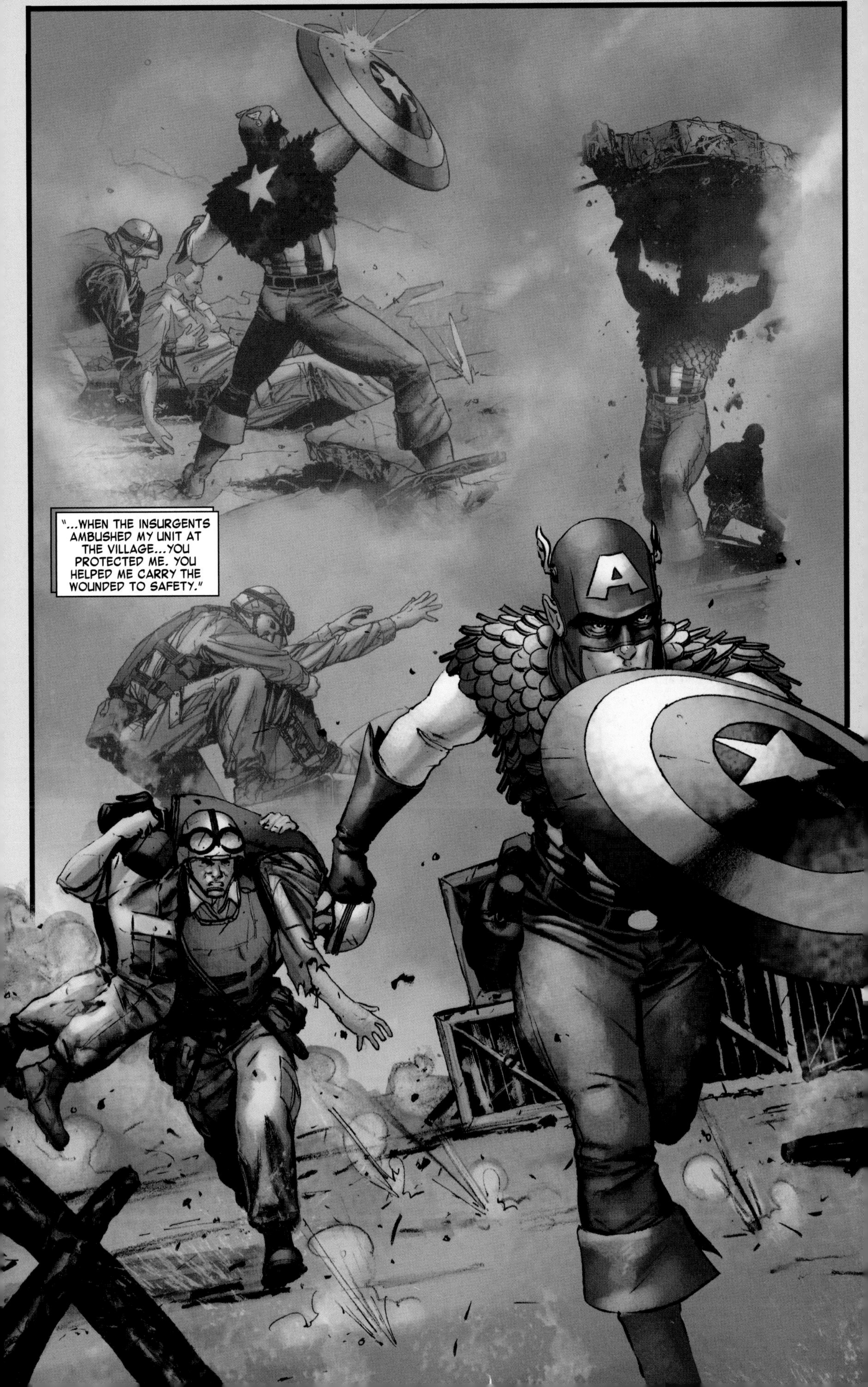
"...WHEN THE INSURGENTS AMBUSHED MY UNIT AT THE VILLAGE...YOU PROTECTED ME. YOU HELPED ME CARRY THE WOUNDED TO SAFETY."

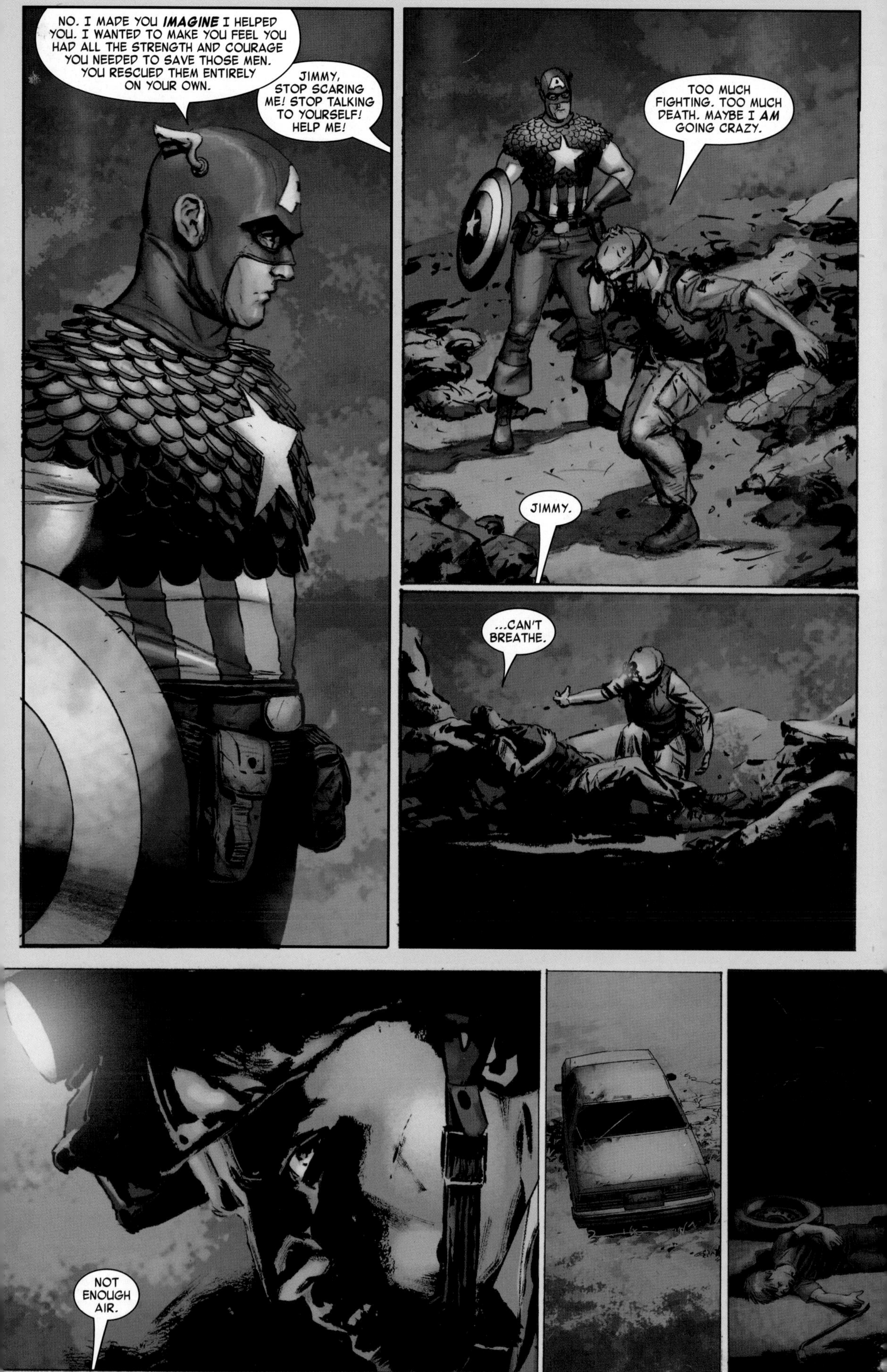

NO. I MADE YOU IMAGINE I HELPED YOU. I WANTED TO MAKE YOU FEEL YOU HAD ALL THE STRENGTH AND COURAGE YOU NEEDED TO SAVE THOSE MEN. YOU RESCUED THEM ENTIRELY ON YOUR OWN.
JIMMY, STOP SCARING ME! STOP TALKING TO YOURSELF! HELP ME!
TOO MUCH FIGHTING. TOO MUCH DEATH. MAYBE I AM GOING CRAZY.
JIMMY.
...CAN'T BREATHE.
NOT ENOUGH AIR.

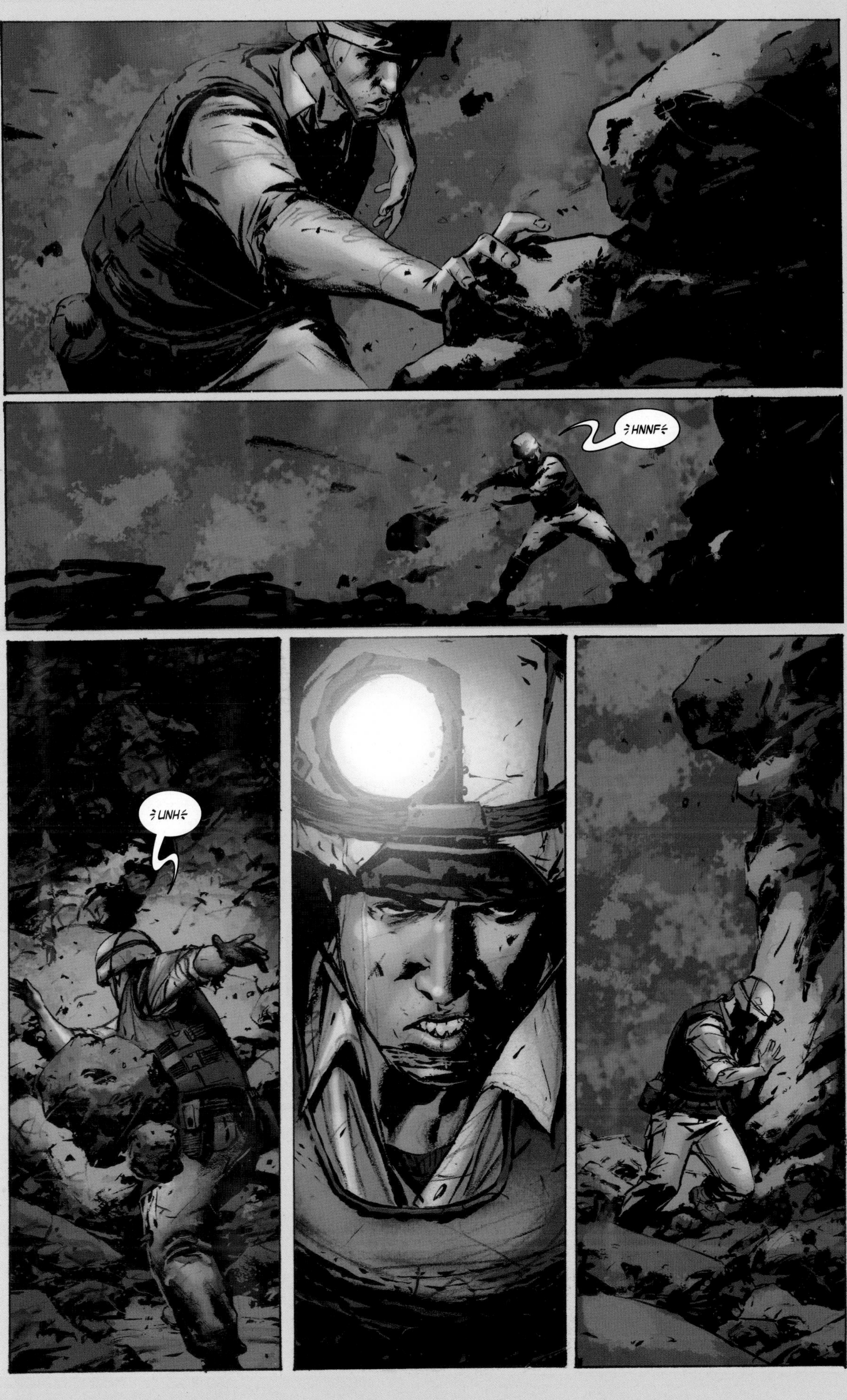
HNNF
UNH

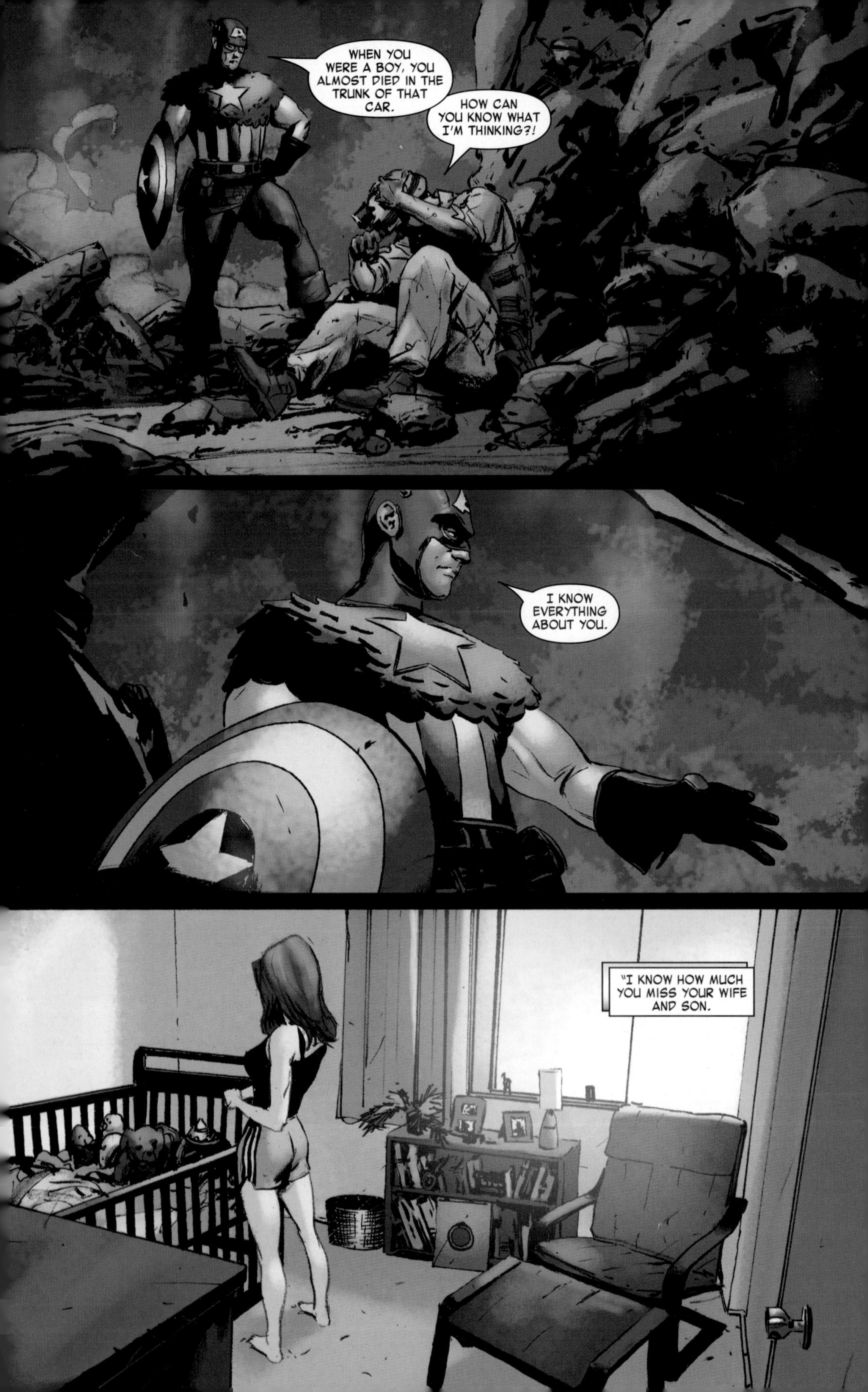
WHEN YOU WERE A BOY, YOU ALMOST DIED IN THE TRUNK OF THAT CAR.
HOW CAN YOU KNOW WHAT I'M THINKING?!
I KNOW EVERYTHING ABOUT YOU.
"I KNOW HOW MUCH YOU MISS YOUR WIFE AND SON.

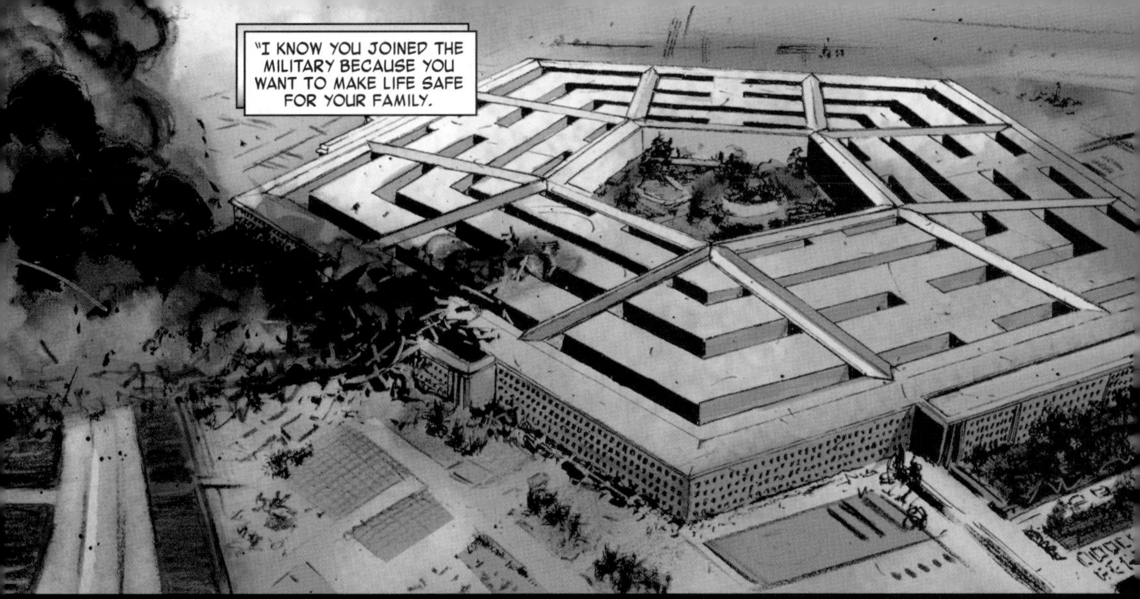
"I KNOW YOU JOINED THE MILITARY BECAUSE YOU WANT TO MAKE LIFE SAFE FOR YOUR FAMILY.

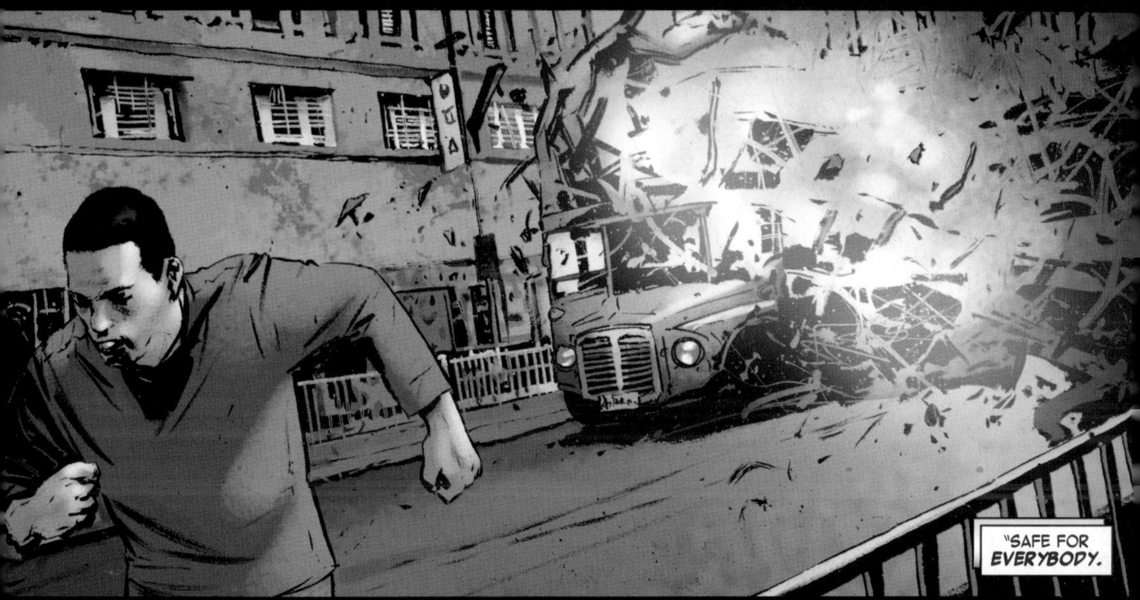
"SAFE FOR *EVERYBODY*.

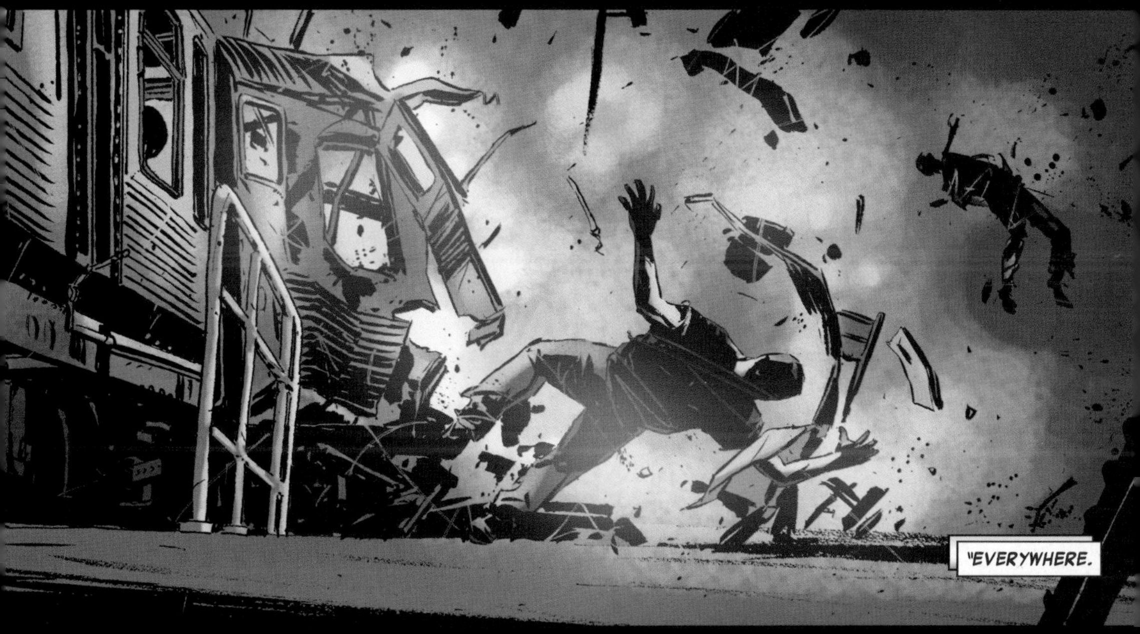
"*EVERYWHERE*.

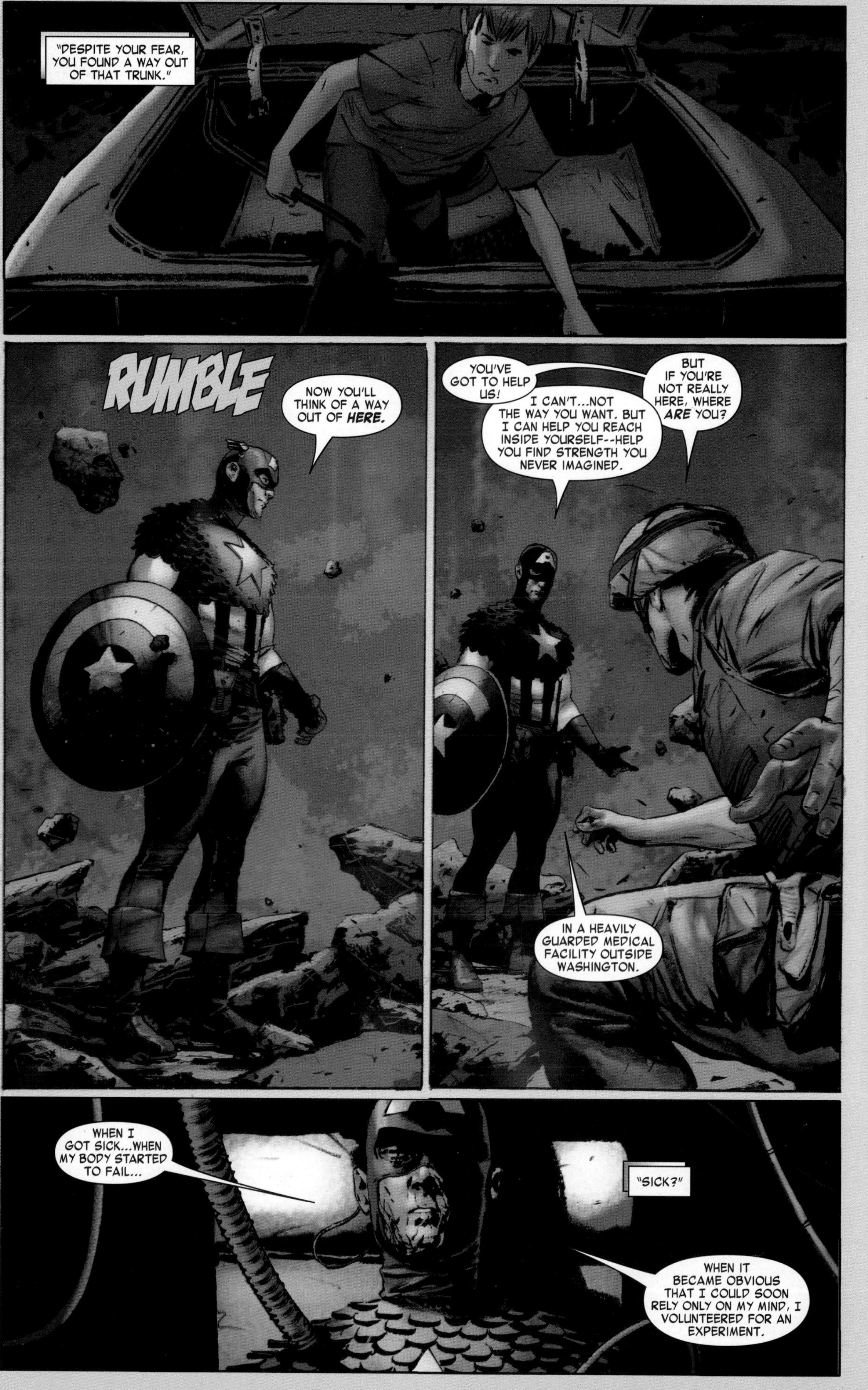
"DESPITE YOUR FEAR, YOU FOUND A WAY OUT OF THAT TRUNK."
RUMBLE
NOW YOU'LL THINK OF A WAY OUT OF HERE.
YOU'VE GOT TO HELP US!
I CAN'T...NOT THE WAY YOU WANT. BUT I CAN HELP YOU REACH INSIDE YOURSELF--HELP YOU FIND STRENGTH YOU NEVER IMAGINED.
BUT IF YOU'RE NOT REALLY HERE, WHERE ARE YOU?
IN A HEAVILY GUARDED MEDICAL FACILITY OUTSIDE WASHINGTON.
WHEN I GOT SICK...WHEN MY BODY STARTED TO FAIL...
"SICK?"
WHEN IT BECAME OBVIOUS THAT I COULD SOON RELY ONLY ON MY MIND, I VOLUNTEERED FOR AN EXPERIMENT.

"IT WAS DANGEROUS, BUT I DIDN'T CARE. ALTHOUGH MY BODY WAS USELESS, I REFUSED TO STOP HELPING PEOPLE.

"THE PROCESS THAT GAVE ME THE PHYSICAL POWER OF CAPTAIN AMERICA ALSO AMPLIFIED THE POWER OF MY BRAIN, AND *THAT* POWER REMAINED STRONG.

"IN MY YOUTH, BEFORE I BECAME WHAT I AM, I WORKED AS A COMMERCIAL ARTIST.

"IT'S AN IDEAL SKILL FOR...

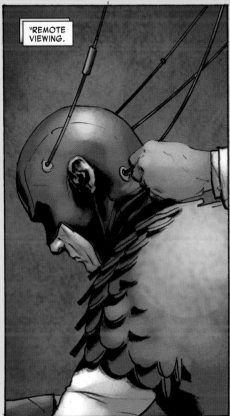

"REMOTE VIEWING.

"IN PROJECTS LIKE SUN STREAK AND GRILL FLAME, OUR SCIENTISTS EXPERIMENTED WITH IT FOR DECADES.

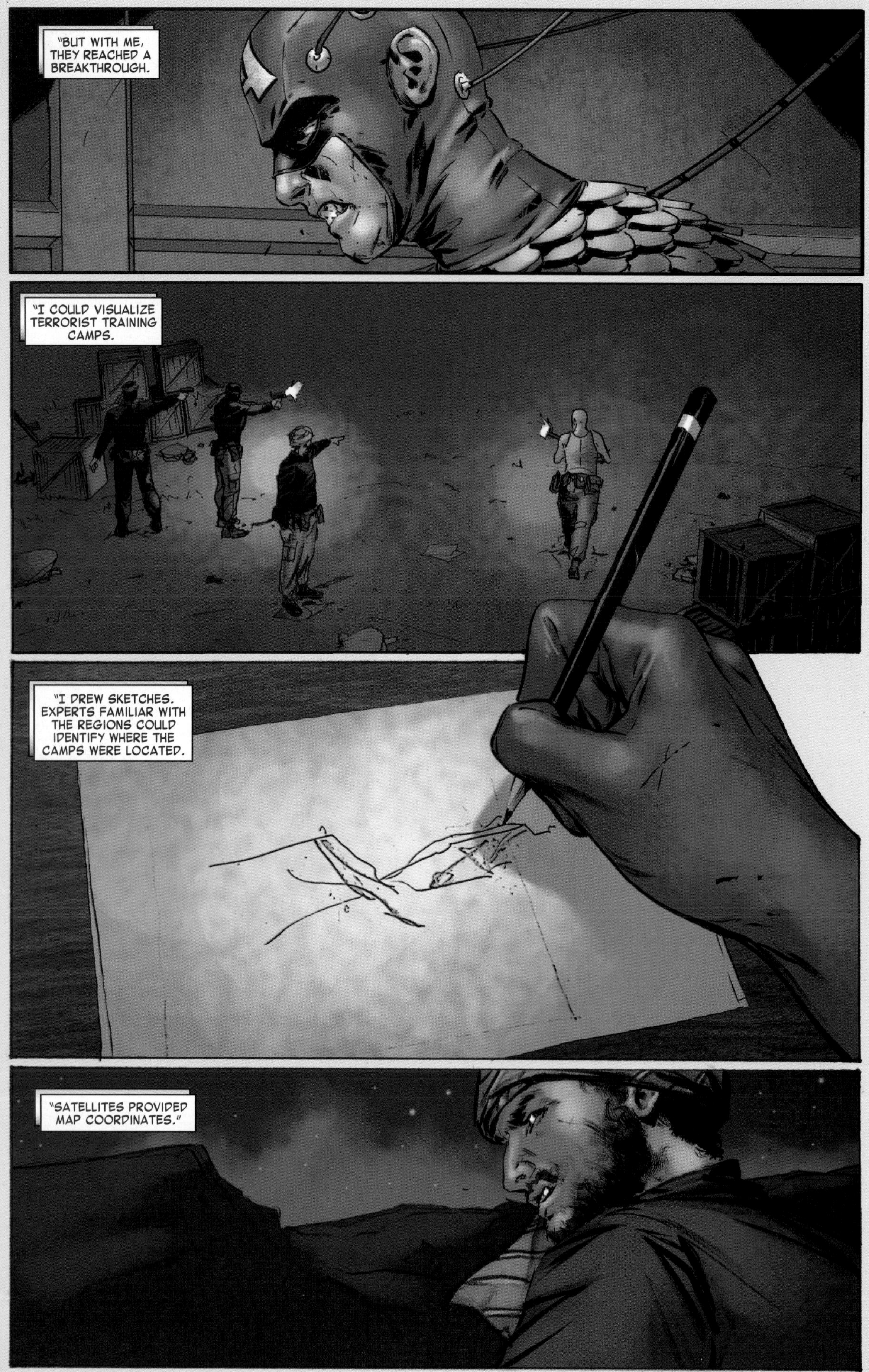
"BUT WITH ME, THEY REACHED A BREAKTHROUGH.
"I COULD VISUALIZE TERRORIST TRAINING CAMPS.
"I DREW SKETCHES. EXPERTS FAMILIAR WITH THE REGIONS COULD IDENTIFY WHERE THE CAMPS WERE LOCATED.
"SATELLITES PROVIDED MAP COORDINATES."

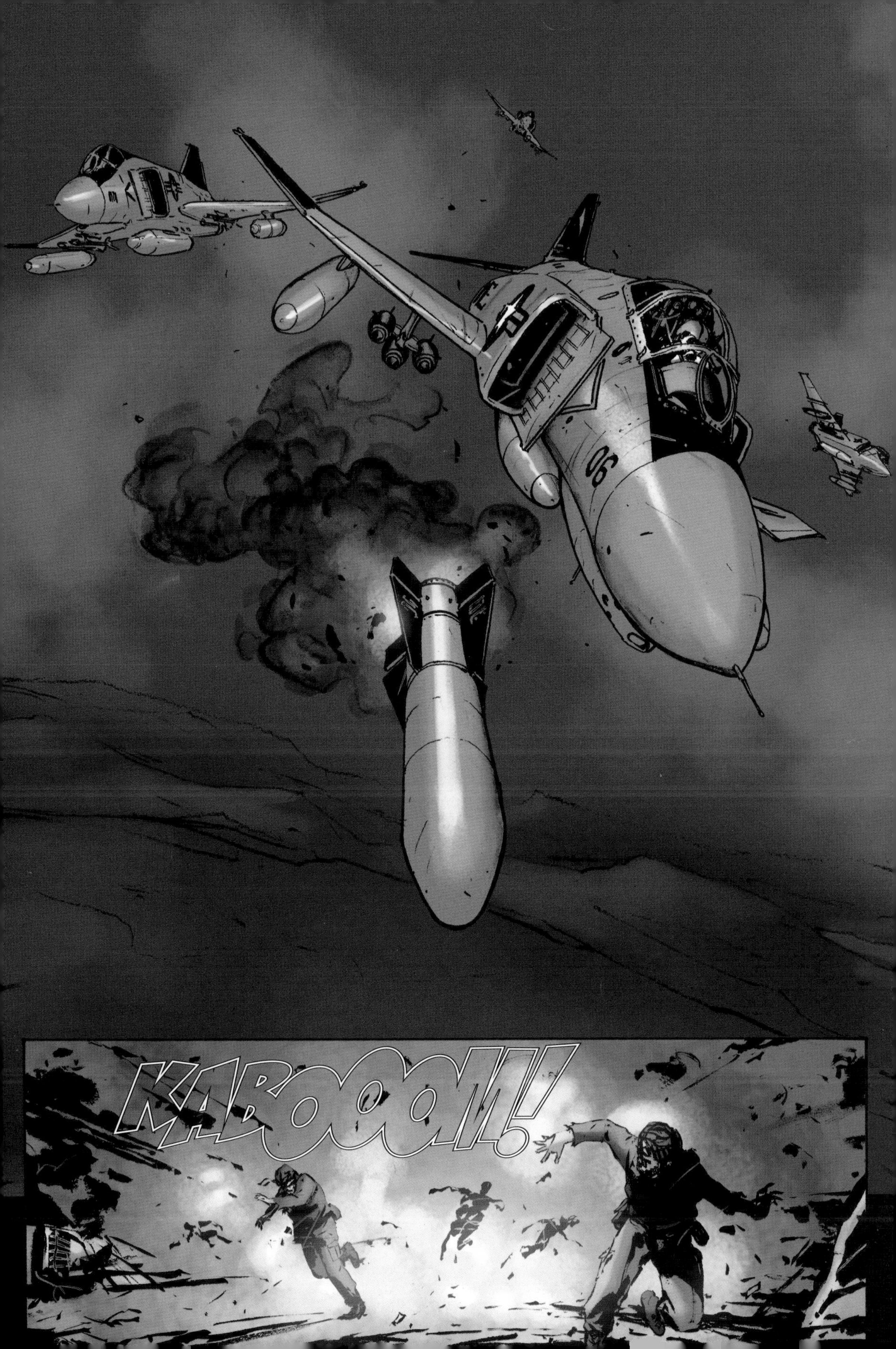
KABOOOM!

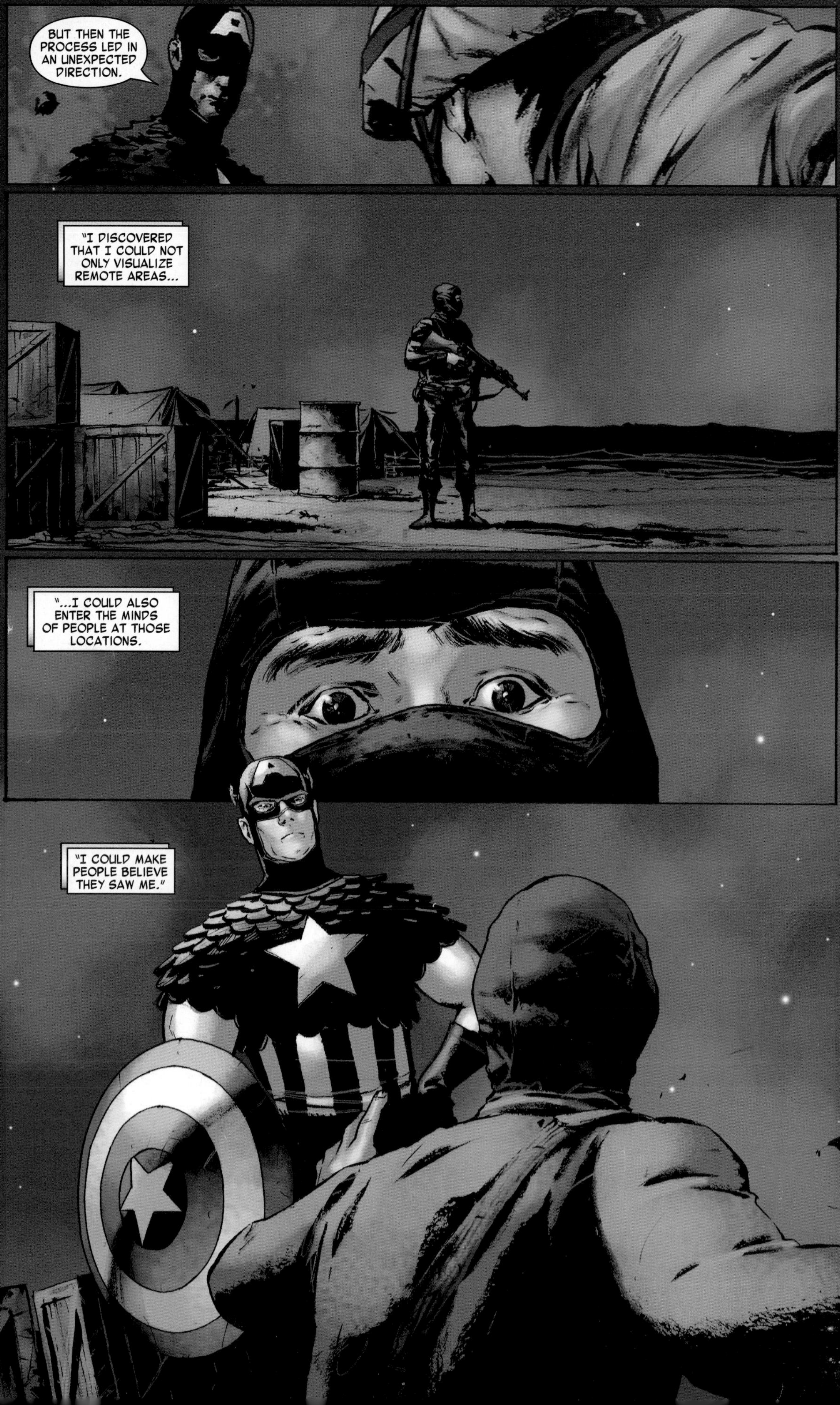
BUT THEN THE PROCESS LED IN AN UNEXPECTED DIRECTION.
"I DISCOVERED THAT I COULD NOT ONLY VISUALIZE REMOTE AREAS...
"...I COULD ALSO ENTER THE MINDS OF PEOPLE AT THOSE LOCATIONS.
"I COULD MAKE PEOPLE BELIEVE THEY SAW ME."

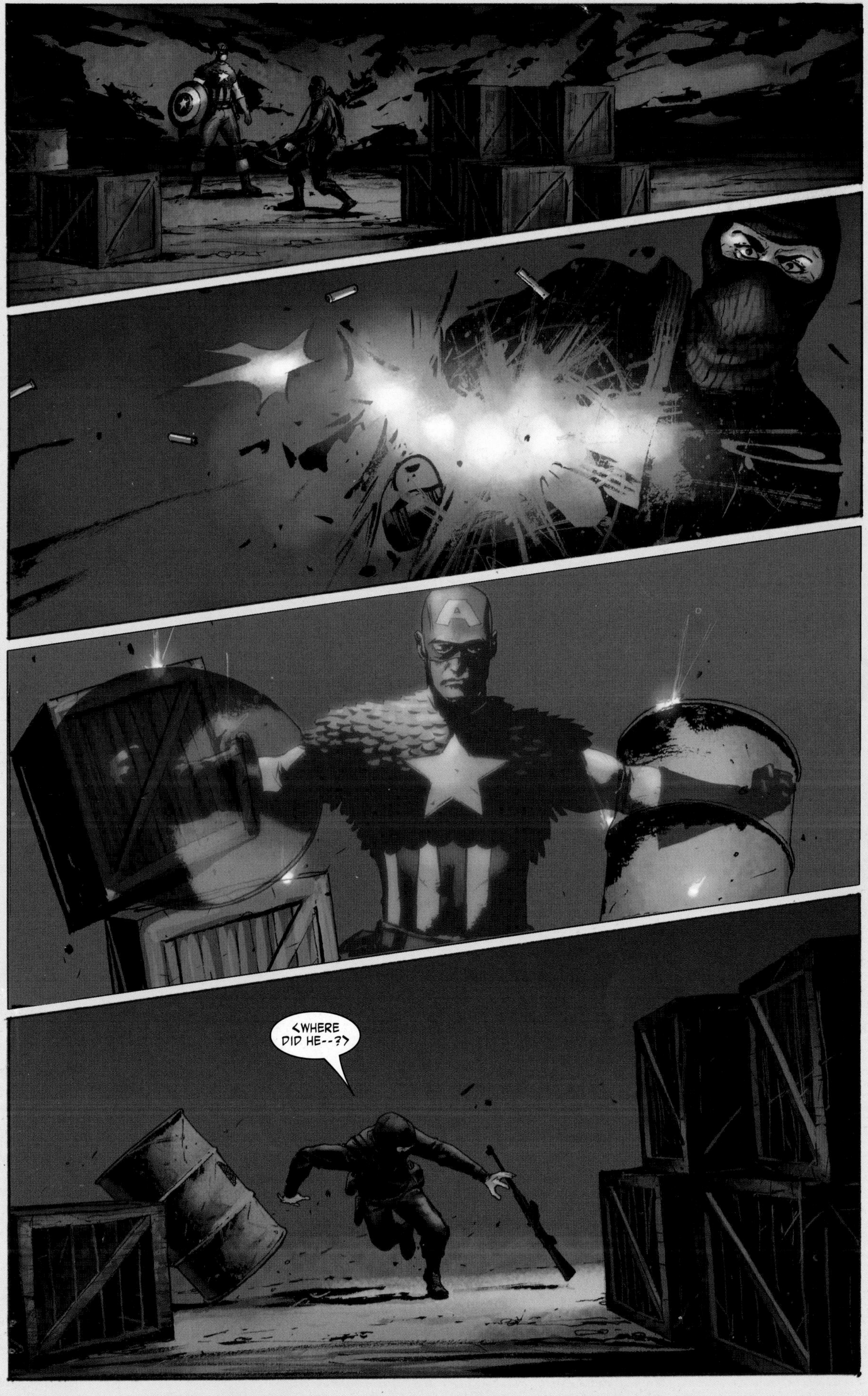
<WHERE DID HE--?>

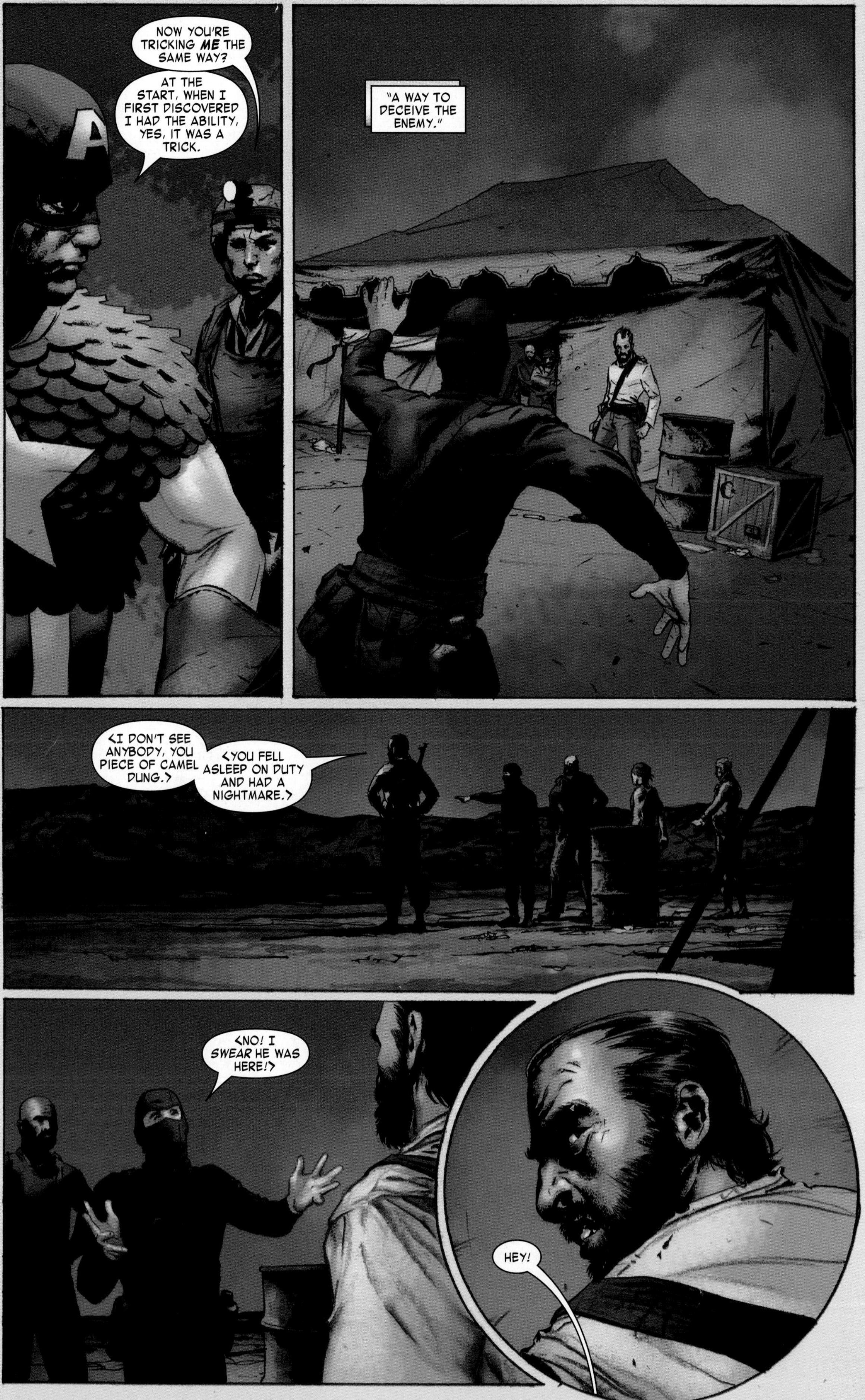
NOW YOU'RE TRICKING *ME* THE SAME WAY?
AT THE START, WHEN I FIRST DISCOVERED I HAD THE ABILITY, YES, IT WAS A TRICK.
"A WAY TO DECEIVE THE ENEMY."
<I DON'T SEE ANYBODY, YOU PIECE OF CAMEL DUNG.>
<YOU FELL ASLEEP ON DUTY AND HAD A NIGHTMARE.>
<NO! I *SWEAR* HE WAS HERE!>
HEY!

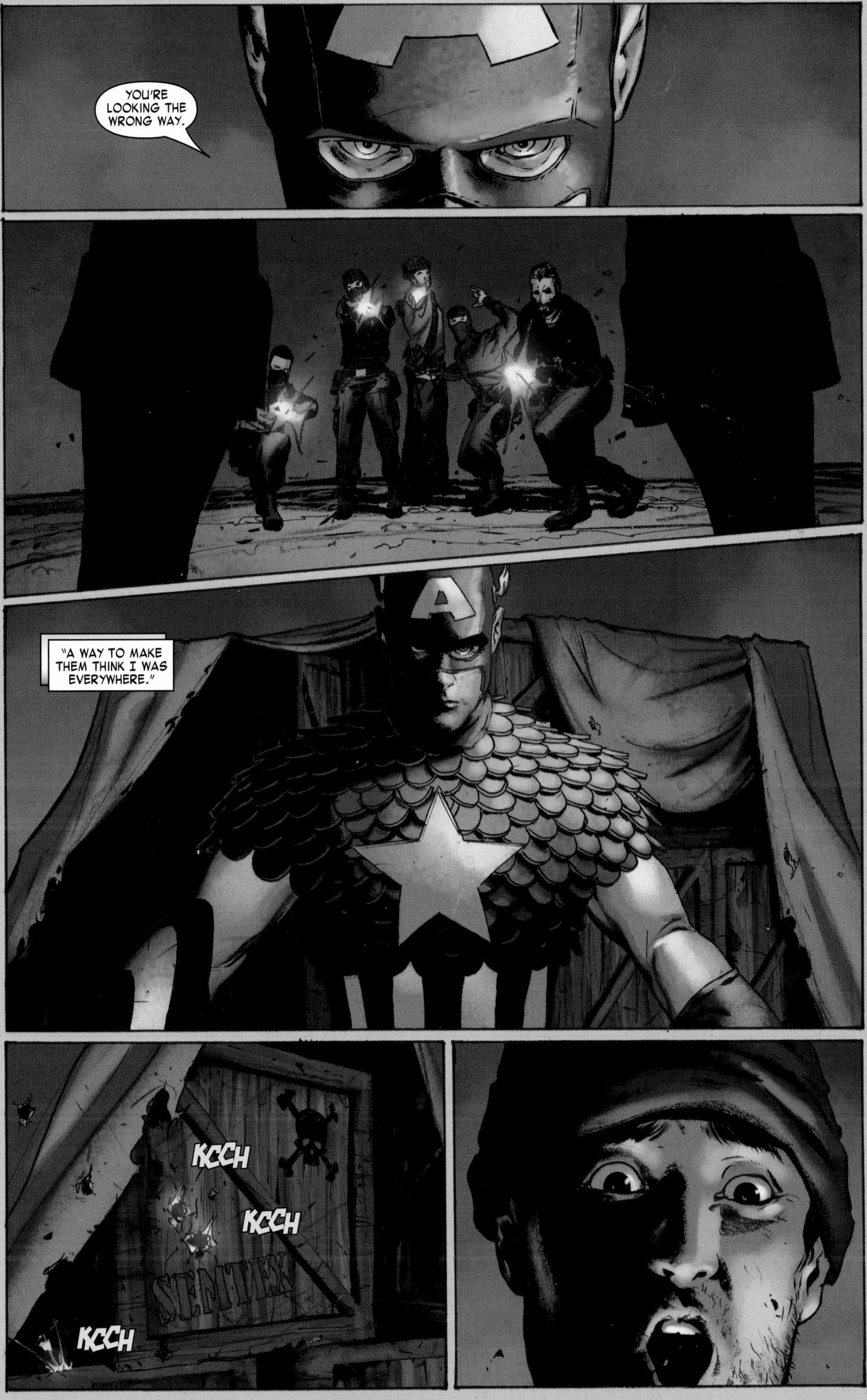
YOU'RE LOOKING THE WRONG WAY.
"A WAY TO MAKE THEM THINK I WAS EVERYWHERE."
KCCH
KCCH
KCCH

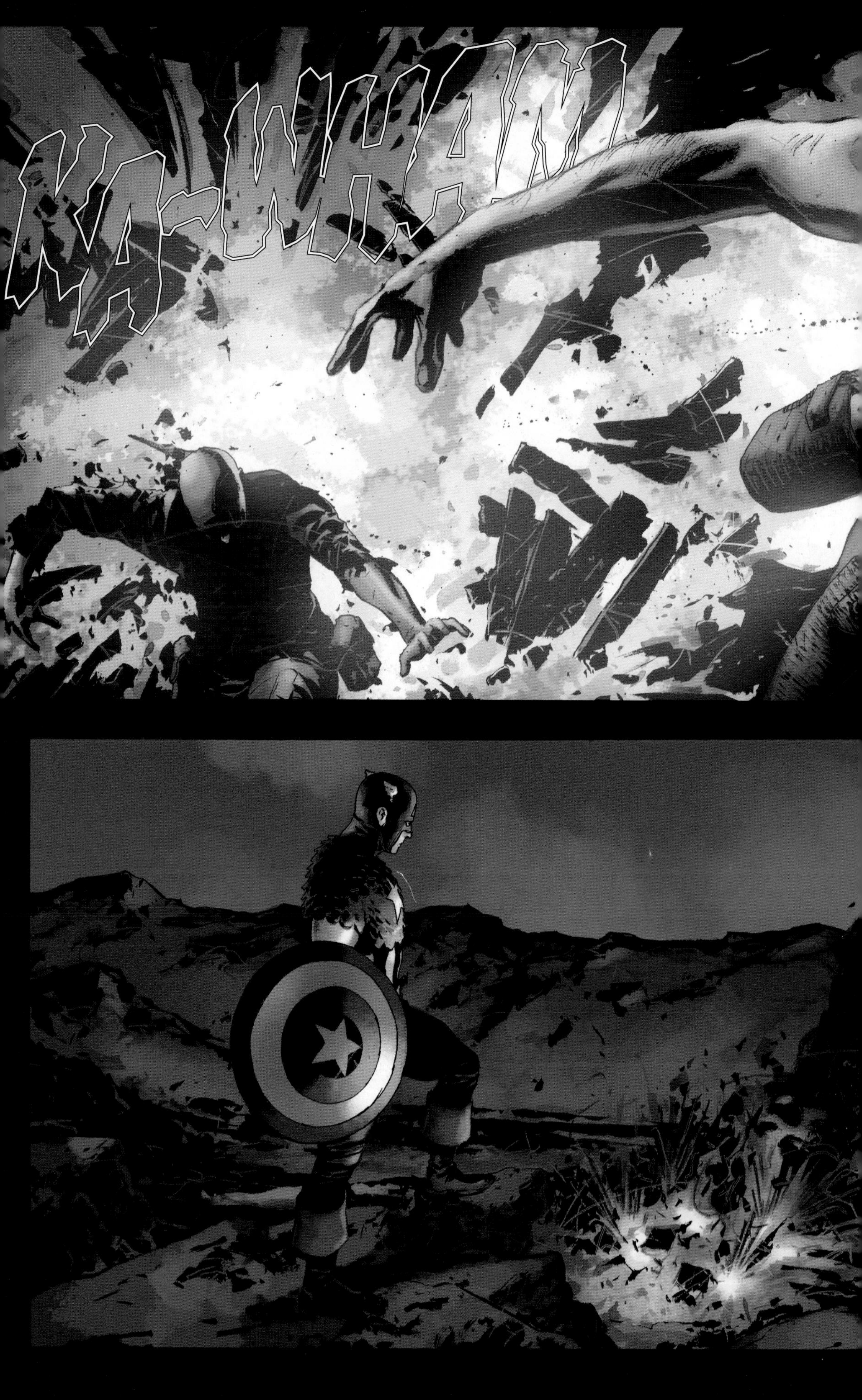
KA-WHAM

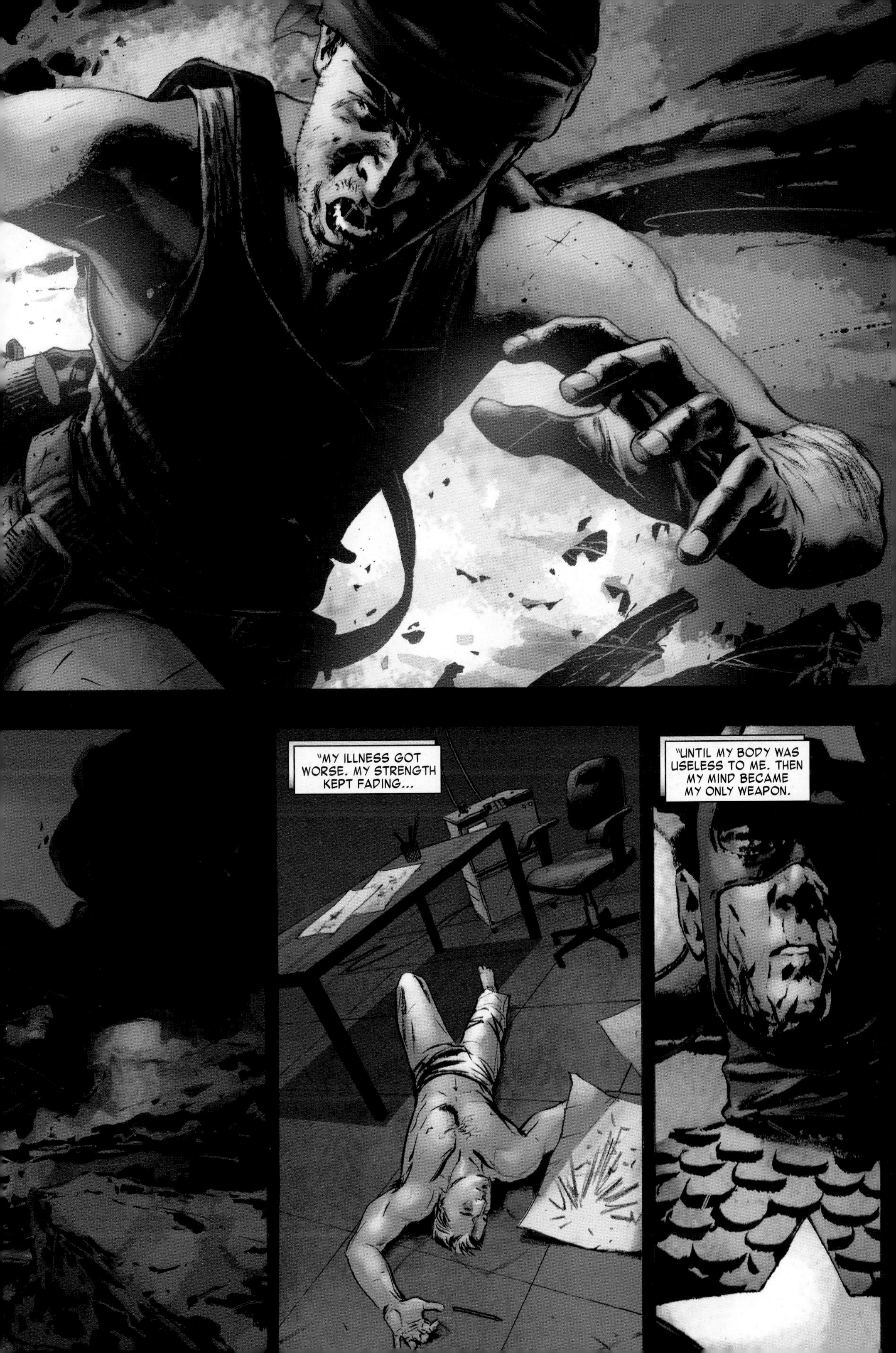
"MY ILLNESS GOT WORSE. MY STRENGTH KEPT FADING...
"UNTIL MY BODY WAS USELESS TO ME. THEN MY MIND BECAME MY ONLY WEAPON.

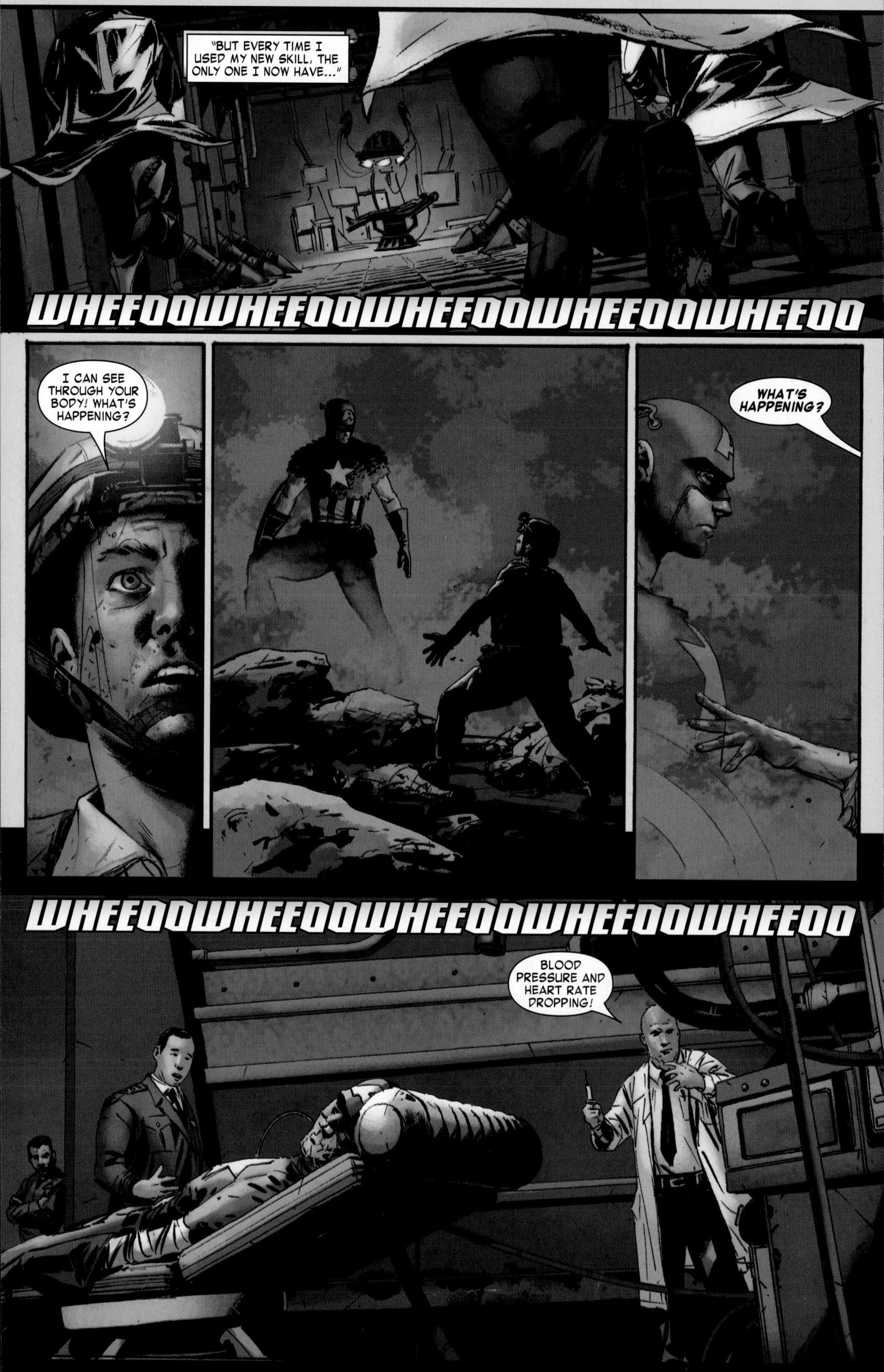
"BUT EVERY TIME I USED MY NEW SKILL, THE ONLY ONE I NOW HAVE..."
WHEEOOWHEEOOWHEEOOWHEEOOWHEEOO
I CAN SEE THROUGH YOUR BODY! WHAT'S HAPPENING?
WHAT'S HAPPENING?
WHEEOOWHEEOOWHEEOOWHEEOOWHEEOO
BLOOD PRESSURE AND HEART RATE DROPPING!

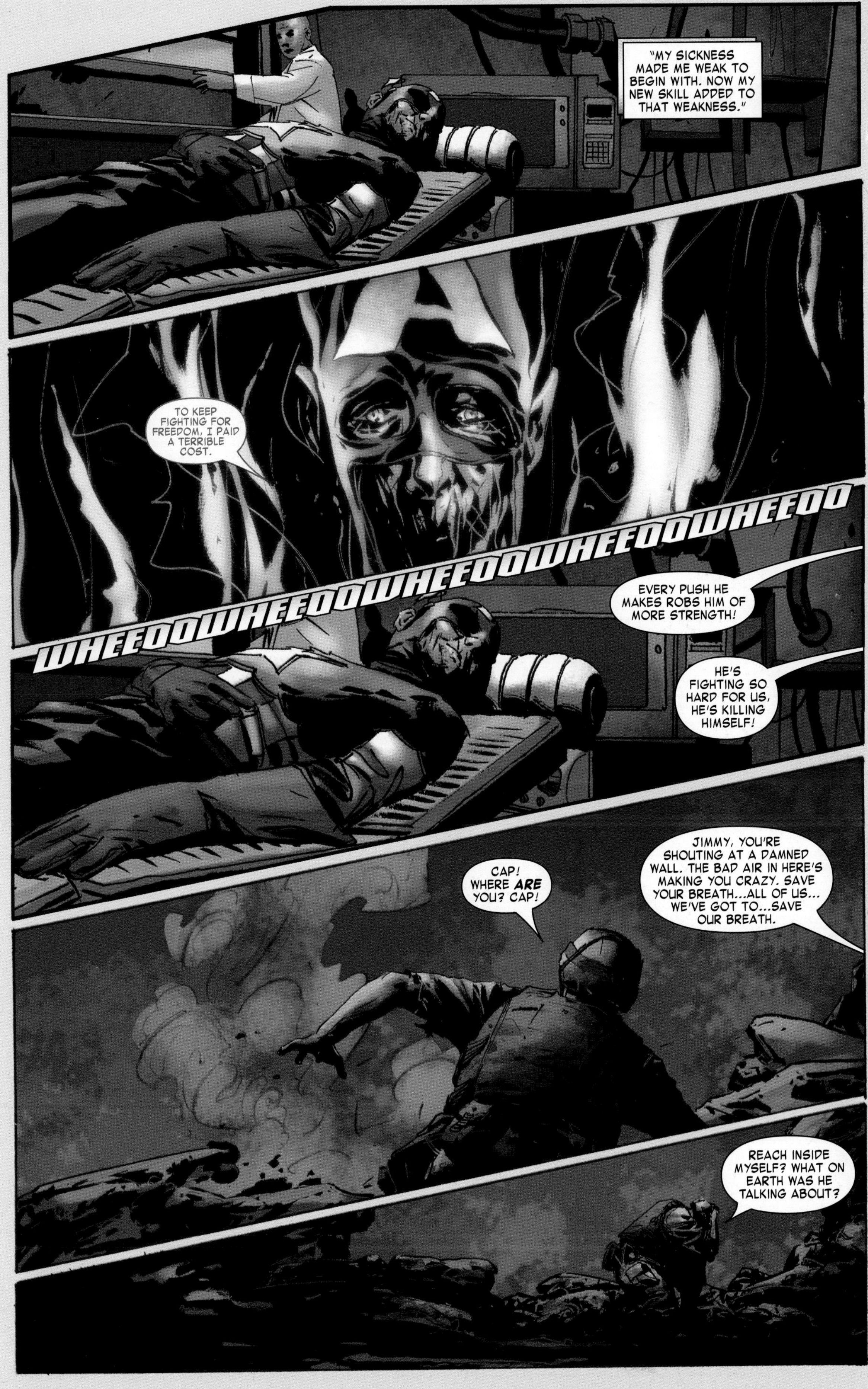
"MY SICKNESS MADE ME WEAK TO BEGIN WITH. NOW MY NEW SKILL ADDED TO THAT WEAKNESS."
TO KEEP FIGHTING FOR FREEDOM, I PAID A TERRIBLE COST.
WHEEOOWHEEOOWHEEOOWHEEOO
EVERY PUSH HE MAKES ROBS HIM OF MORE STRENGTH!
HE'S FIGHTING SO HARD FOR US, HE'S KILLING HIMSELF!
CAP! WHERE ARE YOU? CAP!
JIMMY, YOU'RE SHOUTING AT A DAMNED WALL. THE BAD AIR IN HERE'S MAKING YOU CRAZY. SAVE YOUR BREATH...ALL OF US... WE'VE GOT TO...SAVE OUR BREATH.
REACH INSIDE MYSELF? WHAT ON EARTH WAS HE TALKING ABOUT?

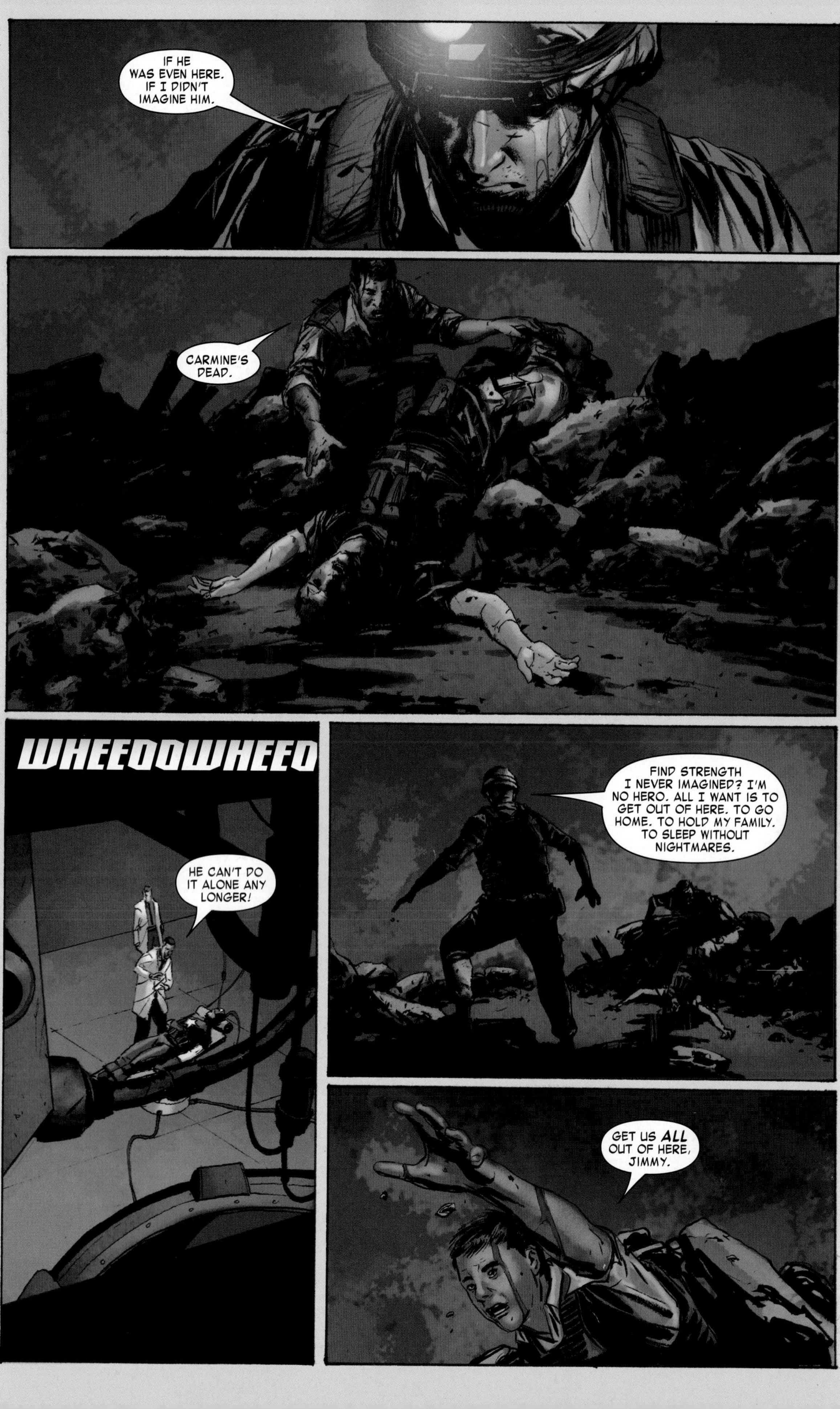
IF HE WAS EVEN HERE. IF I DIDN'T IMAGINE HIM.
CARMINE'S DEAD.
WHEEOOWHEEO
HE CAN'T DO IT ALONE ANY LONGER!
FIND STRENGTH I NEVER IMAGINED? I'M NO HERO. ALL I WANT IS TO GET OUT OF HERE. TO GO HOME. TO HOLD MY FAMILY. TO SLEEP WITHOUT NIGHTMARES.
GET US ALL OUT OF HERE, JIMMY.

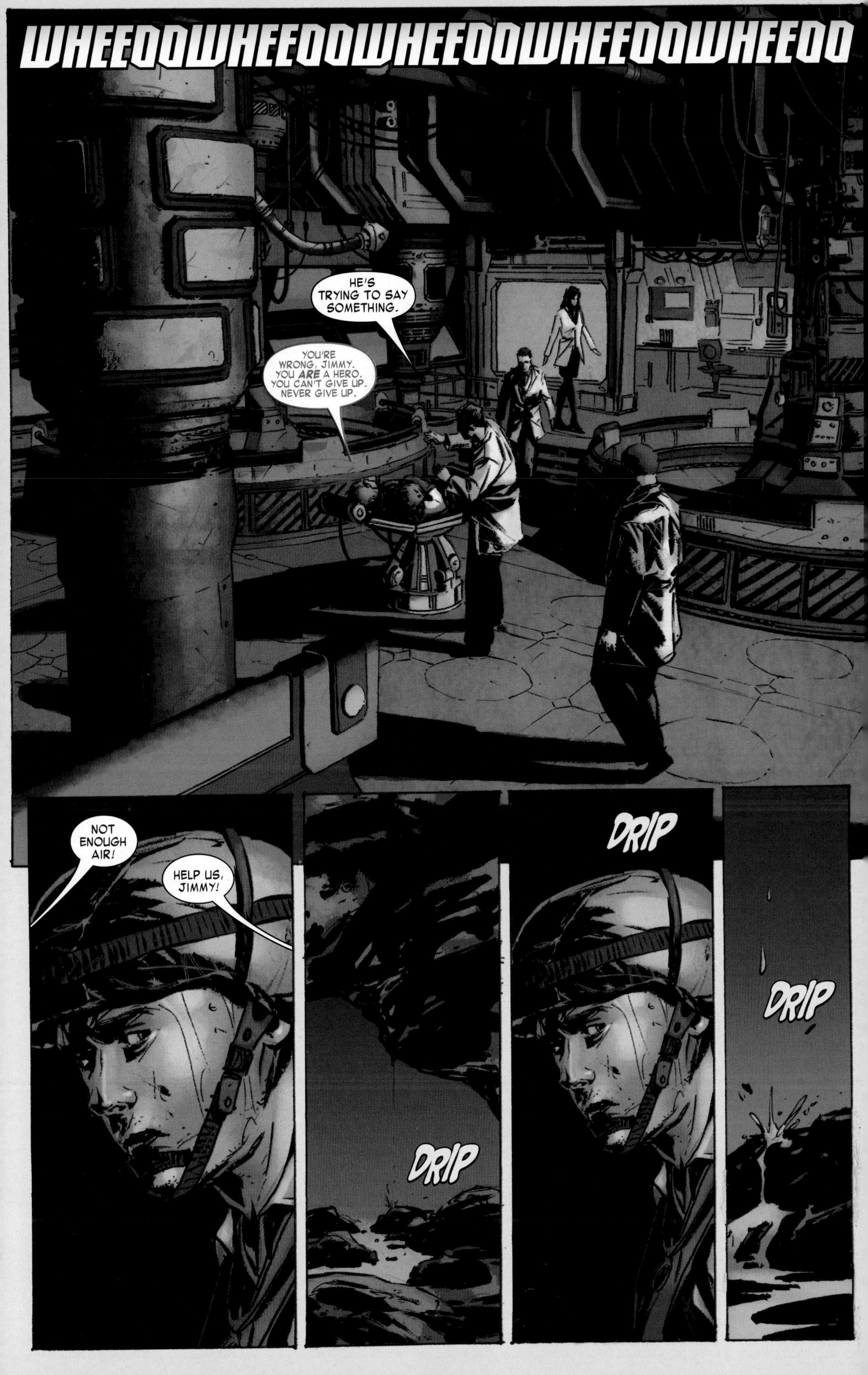
WHEEOOWHEEOOWHEEOOWHEEOOWHEEOO
HE'S TRYING TO SAY SOMETHING.
YOU'RE WRONG, JIMMY. YOU ARE A HERO. YOU CAN'T GIVE UP. NEVER GIVE UP.
NOT ENOUGH AIR!
HELP US, JIMMY!
DRIP
DRIP
DRIP

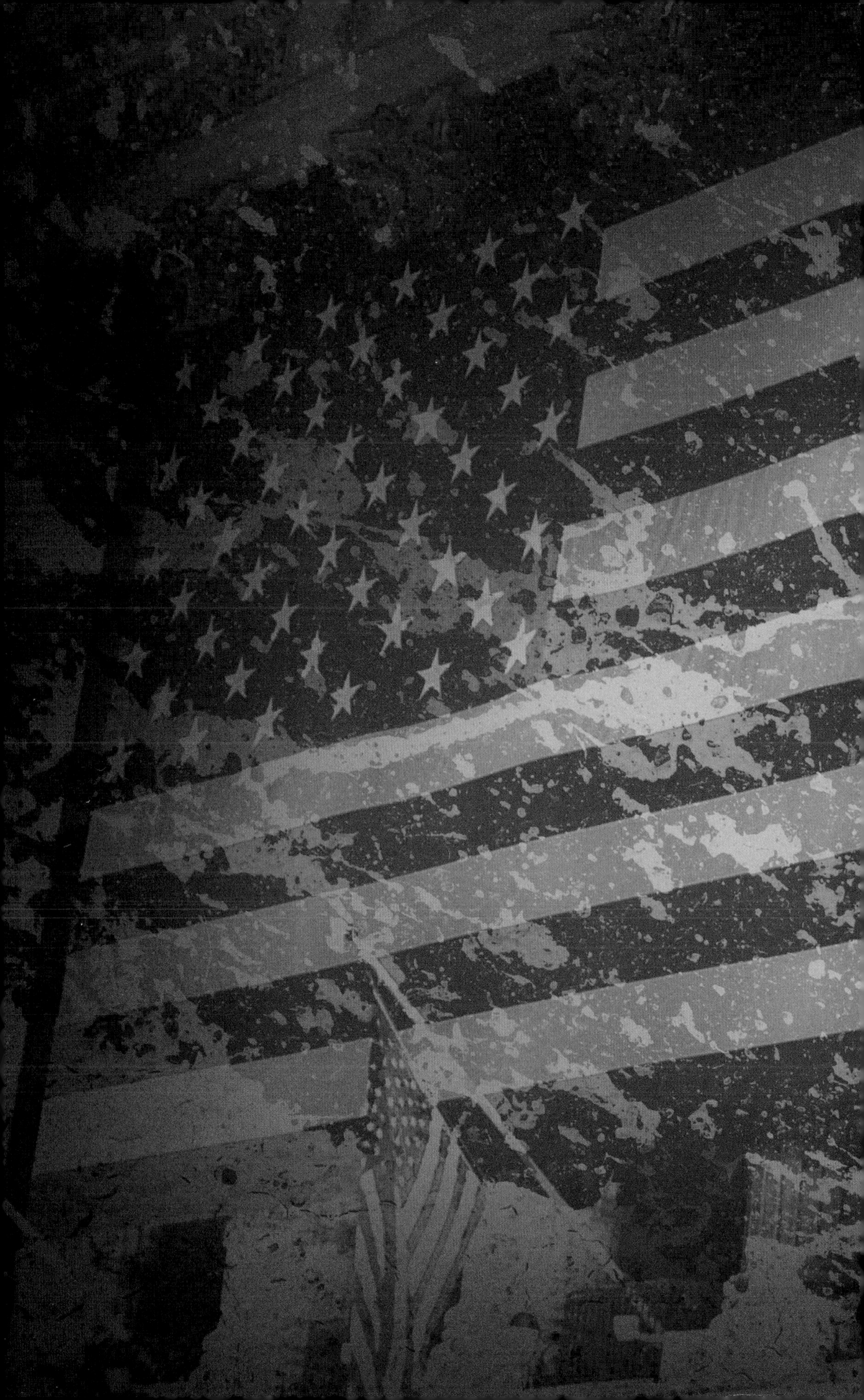

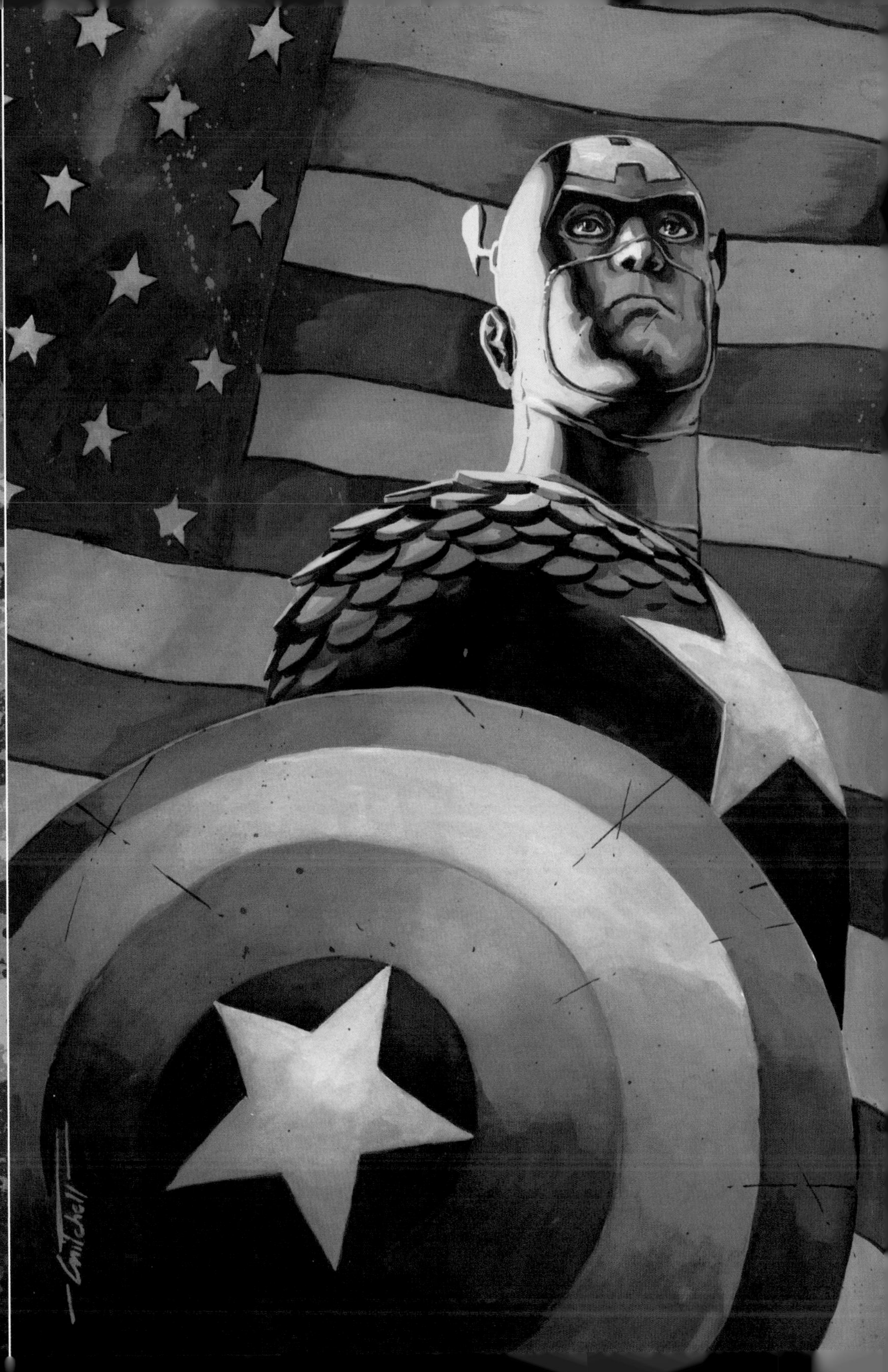

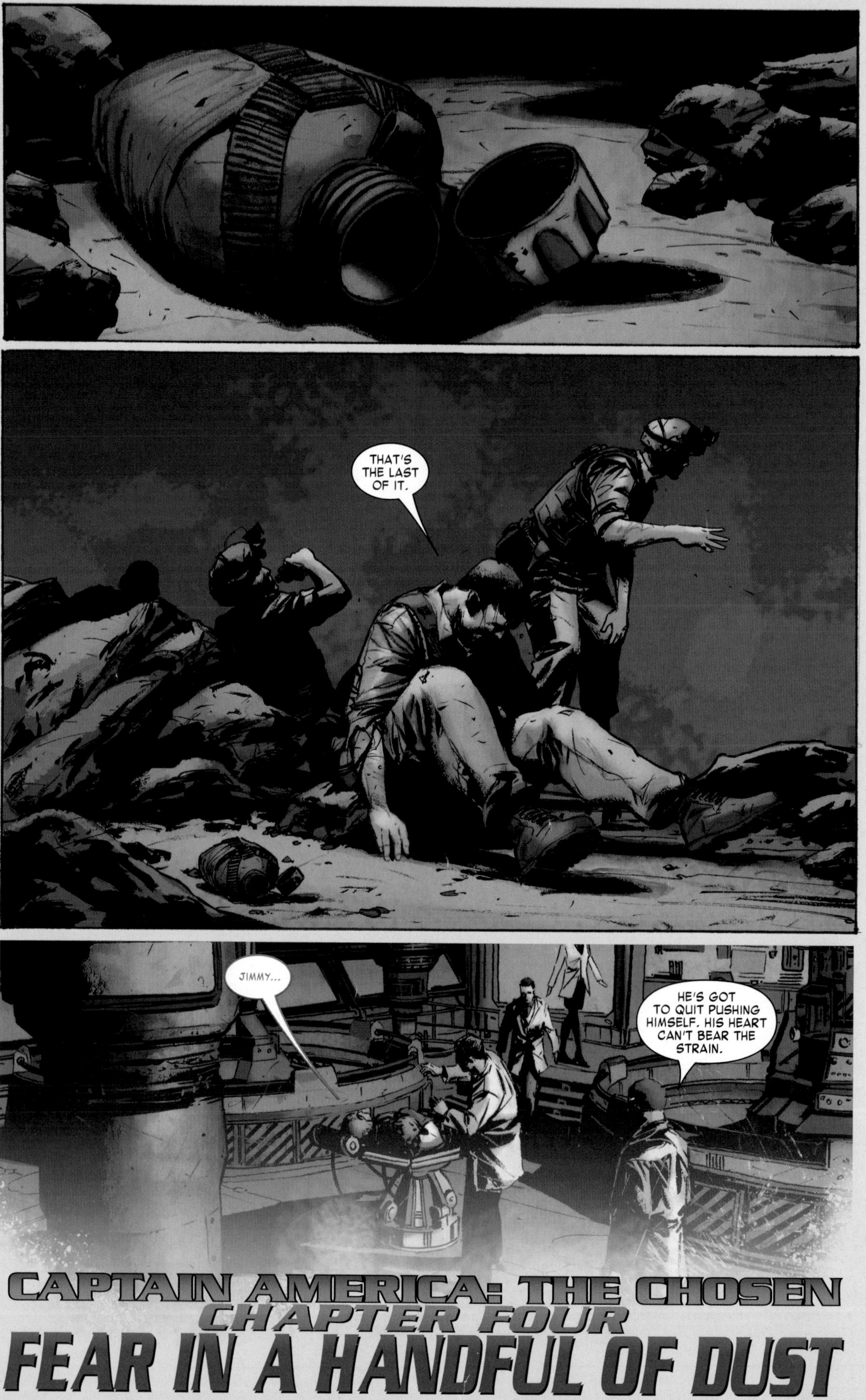
THAT'S THE LAST OF IT.
JIMMY...
HE'S GOT TO QUIT PUSHING HIMSELF. HIS HEART CAN'T BEAR THE STRAIN.

CAPTAIN AMERICA: THE CHOSEN
CHAPTER FOUR
FEAR IN A HANDFUL OF DUST

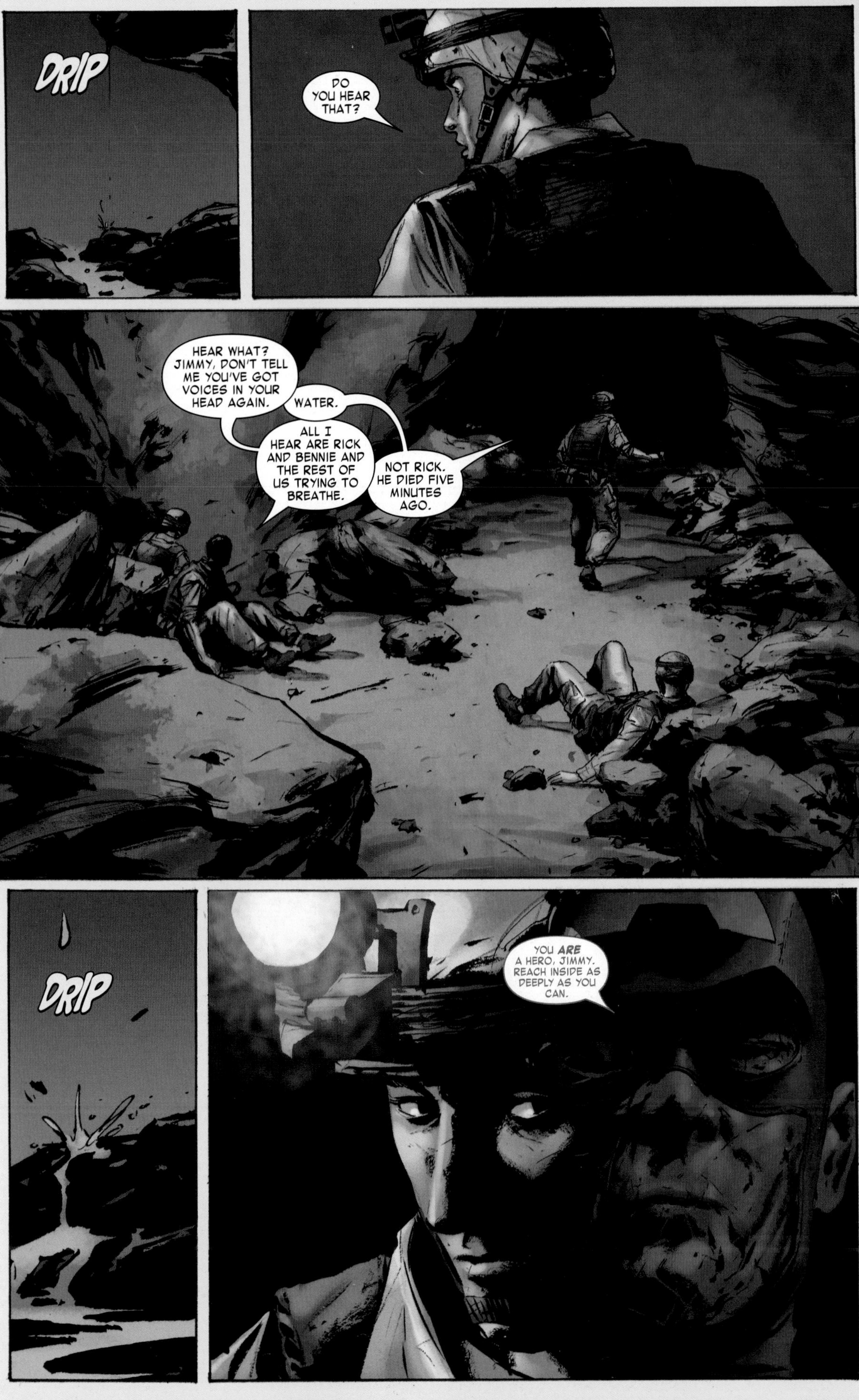
DRIP
DO YOU HEAR THAT?
HEAR WHAT? JIMMY, DON'T TELL ME YOU'VE GOT VOICES IN YOUR HEAD AGAIN.
WATER.
ALL I HEAR ARE RICK AND BENNIE AND THE REST OF US TRYING TO BREATHE.
NOT RICK. HE DIED FIVE MINUTES AGO.
DRIP
YOU ARE A HERO, JIMMY. REACH INSIDE AS DEEPLY AS YOU CAN.

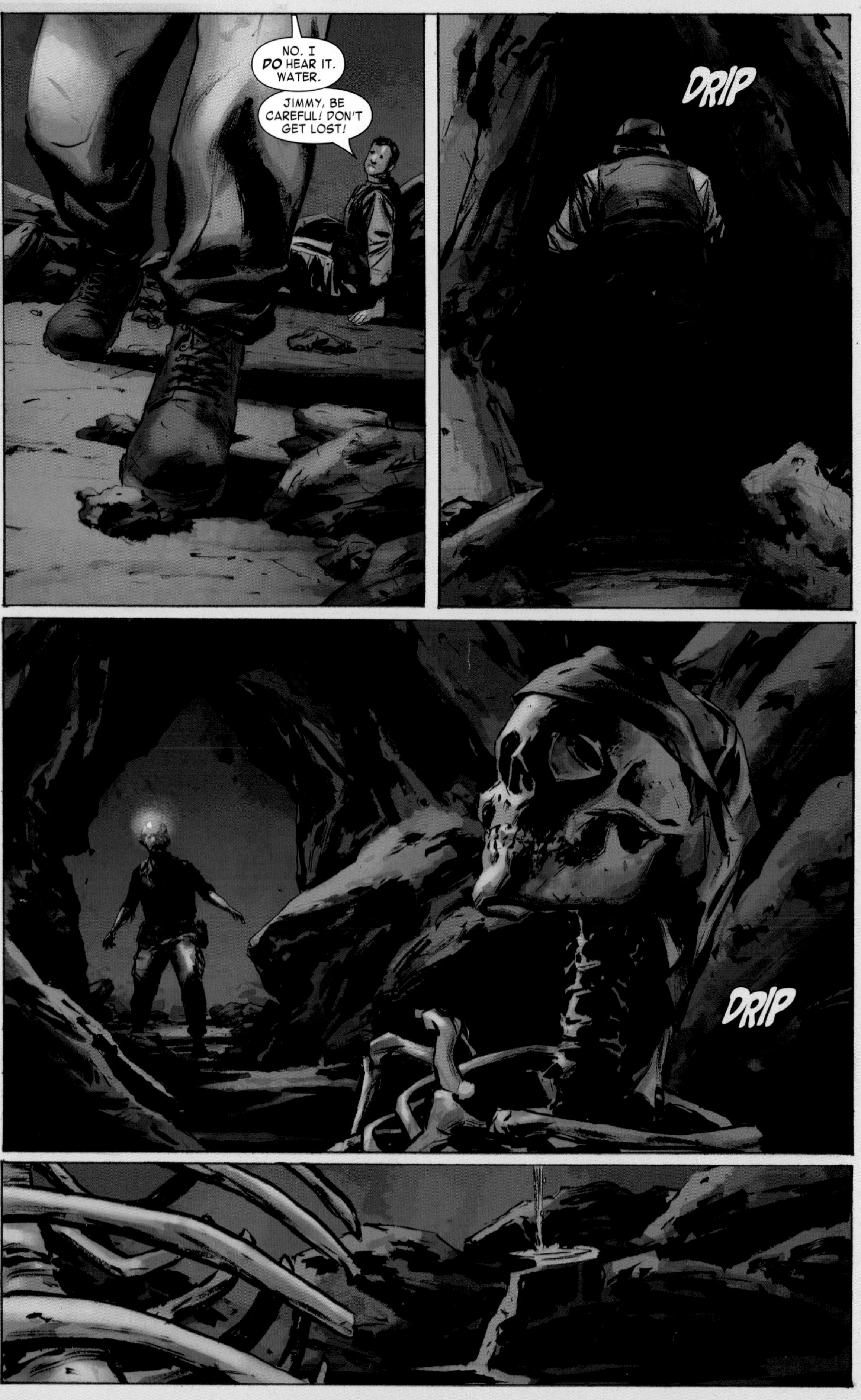
NO. I DO HEAR IT. WATER.
JIMMY, BE CAREFUL! DON'T GET LOST!
DRIP
DRIP

THANK GOD.

WAIT A SECOND.

HOW DID HE DIE?

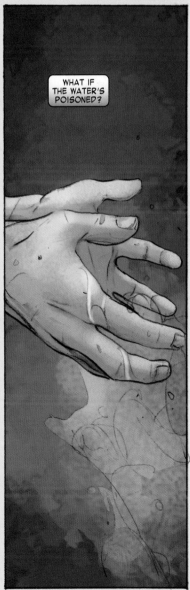

WHAT IF THE WATER'S POISONED?

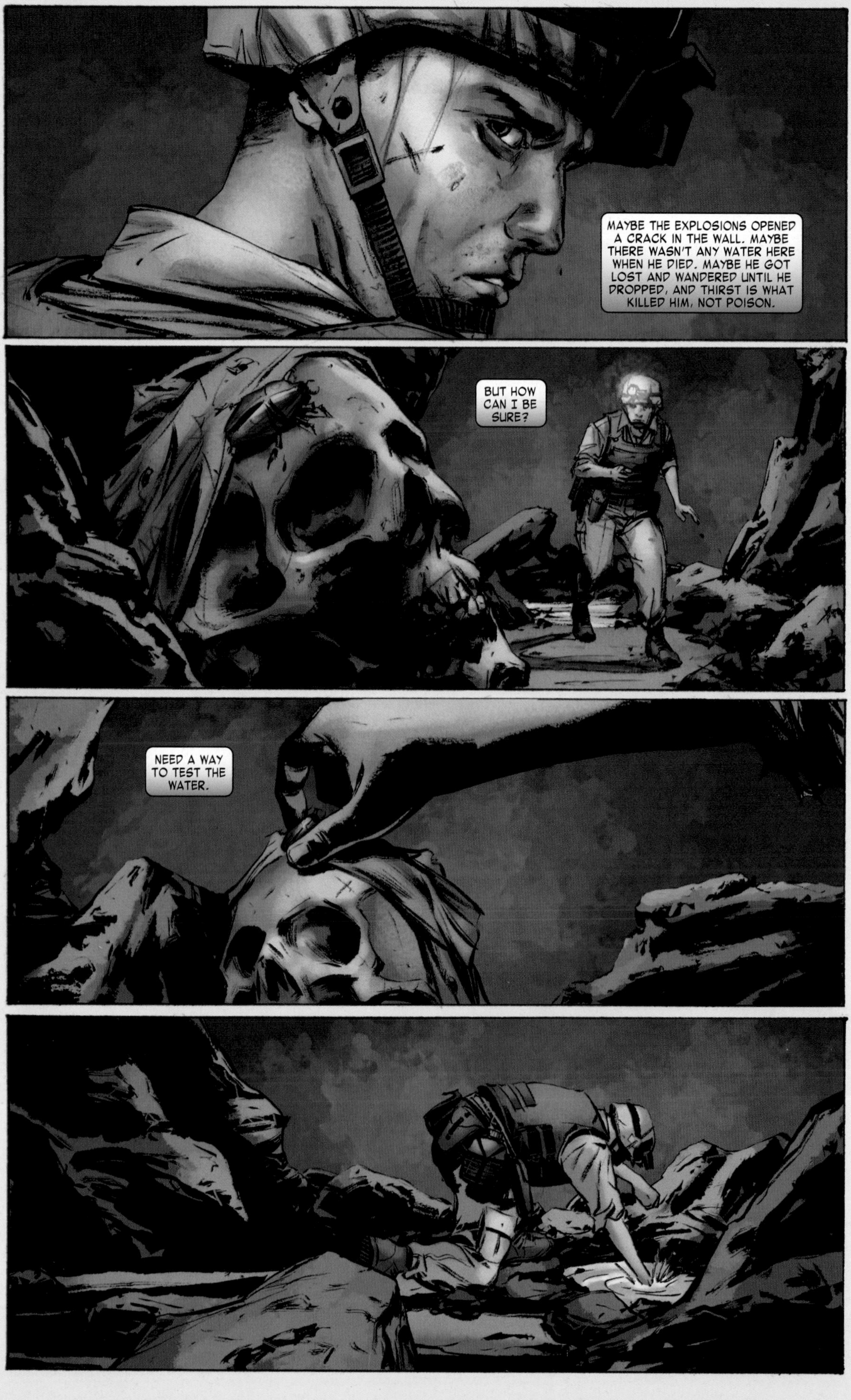
MAYBE THE EXPLOSIONS OPENED A CRACK IN THE WALL. MAYBE THERE WASN'T ANY WATER HERE WHEN HE DIED. MAYBE HE GOT LOST AND WANDERED UNTIL HE DROPPED, AND THIRST IS WHAT KILLED HIM, NOT POISON.
BUT HOW CAN I BE SURE?
NEED A WAY TO TEST THE WATER.

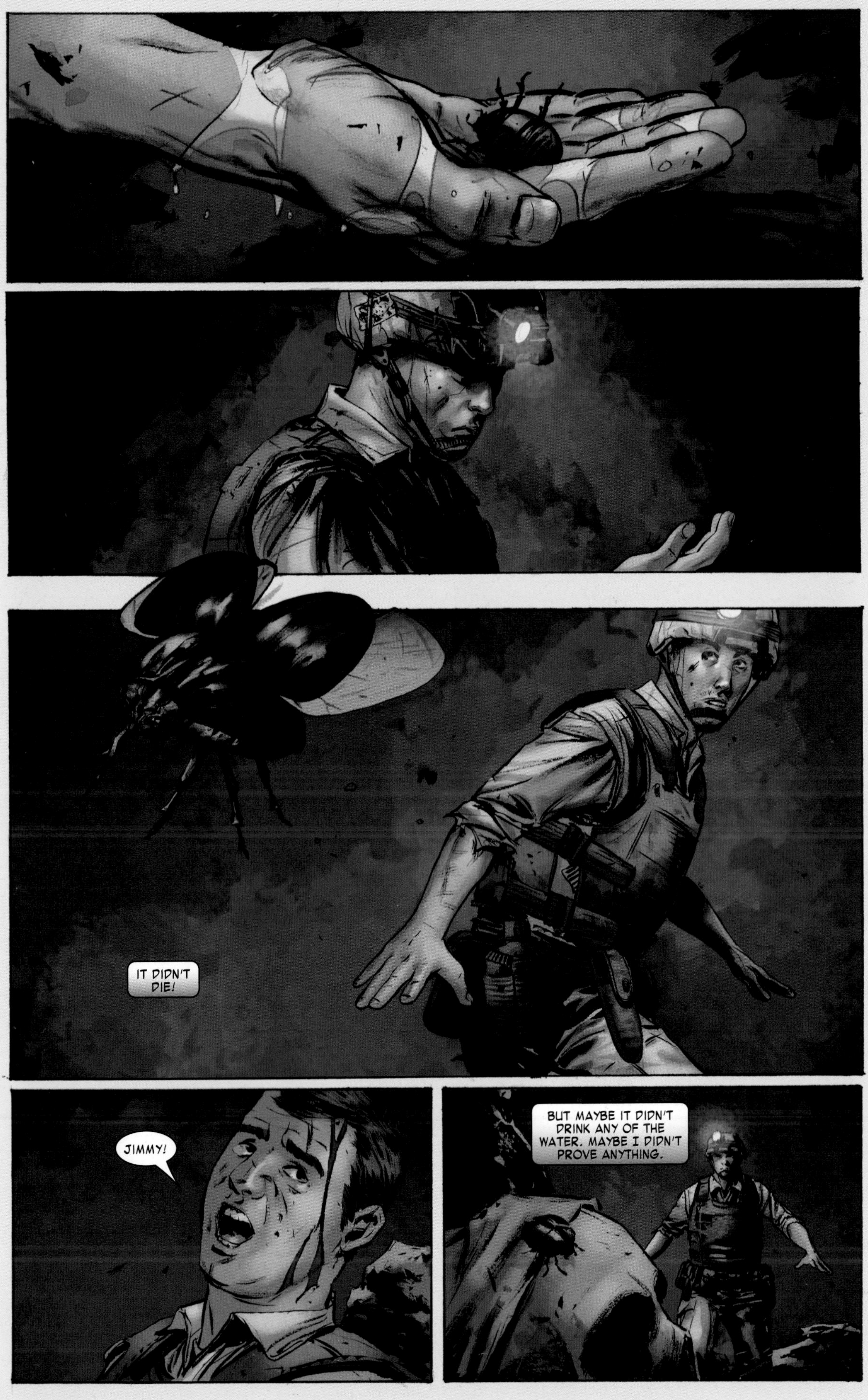
IT DIDN'T DIE!
JIMMY!
BUT MAYBE IT DIDN'T DRINK ANY OF THE WATER. MAYBE I DIDN'T PROVE ANYTHING.

THE MEN ARE SO DEHYDRATED FROM BLEEDING, THEY'LL DIE SOON IF THEY DON'T GET WATER.

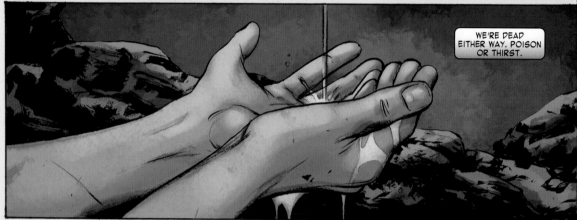

WE'RE DEAD EITHER WAY. POISON OR THIRST.

I'VE GOT TO RISK IT.

HOW LONG WOULD IT TAKE TO KILL ME?

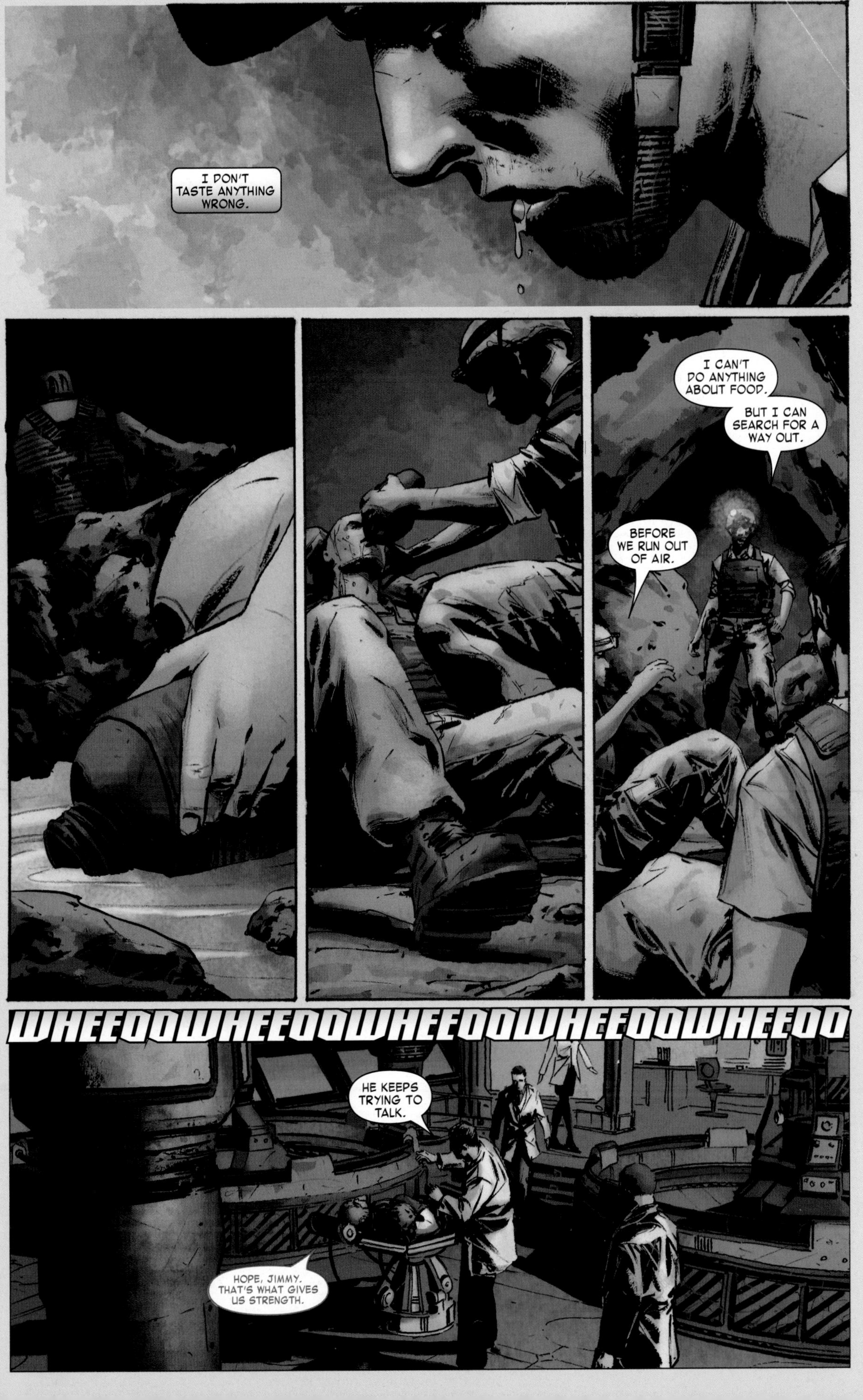
I DON'T TASTE ANYTHING WRONG.
I CAN'T DO ANYTHING ABOUT FOOD.
BUT I CAN SEARCH FOR A WAY OUT.
BEFORE WE RUN OUT OF AIR.
WHEEOOWHEEOOWHEEOOWHEEOOWHEEOO
HE KEEPS TRYING TO TALK.
HOPE, JIMMY. THAT'S WHAT GIVES US STRENGTH.

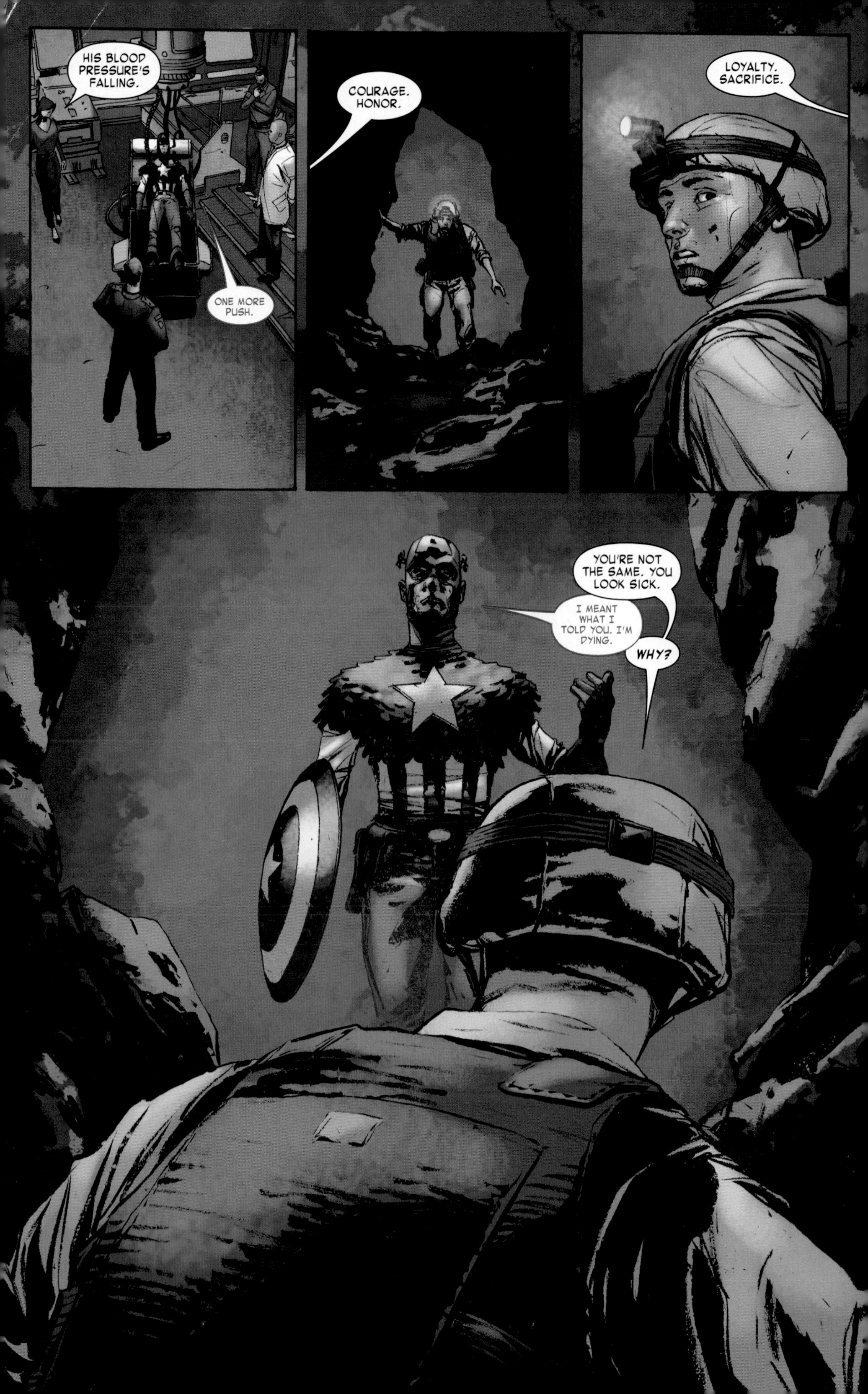
HIS BLOOD PRESSURE'S FALLING.
ONE MORE PUSH.
COURAGE. HONOR.
LOYALTY. SACRIFICE.
YOU'RE NOT THE SAME. YOU LOOK SICK.
I MEANT WHAT I TOLD YOU. I'M DYING.
WHY?

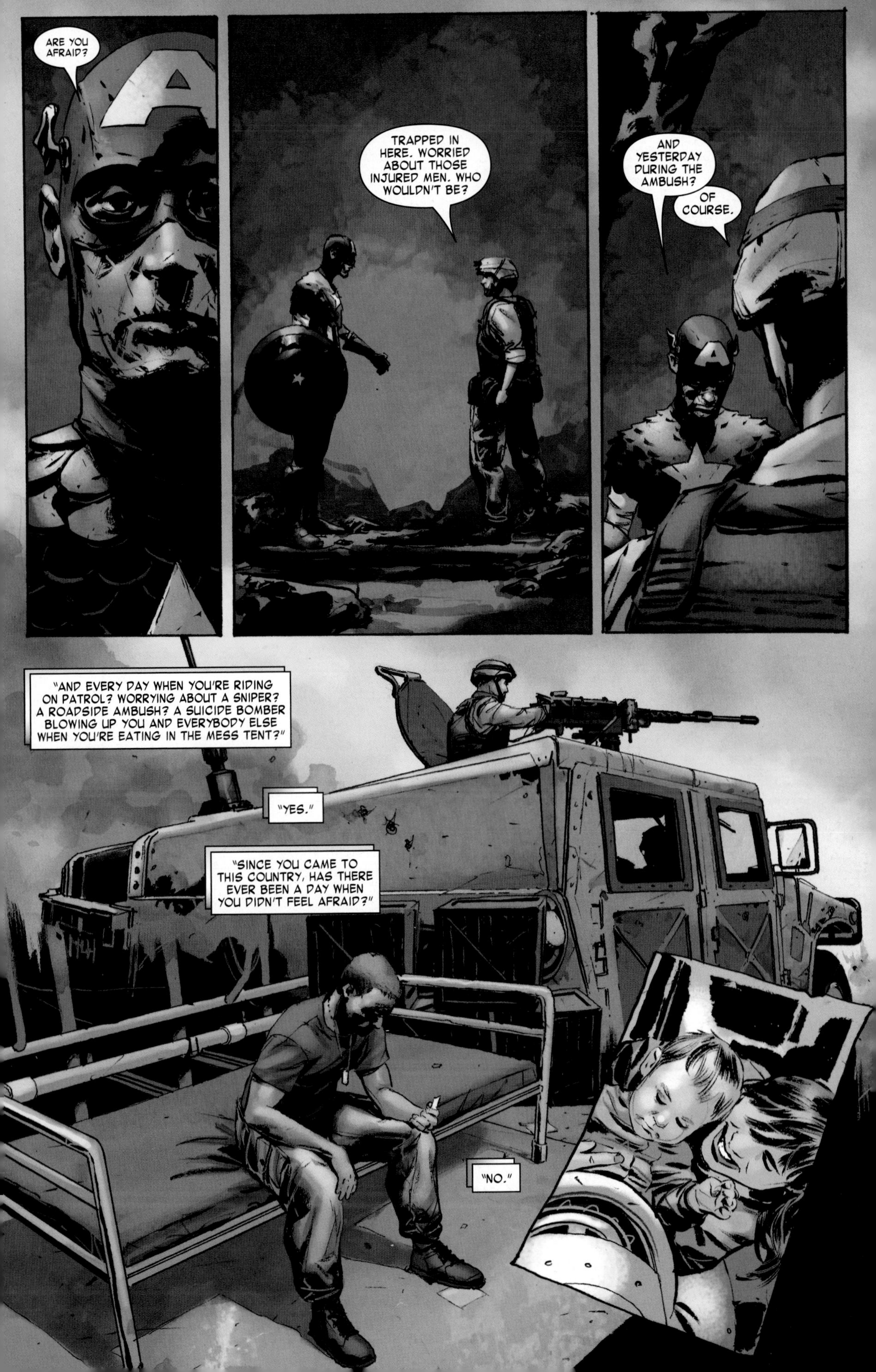
ARE YOU AFRAID?
TRAPPED IN HERE. WORRIED ABOUT THOSE INJURED MEN. WHO WOULDN'T BE?
AND YESTERDAY DURING THE AMBUSH?
OF COURSE.
"AND EVERY DAY WHEN YOU'RE RIDING ON PATROL? WORRYING ABOUT A SNIPER? A ROADSIDE AMBUSH? A SUICIDE BOMBER BLOWING UP YOU AND EVERYBODY ELSE WHEN YOU'RE EATING IN THE MESS TENT?"
"YES."
"SINCE YOU CAME TO THIS COUNTRY, HAS THERE EVER BEEN A DAY WHEN YOU DIDN'T FEEL AFRAID?"
"NO."

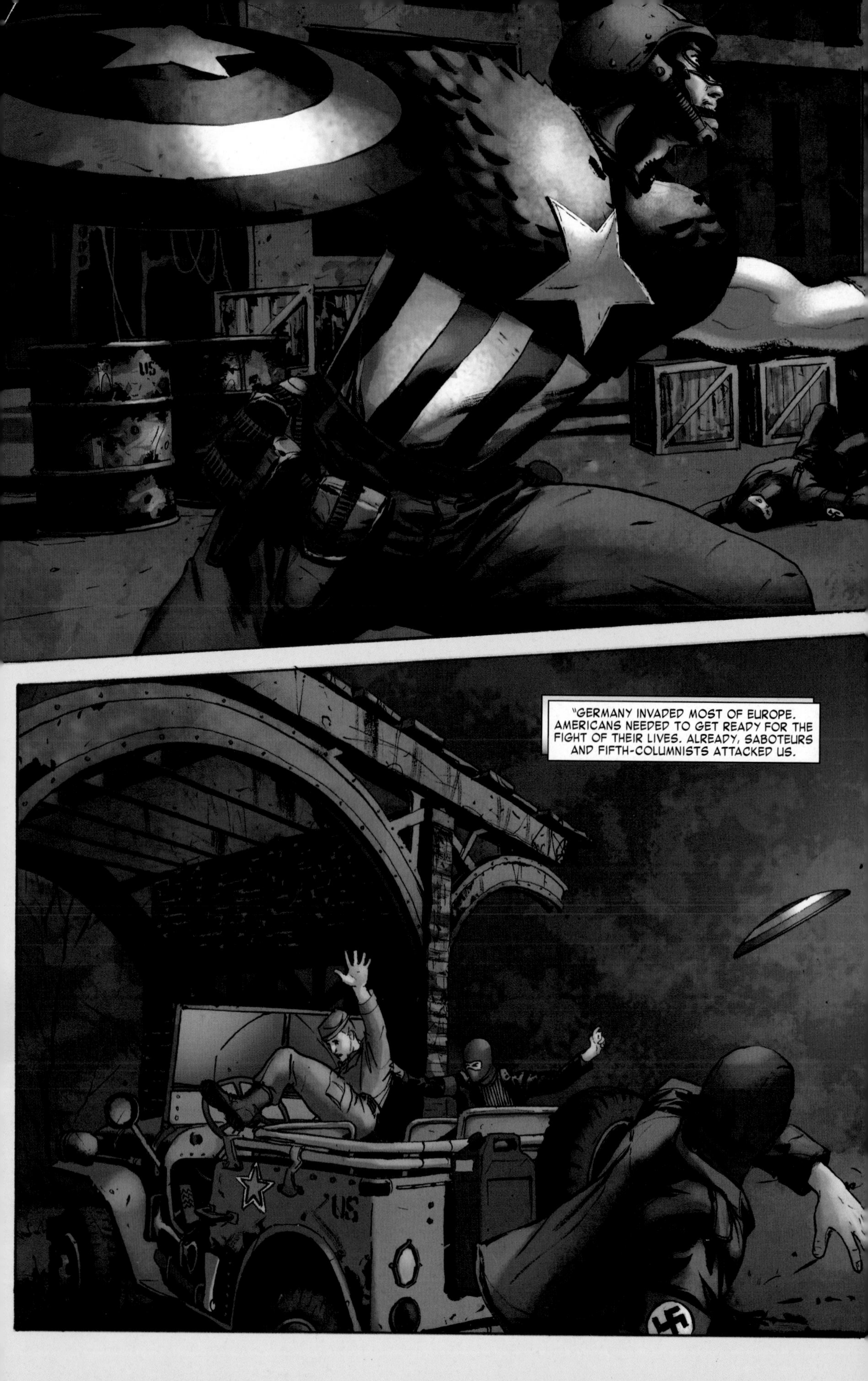
"GERMANY INVADED MOST OF EUROPE. AMERICANS NEEDED TO GET READY FOR THE FIGHT OF THEIR LIVES. ALREADY, SABOTEURS AND FIFTH-COLUMNISTS ATTACKED US.

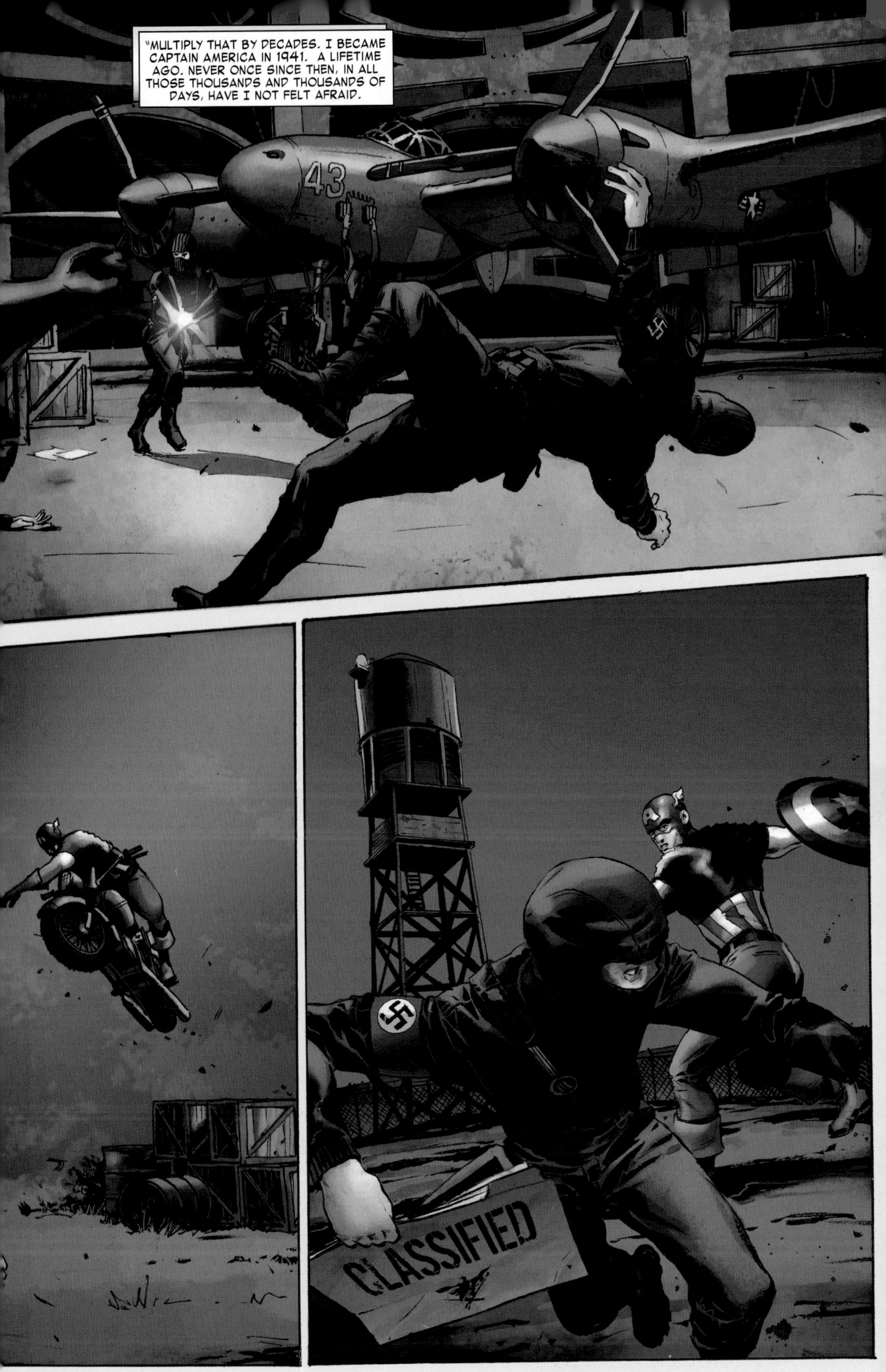

"MULTIPLY THAT BY DECADES. I BECAME CAPTAIN AMERICA IN 1941. A LIFETIME AGO. NEVER ONCE SINCE THEN, IN ALL THOSE THOUSANDS AND THOUSANDS OF DAYS, HAVE I NOT FELT AFRAID.
43
CLASSIFIED

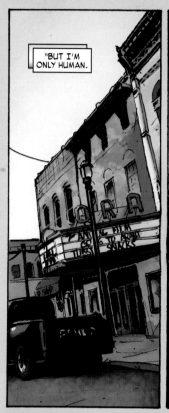

"BUT I'M ONLY HUMAN.

"STEVE ROGERS. AN INSIGNIFICANT NOBODY.

"MY FATHER DIED WHEN I WAS A KID. IT WAS THE DEPRESSION. HE WAS ALWAYS AWAY, LOOKING FOR WORK, TRYING TO SUPPORT US.

"MY MOTHER MANAGED TO FEED US BY TAKING IN LAUNDRY AND MENDING CLOTHES.

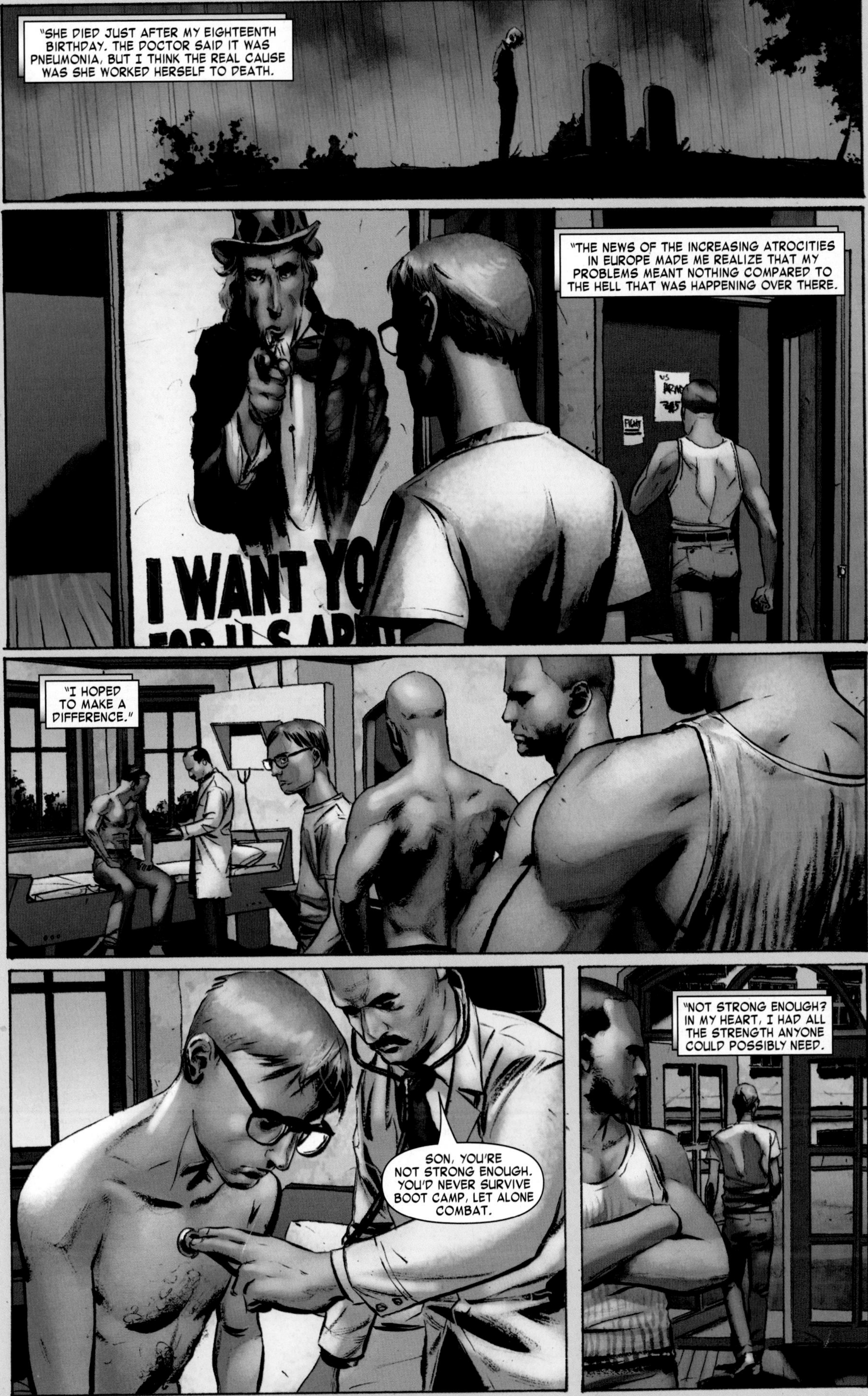
"SHE DIED JUST AFTER MY EIGHTEENTH BIRTHDAY. THE DOCTOR SAID IT WAS PNEUMONIA, BUT I THINK THE REAL CAUSE WAS SHE WORKED HERSELF TO DEATH.
I WANT YO
"THE NEWS OF THE INCREASING ATROCITIES IN EUROPE MADE ME REALIZE THAT MY PROBLEMS MEANT NOTHING COMPARED TO THE HELL THAT WAS HAPPENING OVER THERE.
"I HOPED TO MAKE A DIFFERENCE."
SON, YOU'RE NOT STRONG ENOUGH. YOU'D NEVER SURVIVE BOOT CAMP, LET ALONE COMBAT.
"NOT STRONG ENOUGH? IN MY HEART, I HAD ALL THE STRENGTH ANYONE COULD POSSIBLY NEED.

"THAT'S WHEN I FOUND ANOTHER FATHER. *THREE* OF THEM. PROFESSOR ERSKINE, GENERAL PHILLIPS AND COLONEL FLETCHER.

"OR RATHER, *THEY* FOUND ME.

"THEY NEEDED A CONTROL SUBJECT FOR AN EXPERIMENT CALLED PROJECT REBIRTH. THE GOAL WAS TO BUILD AN ARMY OF SUPER-SOLDIERS THAT WOULD STOP THE RELENTLESS NAZI DOMINATION OF EUROPE.

"THE IDEA WAS TO SATURATE US WITH EXPERIMENTAL CHEMICALS AND HORMONES.

"THEN TO DEVELOP OUR PHYSICAL CAPABILITIES TO THEIR ABSOLUTE LIMITS.

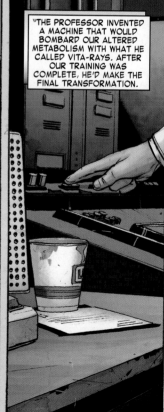

"THE PROFESSOR INVENTED A MACHINE THAT WOULD BOMBARD OUR ALTERED METABOLISM WITH WHAT HE CALLED VITA-RAYS. AFTER OUR TRAINING WAS COMPLETE, HE'D MAKE THE FINAL TRANSFORMATION.

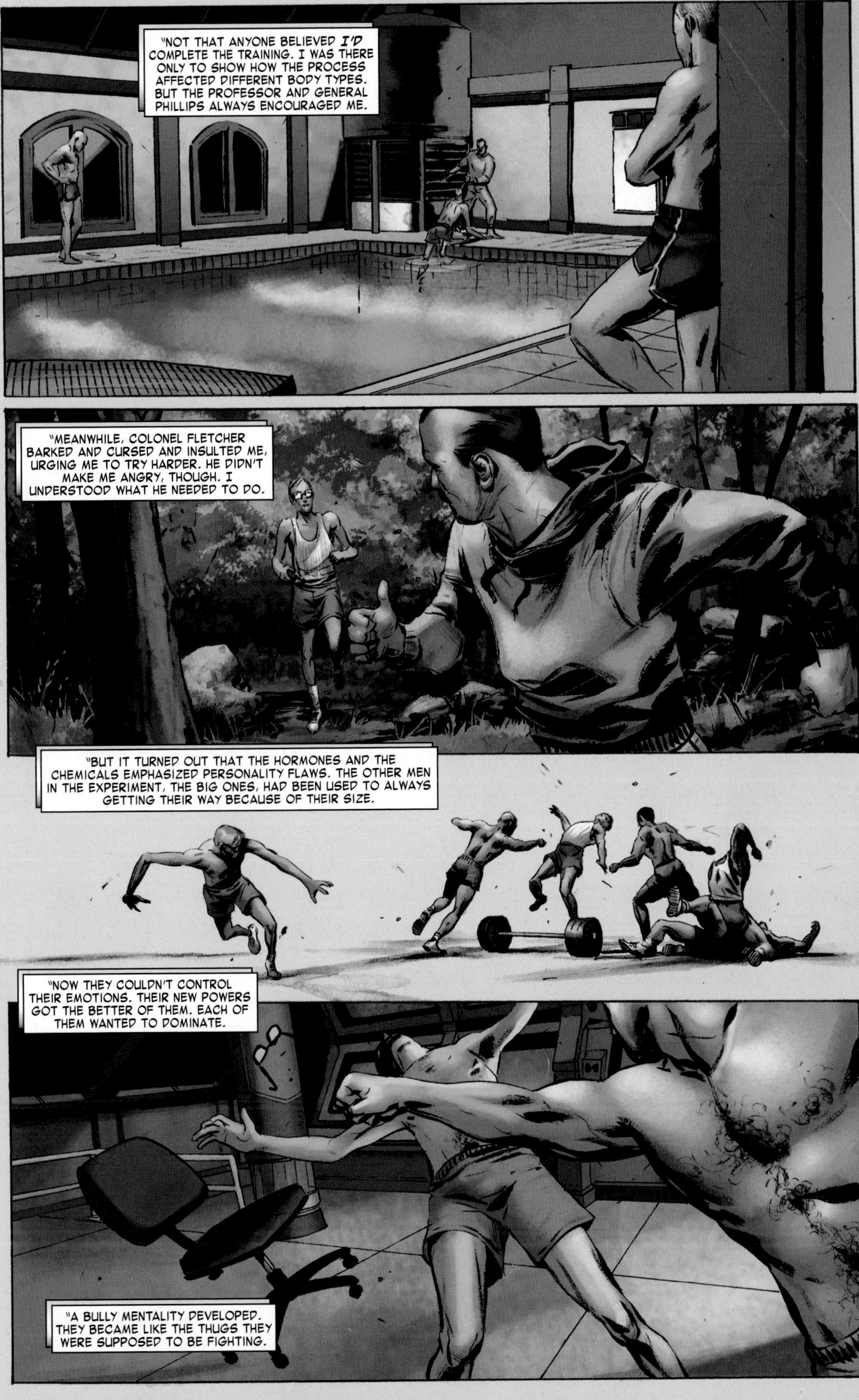
"NOT THAT ANYONE BELIEVED I'D COMPLETE THE TRAINING. I WAS THERE ONLY TO SHOW HOW THE PROCESS AFFECTED DIFFERENT BODY TYPES. BUT THE PROFESSOR AND GENERAL PHILLIPS ALWAYS ENCOURAGED ME.
"MEANWHILE, COLONEL FLETCHER BARKED AND CURSED AND INSULTED ME, URGING ME TO TRY HARDER. HE DIDN'T MAKE ME ANGRY, THOUGH. I UNDERSTOOD WHAT HE NEEDED TO DO.
"BUT IT TURNED OUT THAT THE HORMONES AND THE CHEMICALS EMPHASIZED PERSONALITY FLAWS. THE OTHER MEN IN THE EXPERIMENT, THE BIG ONES, HAD BEEN USED TO ALWAYS GETTING THEIR WAY BECAUSE OF THEIR SIZE.
"NOW THEY COULDN'T CONTROL THEIR EMOTIONS. THEIR NEW POWERS GOT THE BETTER OF THEM. EACH OF THEM WANTED TO DOMINATE.
"A BULLY MENTALITY DEVELOPED. THEY BECAME LIKE THE THUGS THEY WERE SUPPOSED TO BE FIGHTING.

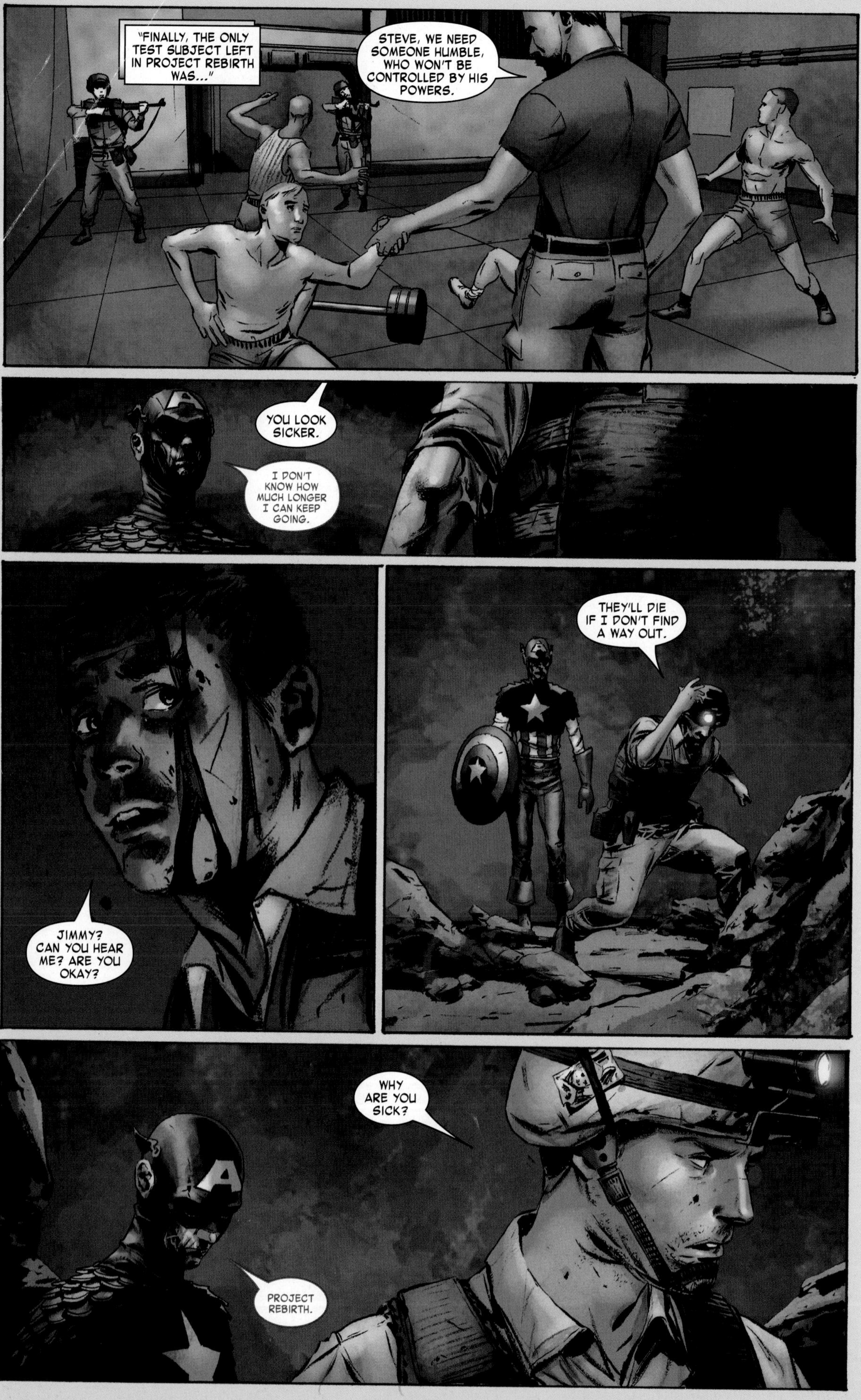
"FINALLY, THE ONLY TEST SUBJECT LEFT IN PROJECT REBIRTH WAS..."
STEVE, WE NEED SOMEONE HUMBLE, WHO WON'T BE CONTROLLED BY HIS POWERS.
YOU LOOK SICKER.
I DON'T KNOW HOW MUCH LONGER I CAN KEEP GOING.
JIMMY? CAN YOU HEAR ME? ARE YOU OKAY?
THEY'LL DIE IF I DON'T FIND A WAY OUT.
WHY ARE YOU SICK?
PROJECT REBIRTH.

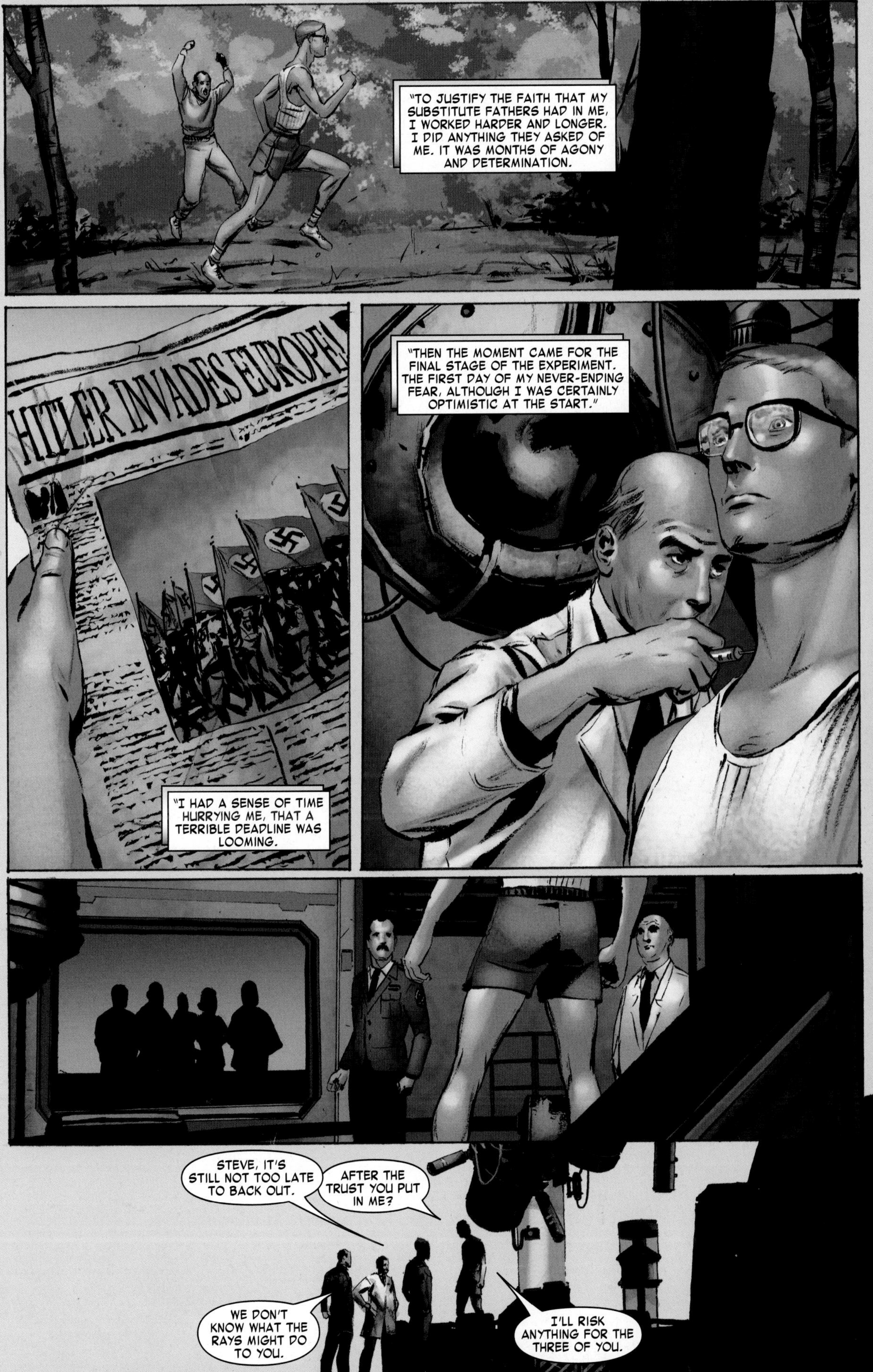
"TO JUSTIFY THE FAITH THAT MY SUBSTITUTE FATHERS HAD IN ME, I WORKED HARDER AND LONGER. I DID ANYTHING THEY ASKED OF ME. IT WAS MONTHS OF AGONY AND DETERMINATION.
HITLER INVADES EUROPE!
"I HAD A SENSE OF TIME HURRYING ME, THAT A TERRIBLE DEADLINE WAS LOOMING.
"THEN THE MOMENT CAME FOR THE FINAL STAGE OF THE EXPERIMENT. THE FIRST DAY OF MY NEVER-ENDING FEAR, ALTHOUGH I WAS CERTAINLY OPTIMISTIC AT THE START."
STEVE, IT'S STILL NOT TOO LATE TO BACK OUT.
AFTER THE TRUST YOU PUT IN ME?
WE DON'T KNOW WHAT THE RAYS MIGHT DO TO YOU.
I'LL RISK ANYTHING FOR THE THREE OF YOU.

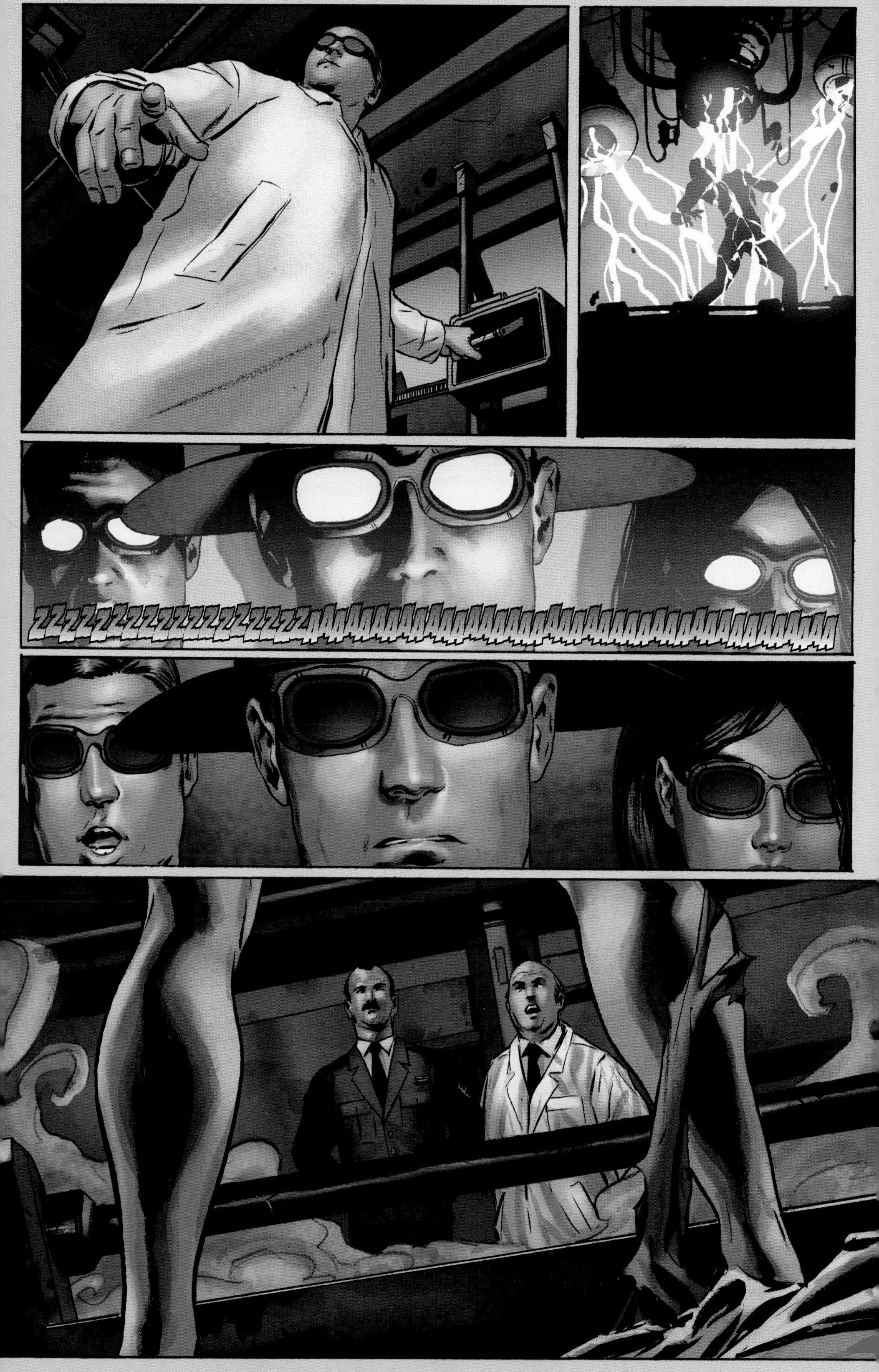
ZZZZZZZZZZZZZZZZZZZZAAAAAAAAAAAAAAAAAAAAAAAAAAAAAAAAAAAAAAAAAAAAA

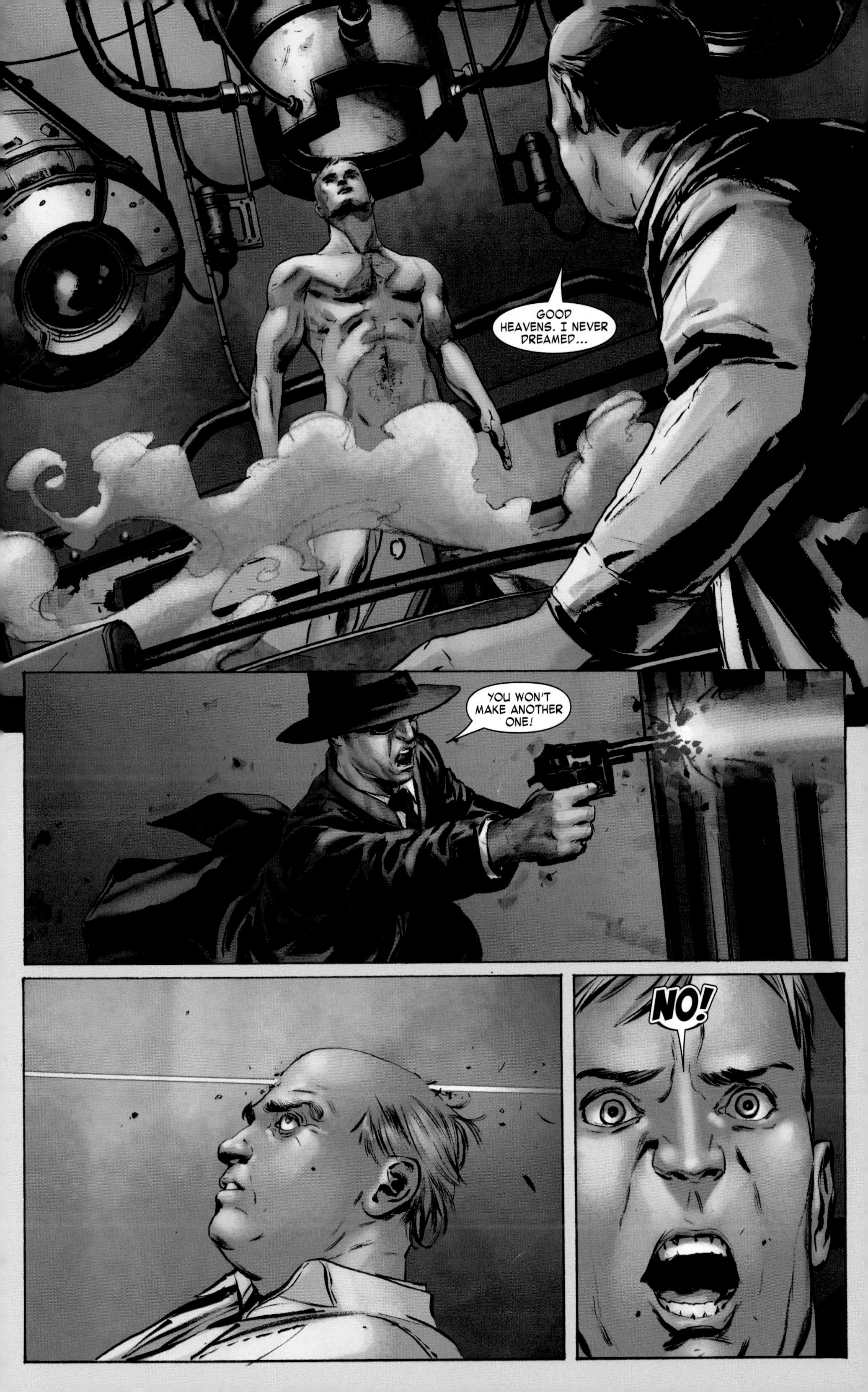
GOOD HEAVENS. I NEVER DREAMED...
YOU WON'T MAKE ANOTHER ONE!
NO!

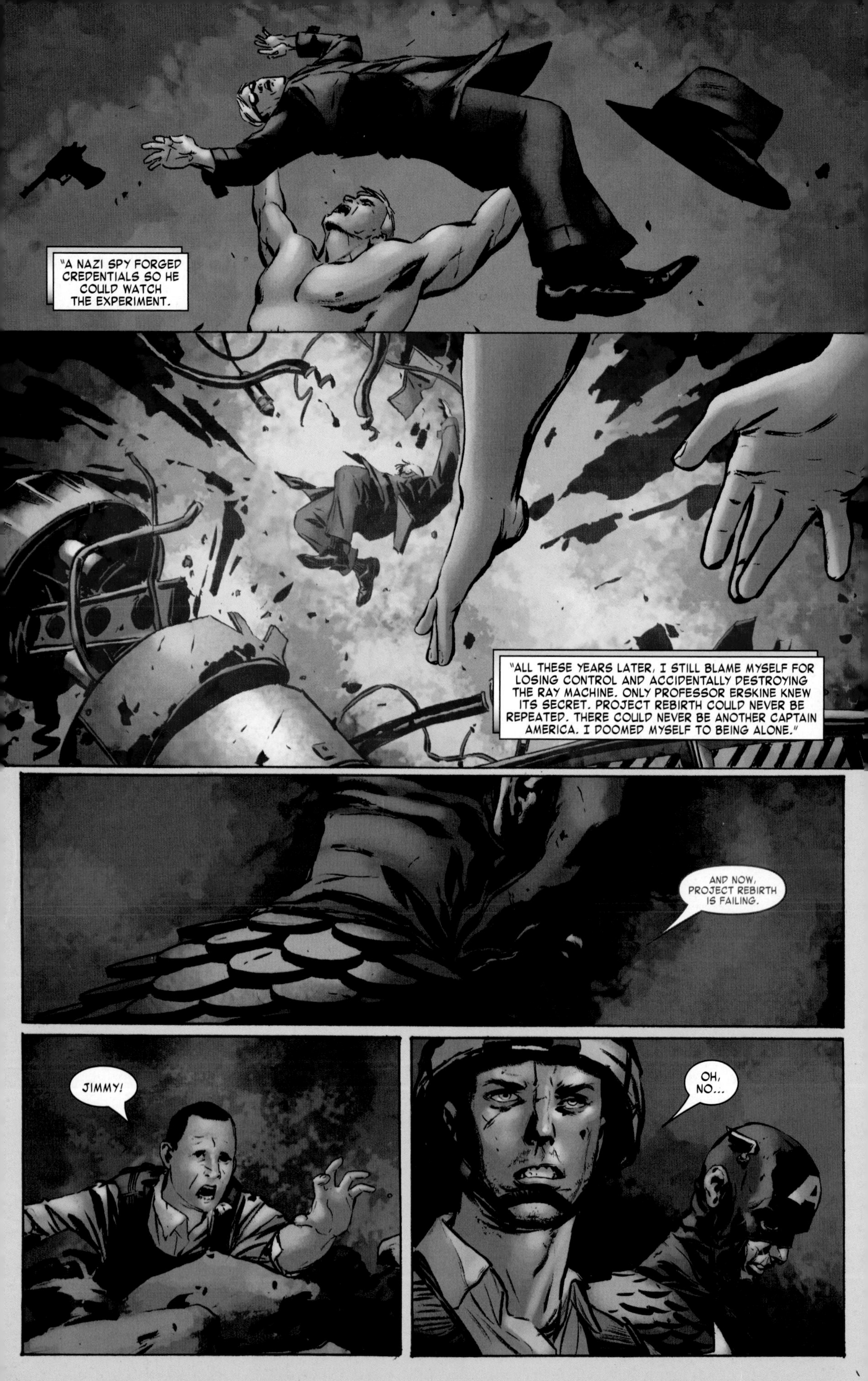
"A NAZI SPY FORGED CREDENTIALS SO HE COULD WATCH THE EXPERIMENT.
"ALL THESE YEARS LATER, I STILL BLAME MYSELF FOR LOSING CONTROL AND ACCIDENTALLY DESTROYING THE RAY MACHINE. ONLY PROFESSOR ERSKINE KNEW ITS SECRET. PROJECT REBIRTH COULD NEVER BE REPEATED. THERE COULD NEVER BE ANOTHER CAPTAIN AMERICA. I DOOMED MYSELF TO BEING ALONE."
AND NOW, PROJECT REBIRTH IS FAILING.
JIMMY!
OH, NO...

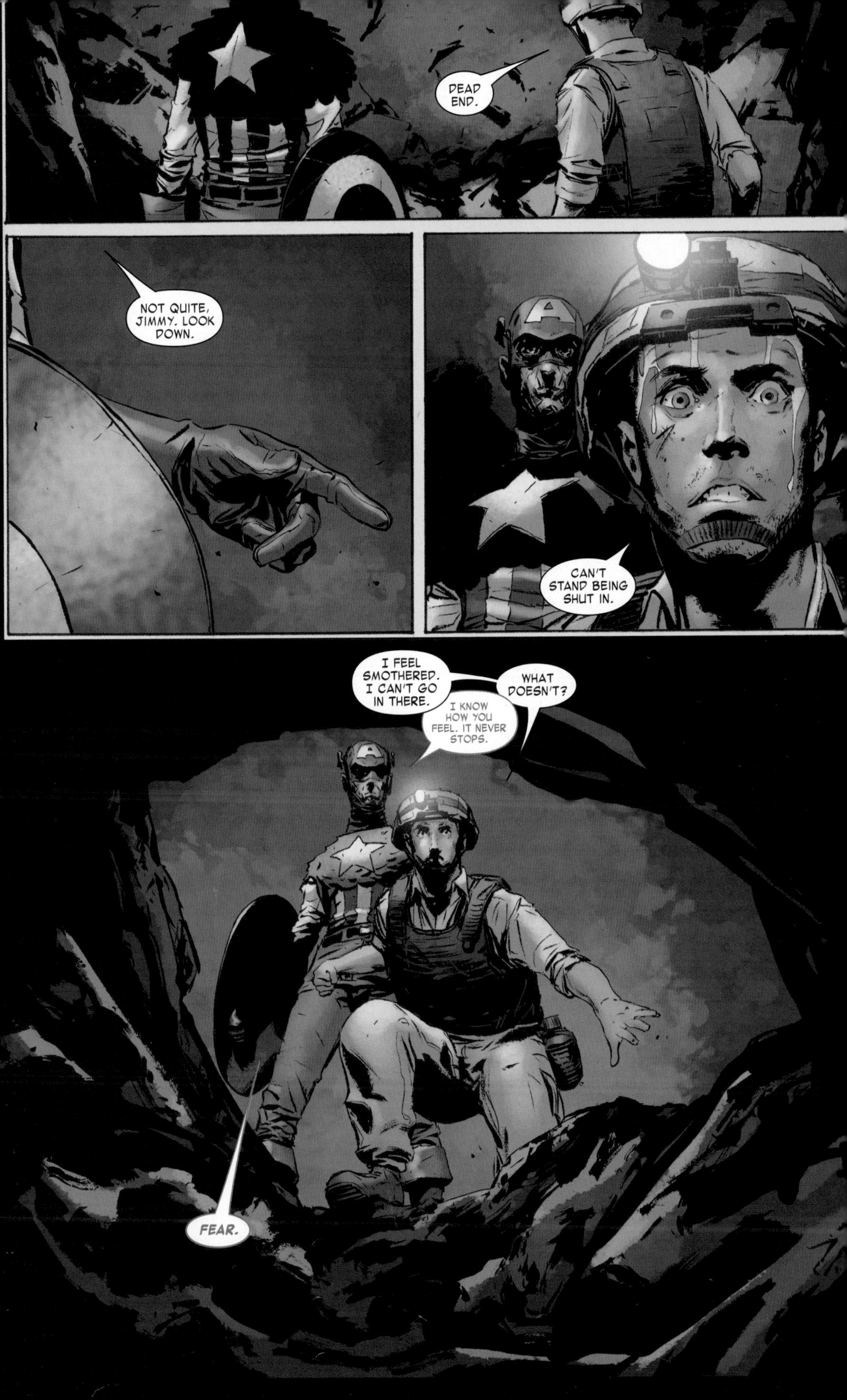
DEAD END.
NOT QUITE, JIMMY. LOOK DOWN.
CAN'T STAND BEING SHUT IN.
I FEEL SMOTHERED. I CAN'T GO IN THERE.
WHAT DOESN'T?
I KNOW HOW YOU FEEL. IT NEVER STOPS.
FEAR.

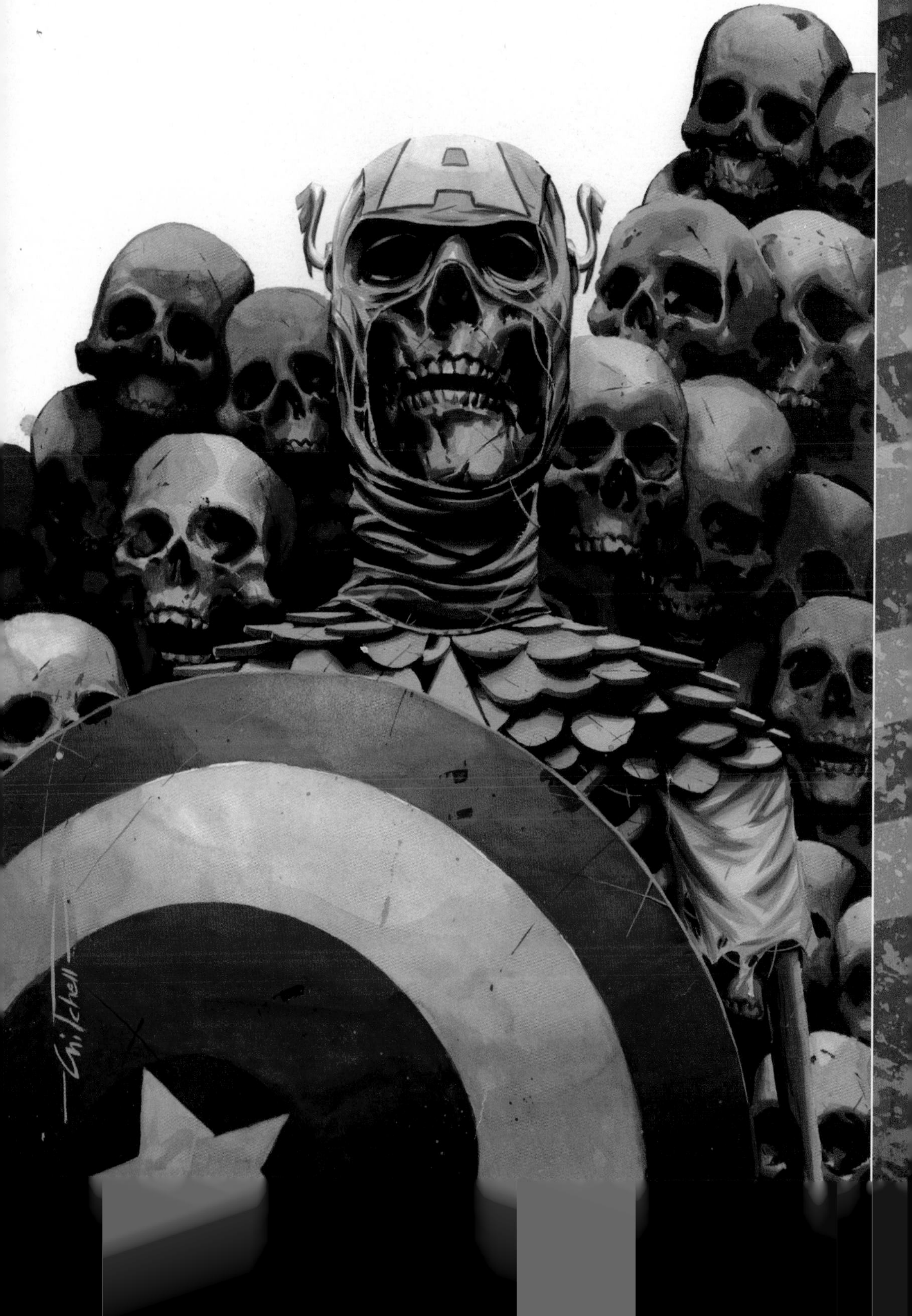

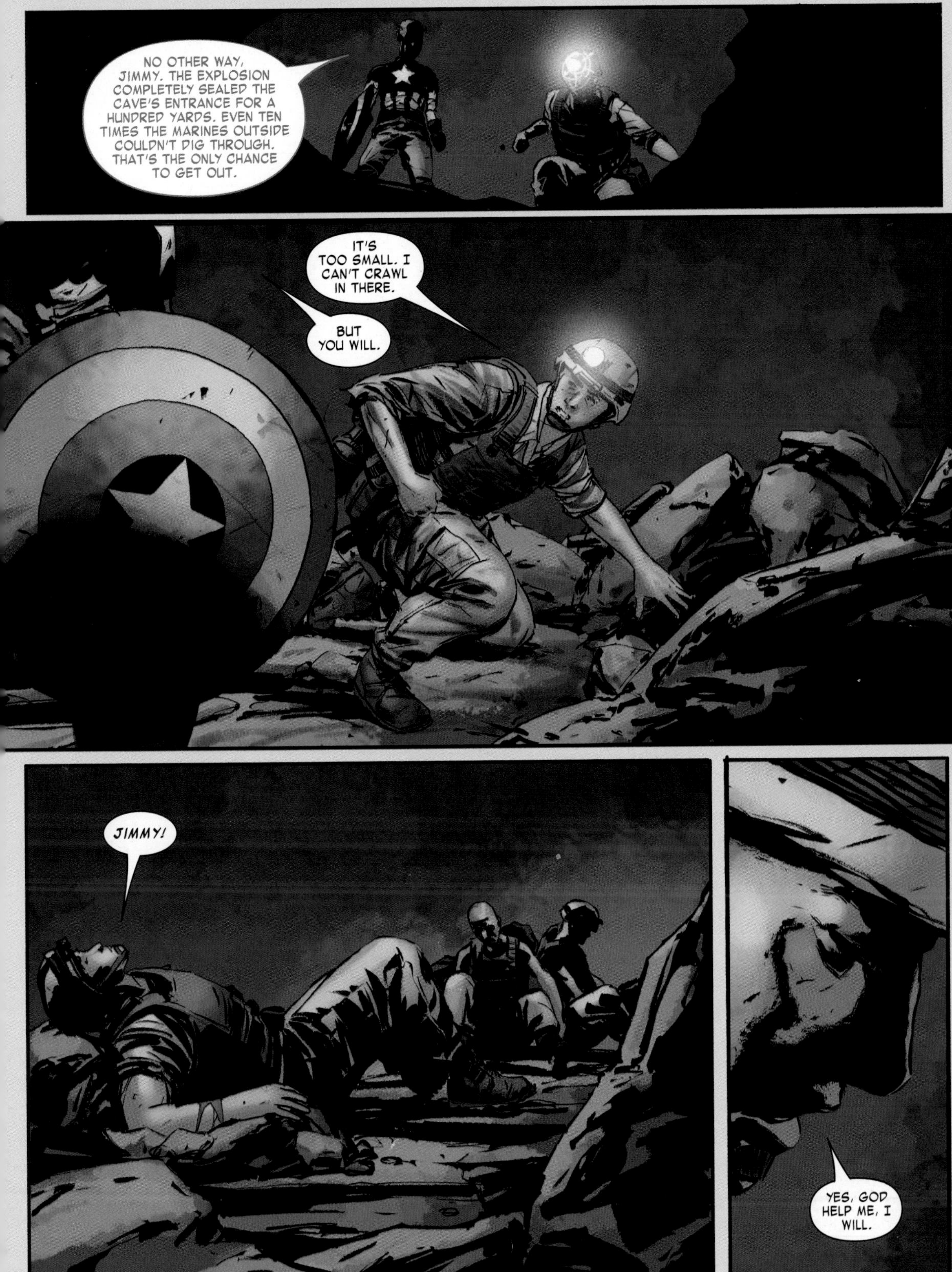
NO OTHER WAY, JIMMY. THE EXPLOSION COMPLETELY SEALED THE CAVE'S ENTRANCE FOR A HUNDRED YARDS. EVEN TEN TIMES THE MARINES OUTSIDE COULDN'T DIG THROUGH. THAT'S THE ONLY CHANCE TO GET OUT.
IT'S TOO SMALL. I CAN'T CRAWL IN THERE.
BUT YOU WILL.
JIMMY!
YES, GOD HELP ME, I WILL.

CAPTAIN AMERICA: THE CHOSEN
CHAPTER 5:
THE CRUCIBLE

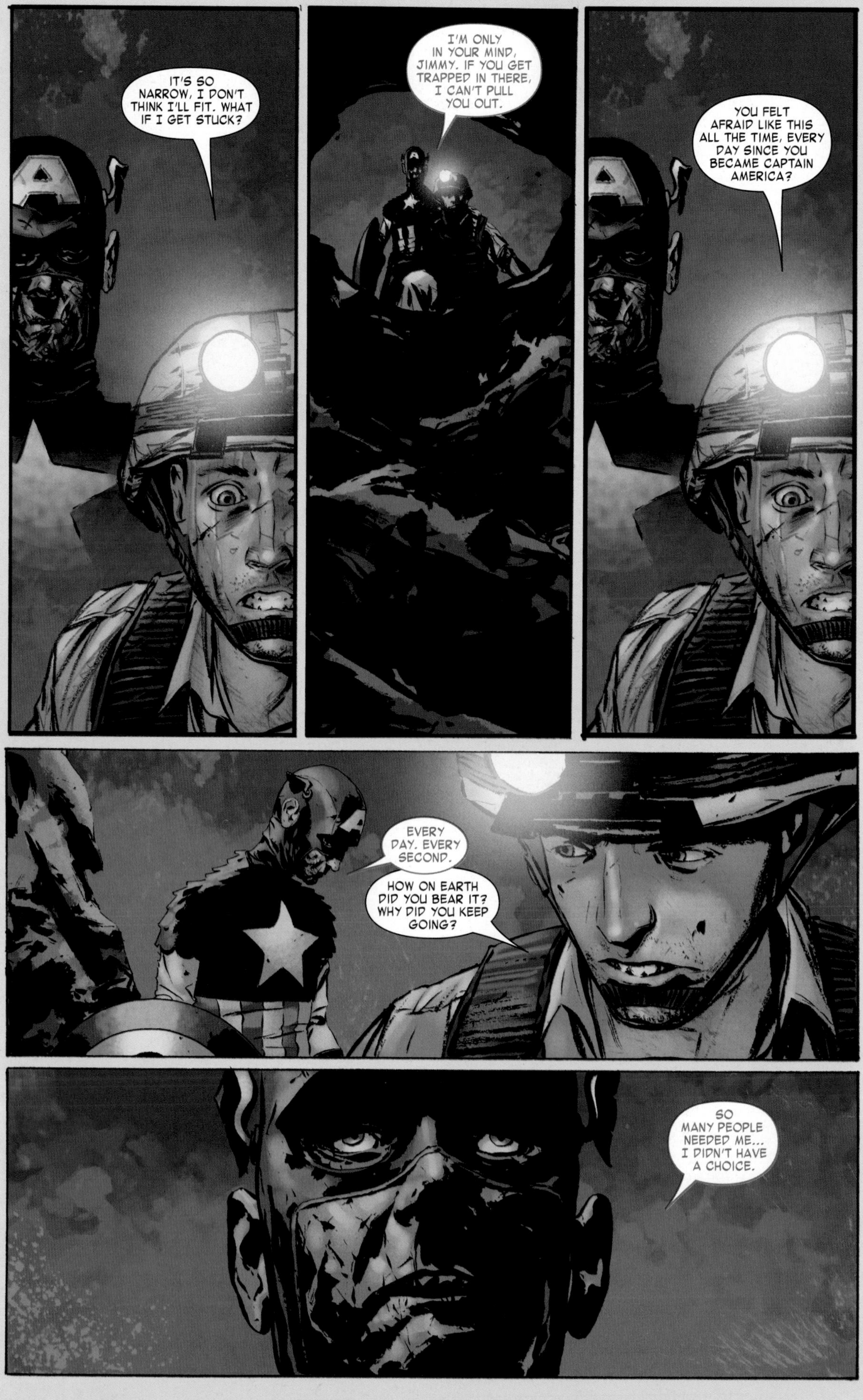
IT'S SO NARROW, I DON'T THINK I'LL FIT. WHAT IF I GET STUCK?
I'M ONLY IN YOUR MIND, JIMMY. IF YOU GET TRAPPED IN THERE, I CAN'T PULL YOU OUT.
YOU FELT AFRAID LIKE THIS ALL THE TIME, EVERY DAY SINCE YOU BECAME CAPTAIN AMERICA?
EVERY DAY. EVERY SECOND.
HOW ON EARTH DID YOU BEAR IT? WHY DID YOU KEEP GOING?
SO MANY PEOPLE NEEDED ME... I DIDN'T HAVE A CHOICE.

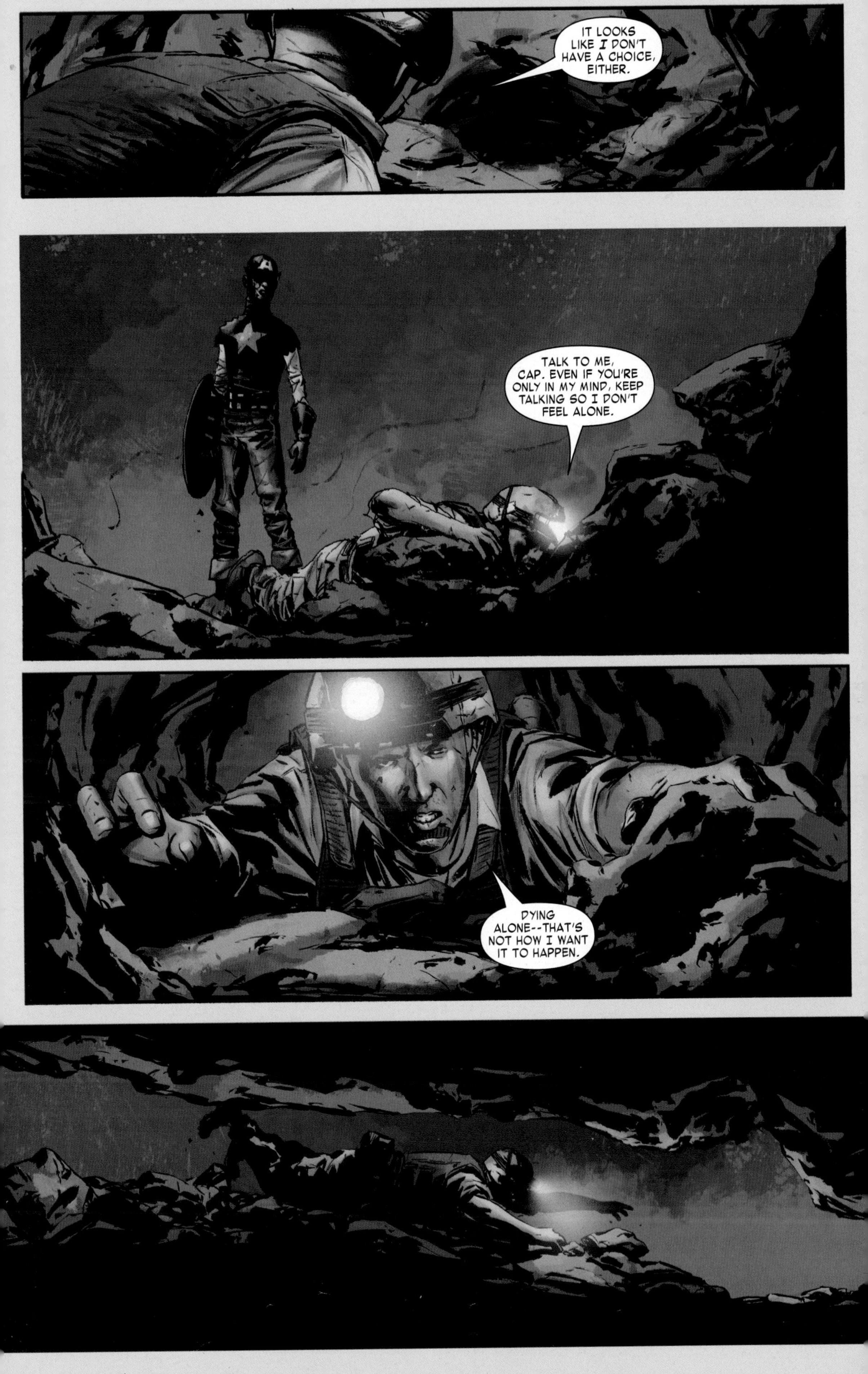
IT LOOKS LIKE *I* DON'T HAVE A CHOICE, EITHER.
TALK TO ME, CAP. EVEN IF YOU'RE ONLY IN MY MIND, KEEP TALKING SO I DON'T FEEL ALONE.
DYING ALONE--THAT'S NOT HOW I WANT IT TO HAPPEN.

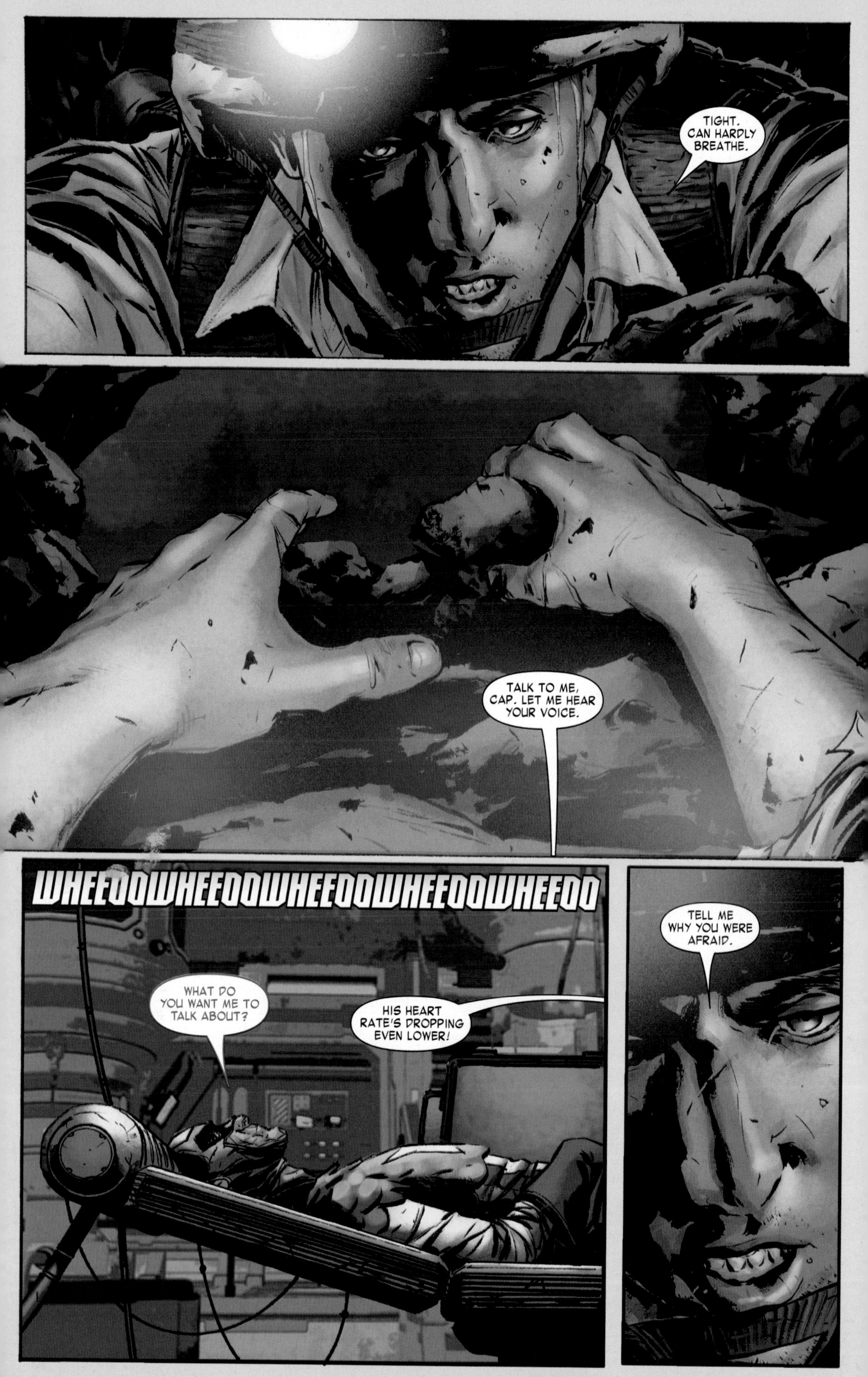

TIGHT. CAN HARDLY BREATHE.
TALK TO ME, CAP. LET ME HEAR YOUR VOICE.
WHEEOOWHEEOOWHEEOOWHEEOOWHEEOO
WHAT DO YOU WANT ME TO TALK ABOUT?
HIS HEART RATE'S DROPPING EVEN LOWER!
TELL ME WHY YOU WERE AFRAID.

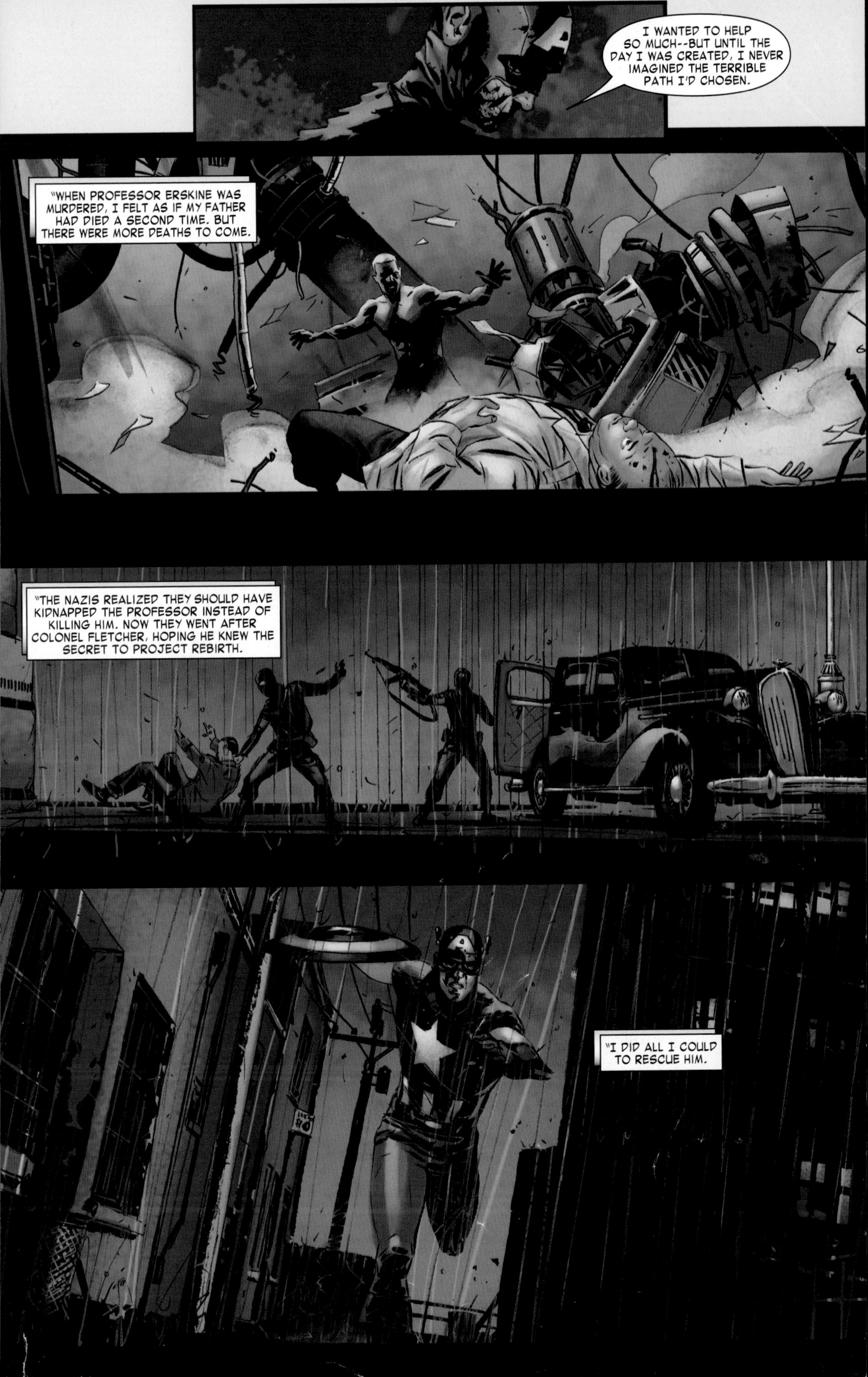
I WANTED TO HELP SO MUCH--BUT UNTIL THE DAY I WAS CREATED, I NEVER IMAGINED THE TERRIBLE PATH I'D CHOSEN.
"WHEN PROFESSOR ERSKINE WAS MURDERED, I FELT AS IF MY FATHER HAD DIED A SECOND TIME. BUT THERE WERE MORE DEATHS TO COME.
"THE NAZIS REALIZED THEY SHOULD HAVE KIDNAPPED THE PROFESSOR INSTEAD OF KILLING HIM. NOW THEY WENT AFTER COLONEL FLETCHER, HOPING HE KNEW THE SECRET TO PROJECT REBIRTH.
"I DID ALL I COULD TO RESCUE HIM.

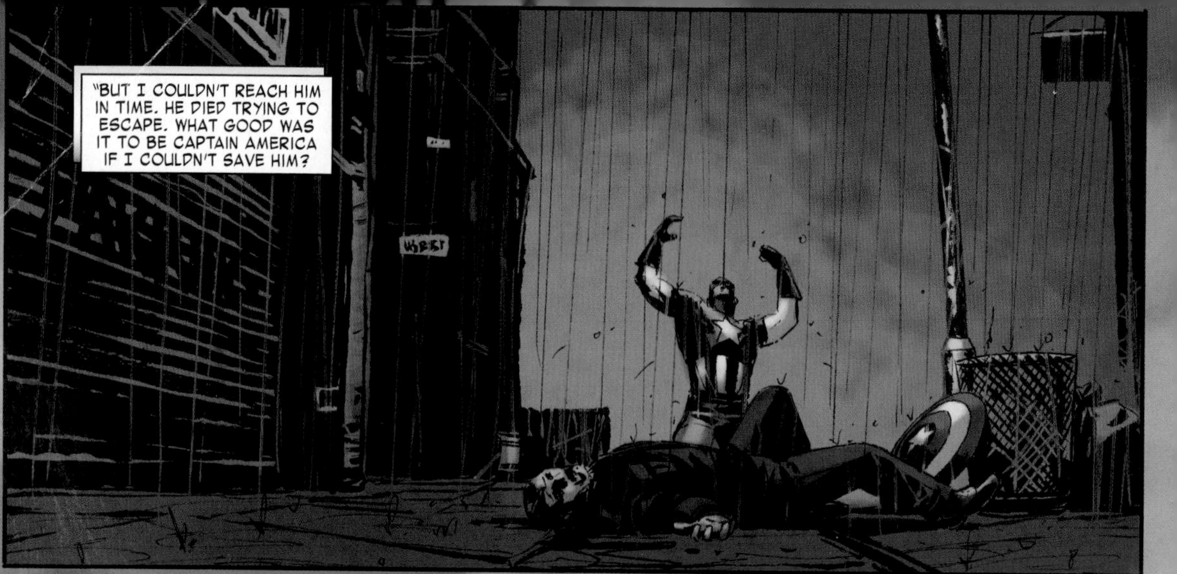
"BUT I COULDN'T REACH HIM IN TIME. HE DIED TRYING TO ESCAPE. WHAT GOOD WAS IT TO BE CAPTAIN AMERICA IF I COULDN'T SAVE HIM?

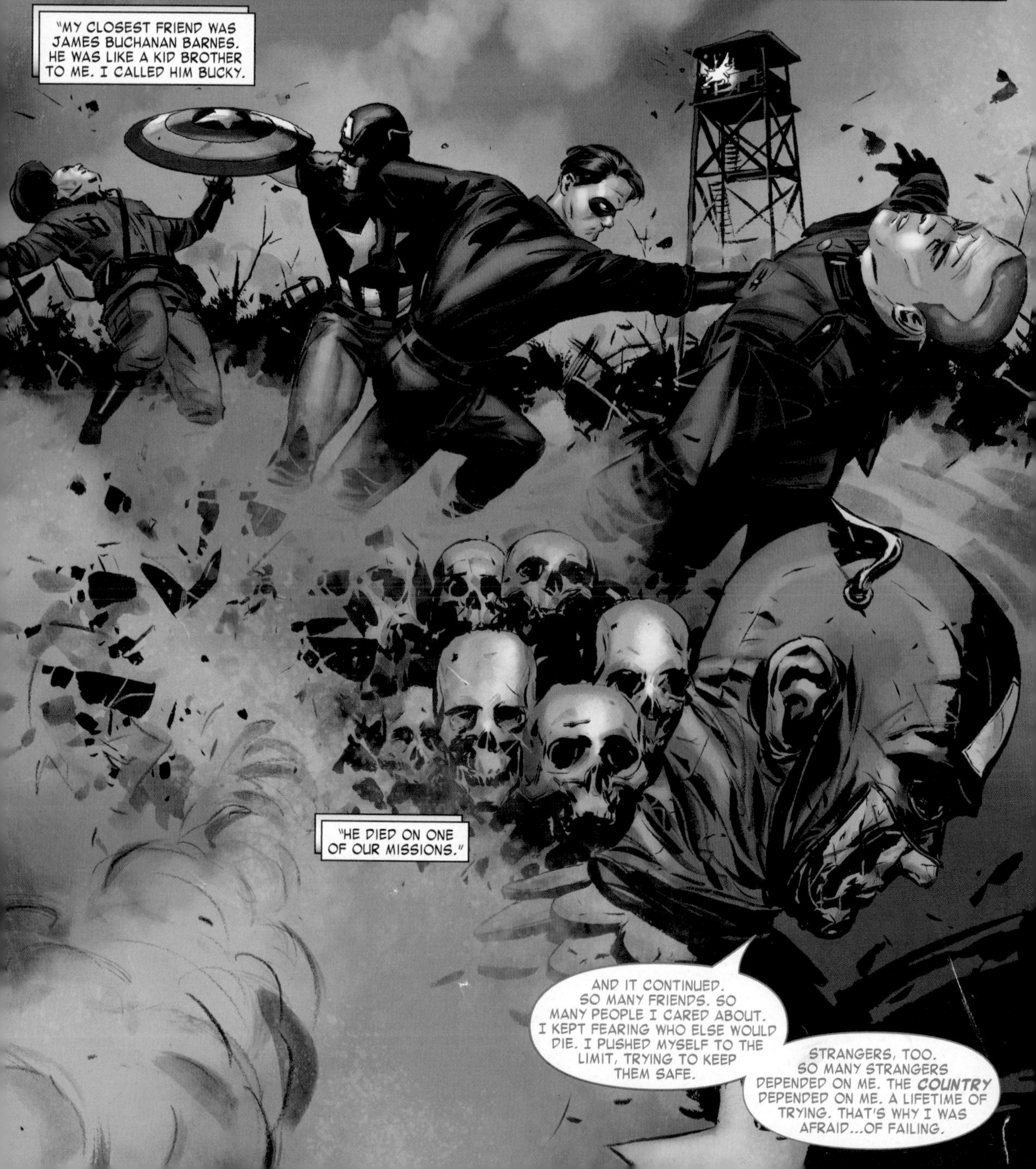
"MY CLOSEST FRIEND WAS JAMES BUCHANAN BARNES. HE WAS LIKE A KID BROTHER TO ME. I CALLED HIM BUCKY.
"HE DIED ON ONE OF OUR MISSIONS."
AND IT CONTINUED. SO MANY FRIENDS. SO MANY PEOPLE I CARED ABOUT. I KEPT FEARING WHO ELSE WOULD DIE. I PUSHED MYSELF TO THE LIMIT, TRYING TO KEEP THEM SAFE.
STRANGERS, TOO. SO MANY STRANGERS DEPENDED ON ME. THE *COUNTRY* DEPENDED ON ME. A LIFETIME OF TRYING. THAT'S WHY I WAS AFRAID...OF FAILING.

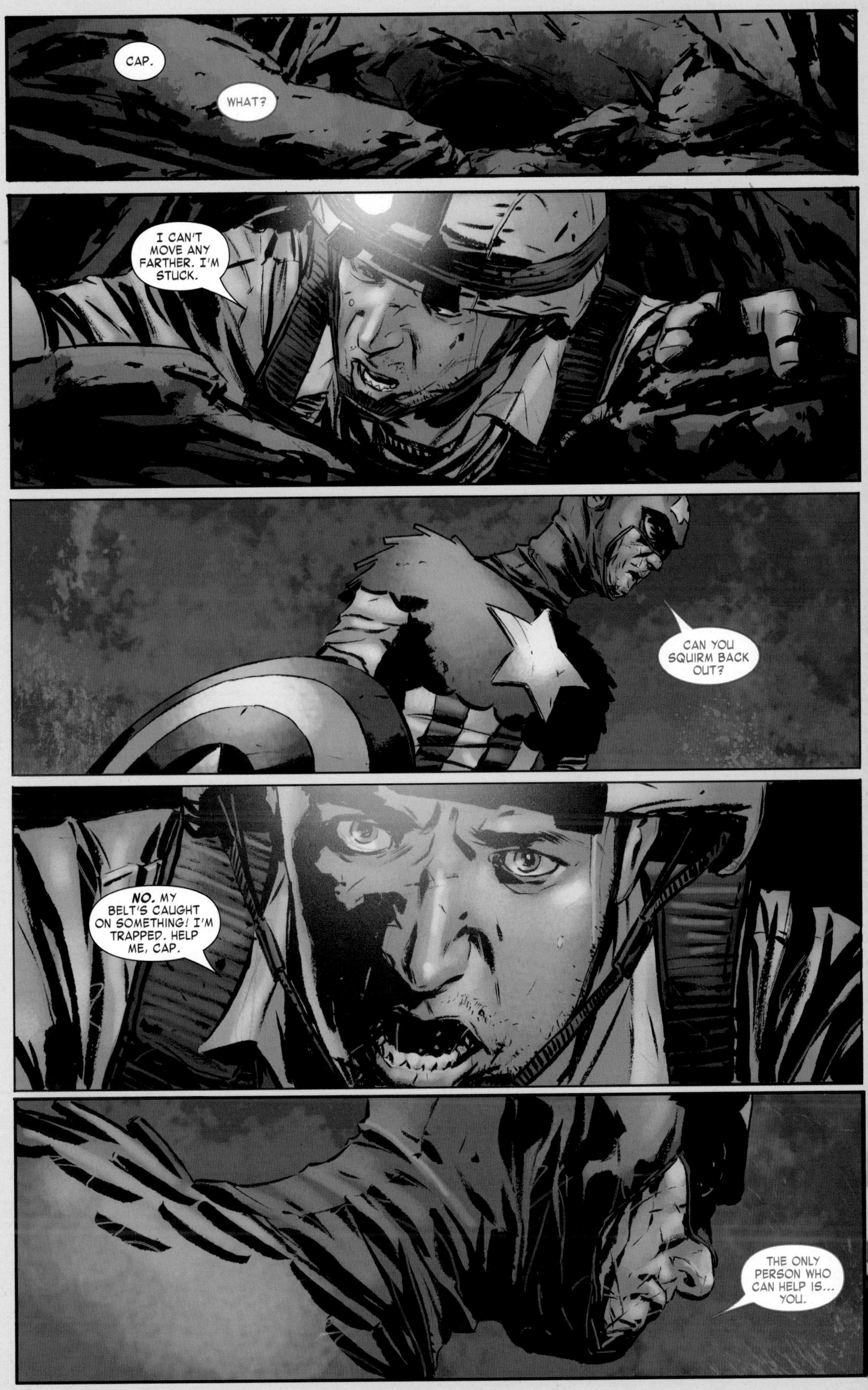
CAP.
WHAT?
I CAN'T MOVE ANY FARTHER. I'M STUCK.
CAN YOU SQUIRM BACK OUT?
NO. MY BELT'S CAUGHT ON SOMETHING! I'M TRAPPED. HELP ME, CAP.
THE ONLY PERSON WHO CAN HELP IS... YOU.

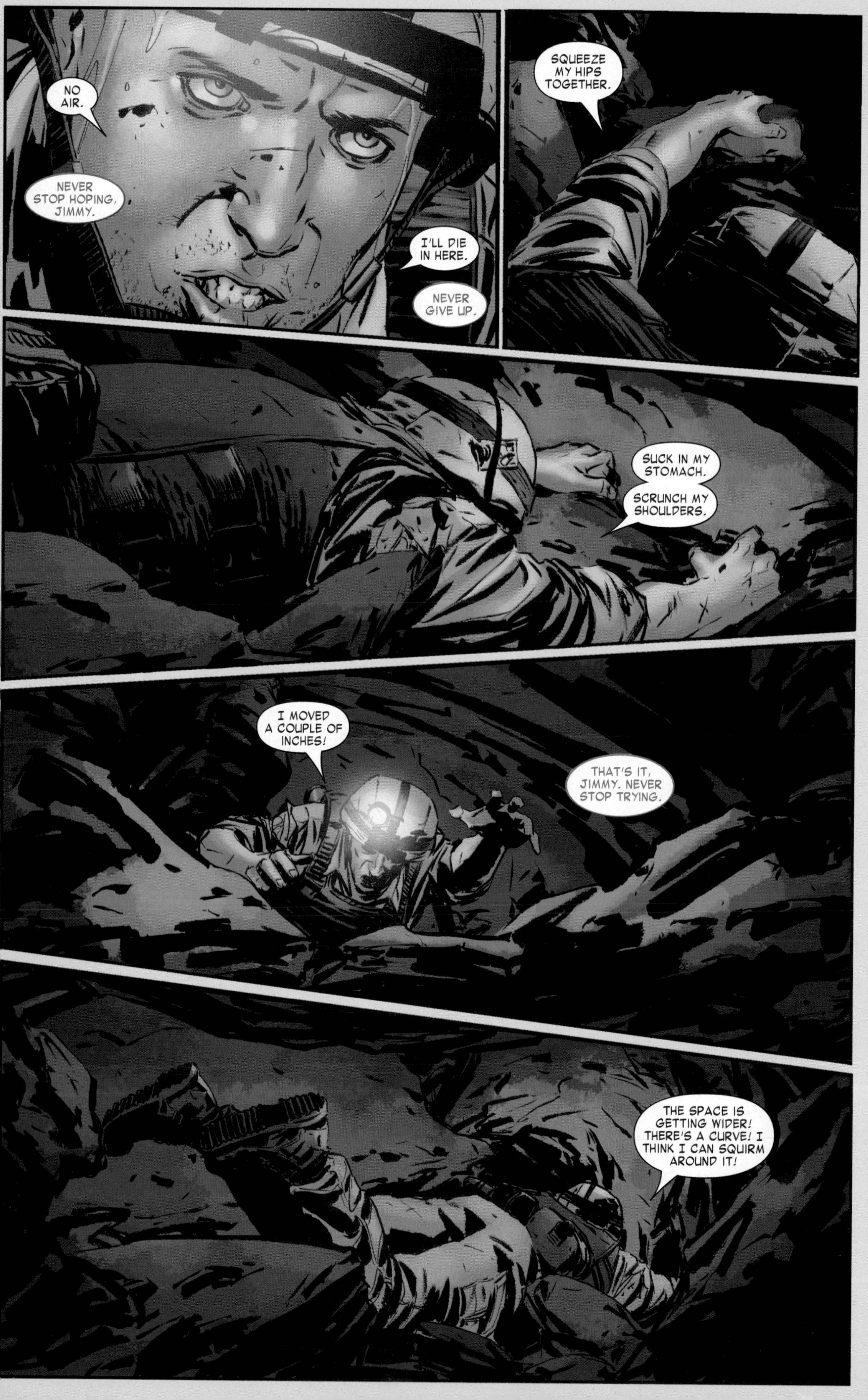
NO AIR.
NEVER STOP HOPING, JIMMY.
I'LL DIE IN HERE.
NEVER GIVE UP.
SQUEEZE MY HIPS TOGETHER.
SUCK IN MY STOMACH.
SCRUNCH MY SHOULDERS.
I MOVED A COUPLE OF INCHES!
THAT'S IT, JIMMY. NEVER STOP TRYING.
THE SPACE IS GETTING WIDER! THERE'S A CURVE! I THINK I CAN SQUIRM AROUND IT!

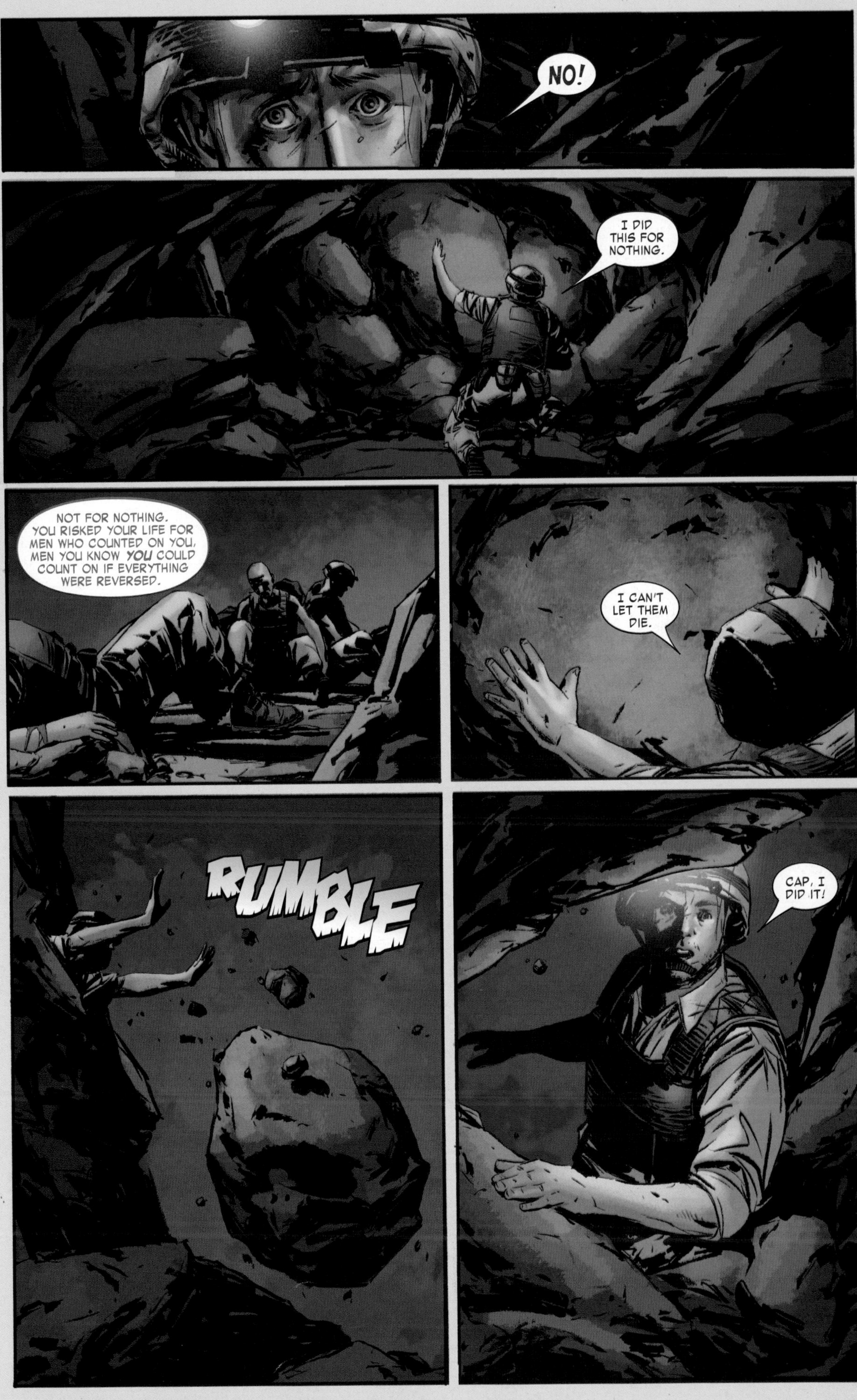
NO!
I DID THIS FOR NOTHING.
NOT FOR NOTHING. YOU RISKED YOUR LIFE FOR MEN WHO COUNTED ON YOU, MEN YOU KNOW *YOU* COULD COUNT ON IF EVERYTHING WERE REVERSED.
I CAN'T LET THEM DIE.
RUMBLE
CAP, I DID IT!

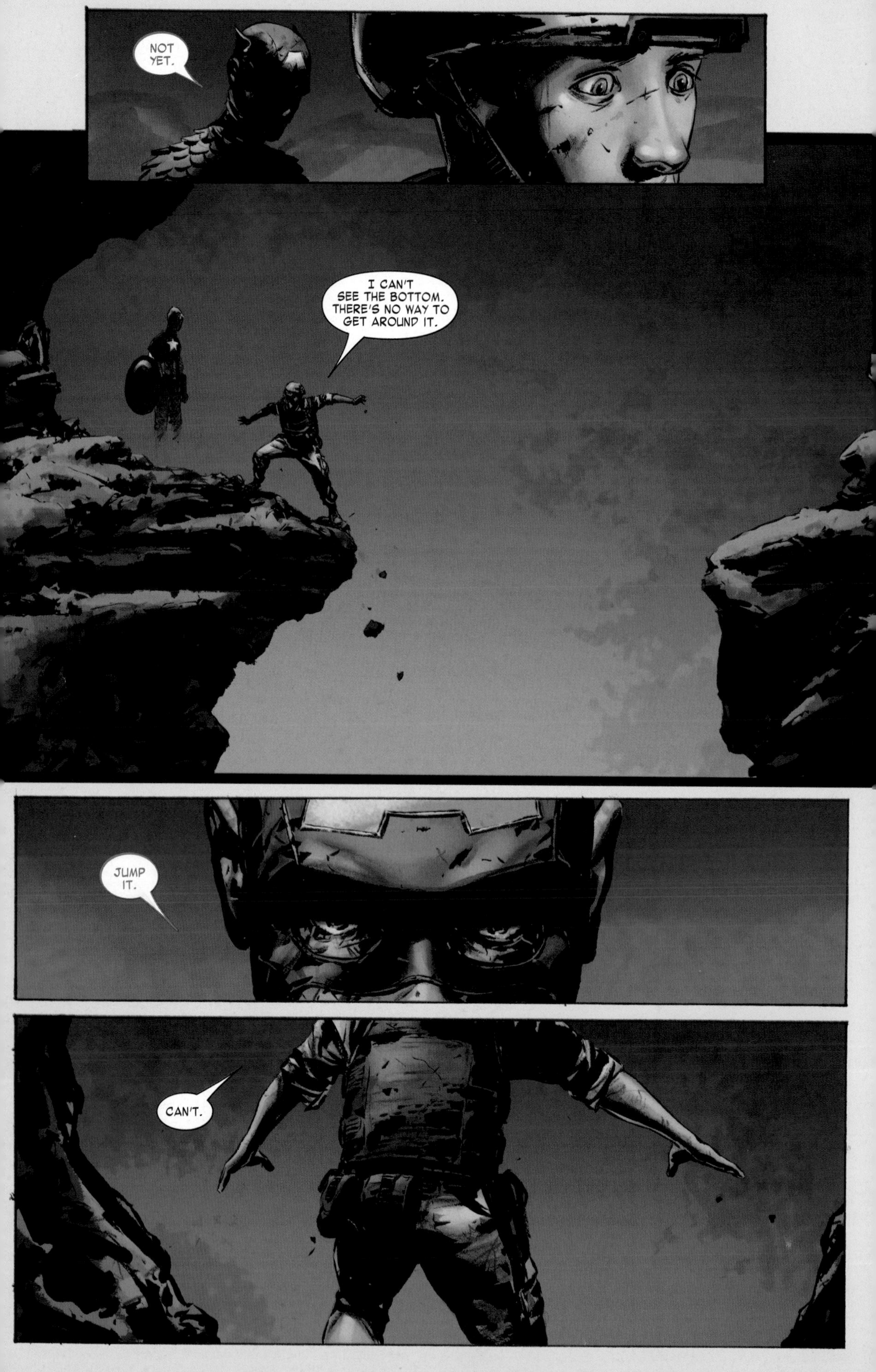
NOT YET.
I CAN'T SEE THE BOTTOM. THERE'S NO WAY TO GET AROUND IT.
JUMP IT.
CAN'T.

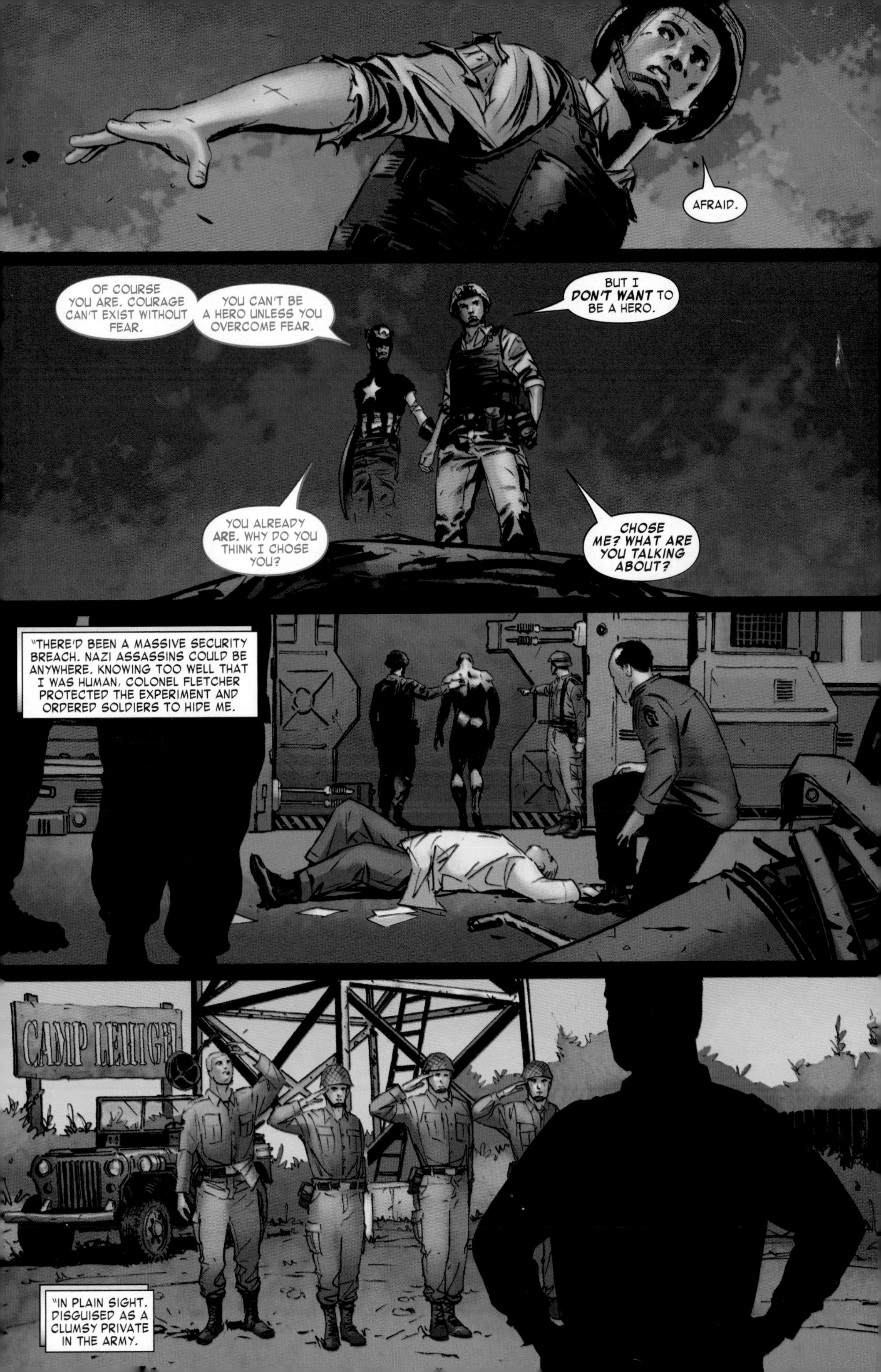
AFRAID.
OF COURSE YOU ARE. COURAGE CAN'T EXIST WITHOUT FEAR.
YOU CAN'T BE A HERO UNLESS YOU OVERCOME FEAR.
BUT I DON'T WANT TO BE A HERO.
YOU ALREADY ARE. WHY DO YOU THINK I CHOSE YOU?
CHOSE ME? WHAT ARE YOU TALKING ABOUT?
"THERE'D BEEN A MASSIVE SECURITY BREACH. NAZI ASSASSINS COULD BE ANYWHERE. KNOWING TOO WELL THAT I WAS HUMAN, COLONEL FLETCHER PROTECTED THE EXPERIMENT AND ORDERED SOLDIERS TO HIDE ME.
CAMP LEHIGH
"IN PLAIN SIGHT. DISGUISED AS A CLUMSY PRIVATE IN THE ARMY.

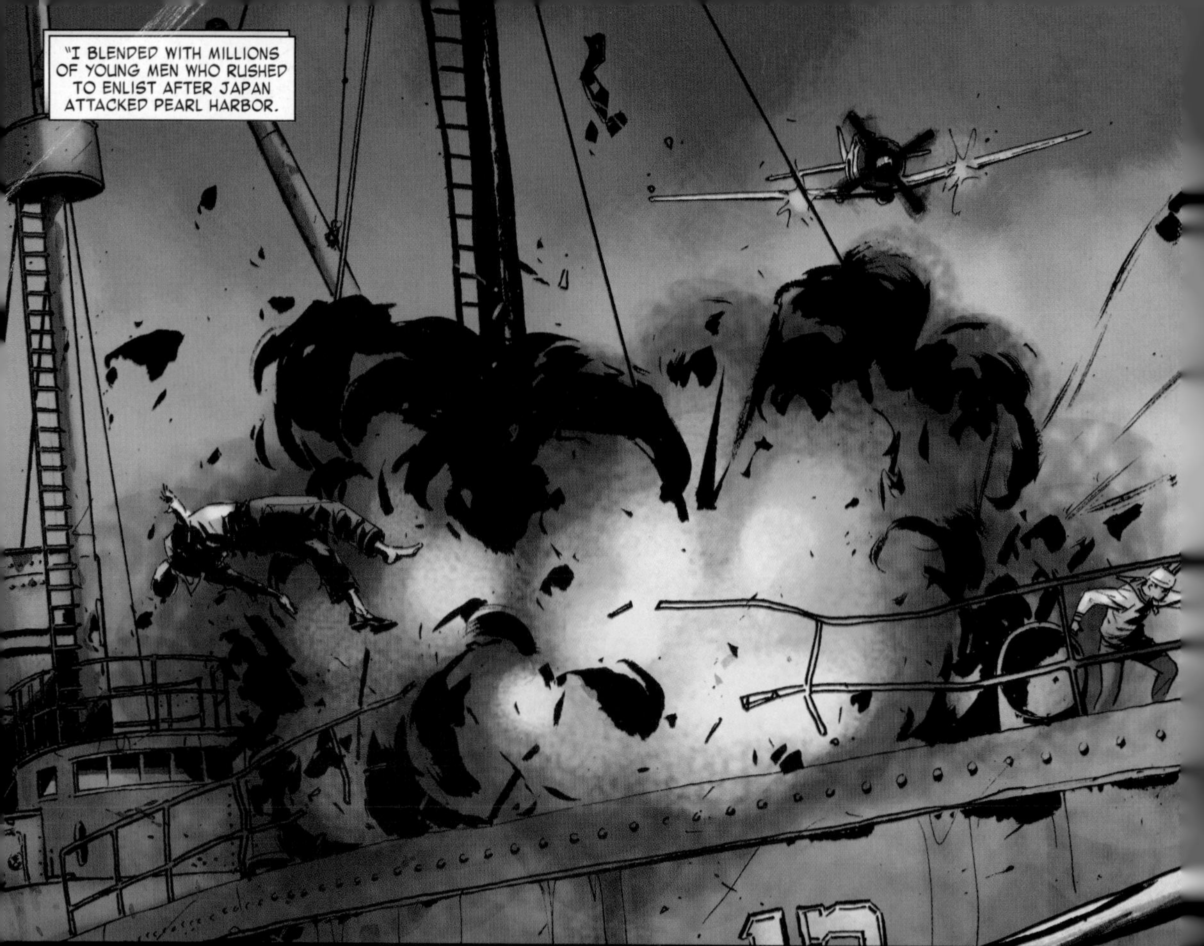
"I BLENDED WITH MILLIONS OF YOUNG MEN WHO RUSHED TO ENLIST AFTER JAPAN ATTACKED PEARL HARBOR.

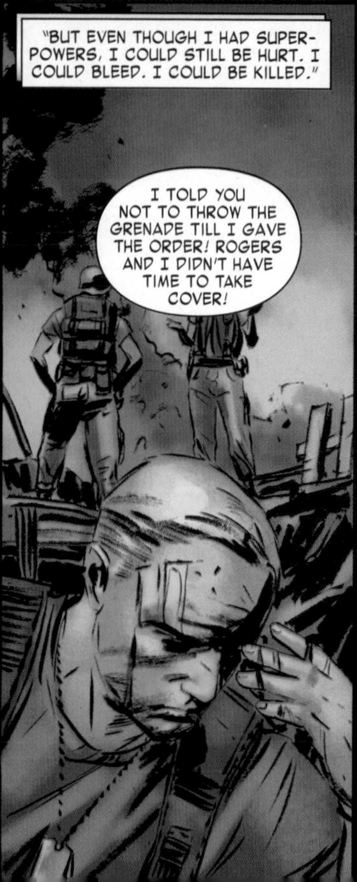
"BUT EVEN THOUGH I HAD SUPER-POWERS, I COULD STILL BE HURT. I COULD BLEED. I COULD BE KILLED."
I TOLD YOU NOT TO THROW THE GRENADE TILL I GAVE THE ORDER! ROGERS AND I DIDN'T HAVE TIME TO TAKE COVER!

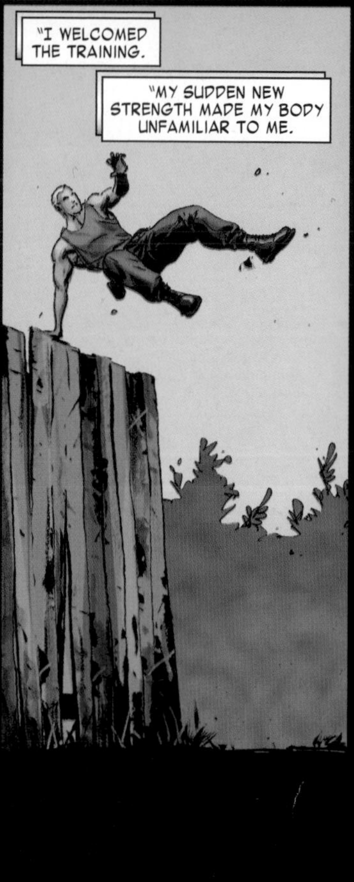
"I WELCOMED THE TRAINING.
"MY SUDDEN NEW STRENGTH MADE MY BODY UNFAMILIAR TO ME.

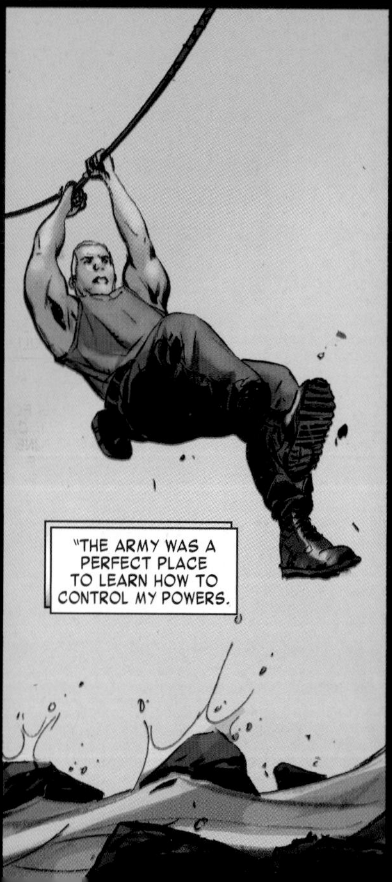
"THE ARMY WAS A PERFECT PLACE TO LEARN HOW TO CONTROL MY POWERS.

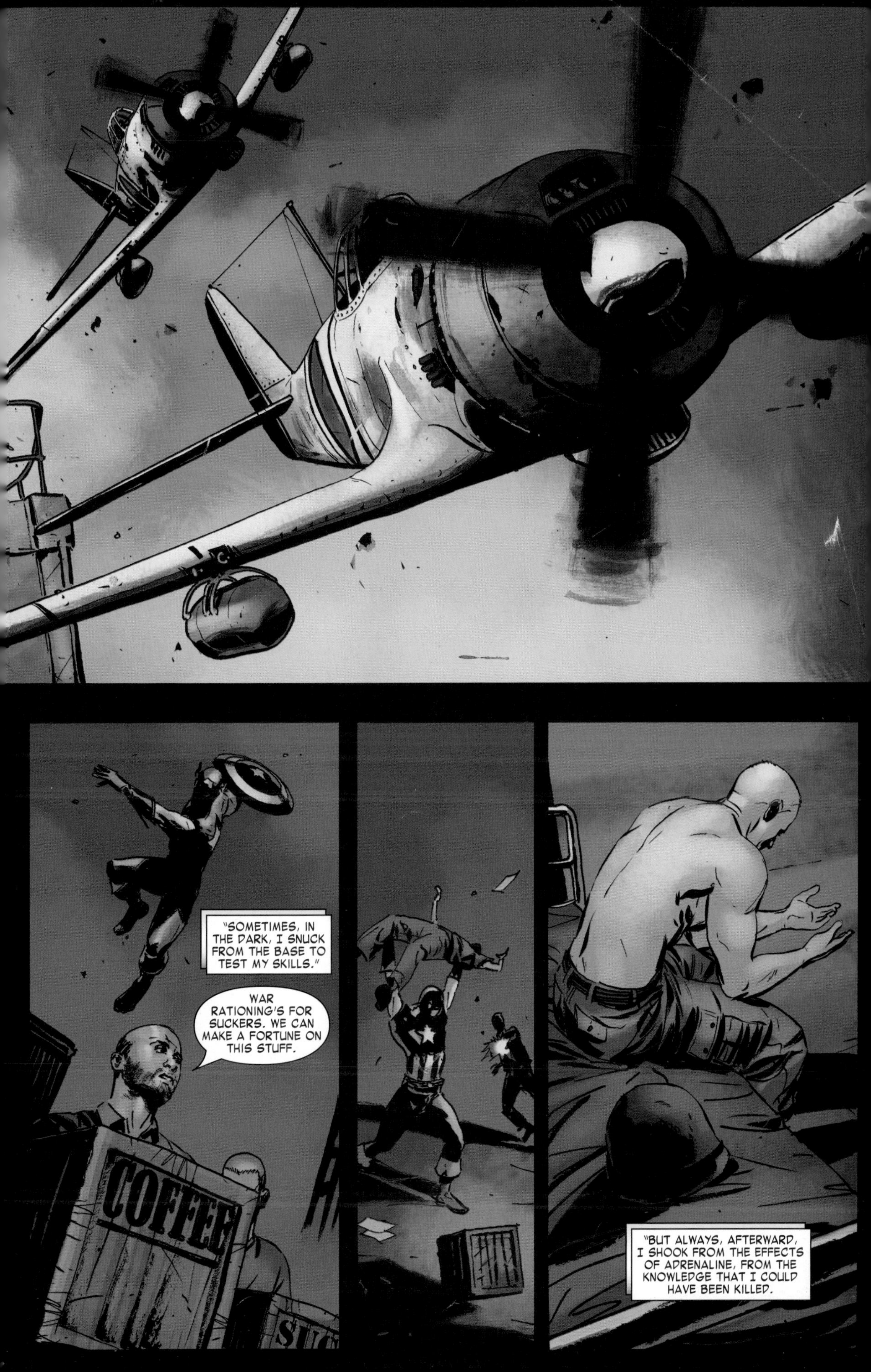
"SOMETIMES, IN THE DARK, I SNUCK FROM THE BASE TO TEST MY SKILLS."
WAR RATIONING'S FOR SUCKERS. WE CAN MAKE A FORTUNE ON THIS STUFF.
COFFEE
"BUT ALWAYS, AFTERWARD, I SHOOK FROM THE EFFECTS OF ADRENALINE, FROM THE KNOWLEDGE THAT I COULD HAVE BEEN KILLED.

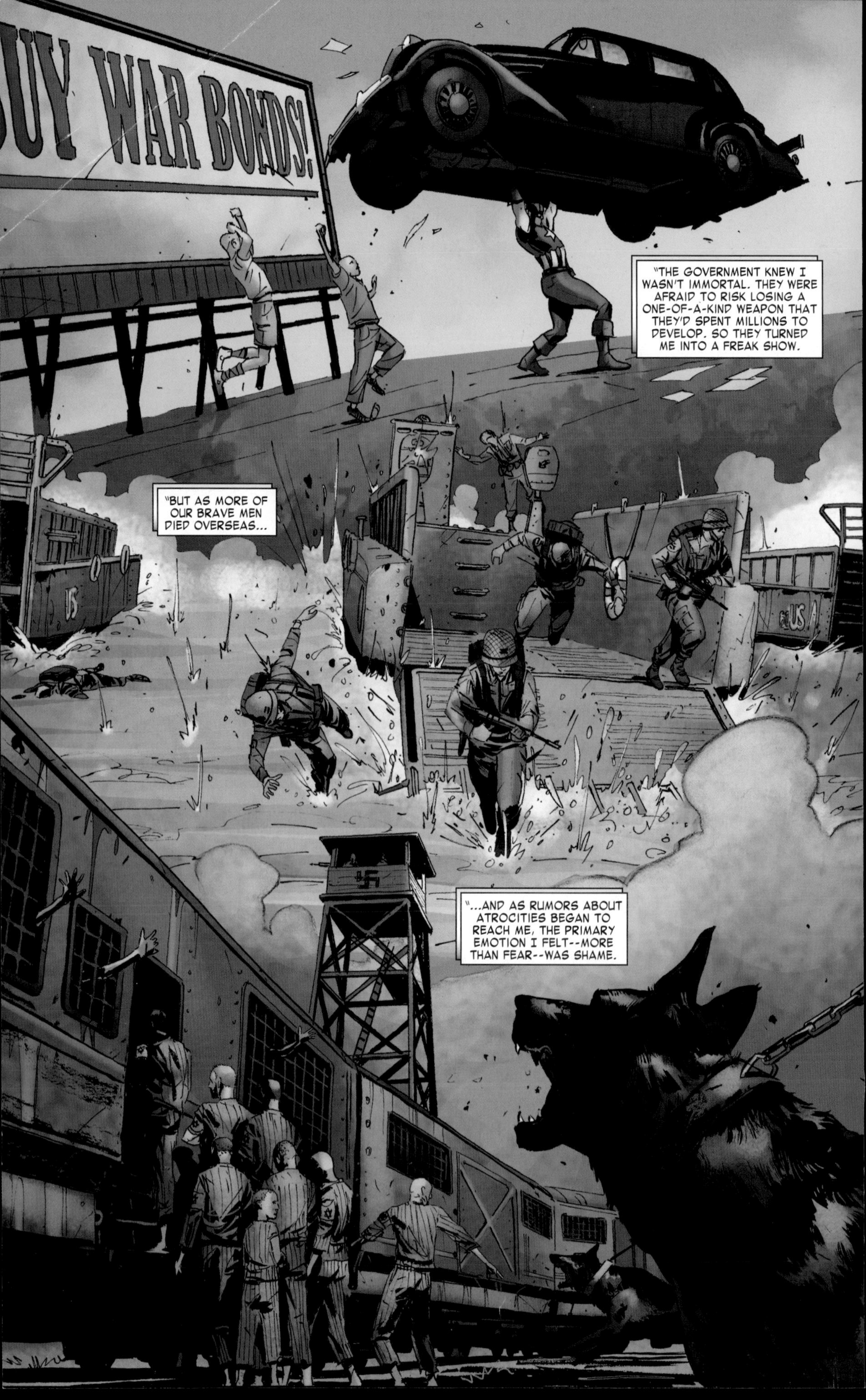
BUY WAR BONDS!
"THE GOVERNMENT KNEW I WASN'T IMMORTAL. THEY WERE AFRAID TO RISK LOSING A ONE-OF-A-KIND WEAPON THAT THEY'D SPENT MILLIONS TO DEVELOP. SO THEY TURNED ME INTO A FREAK SHOW.
"BUT AS MORE OF OUR BRAVE MEN DIED OVERSEAS...
"...AND AS RUMORS ABOUT ATROCITIES BEGAN TO REACH ME, THE PRIMARY EMOTION I FELT--MORE THAN FEAR--WAS SHAME.

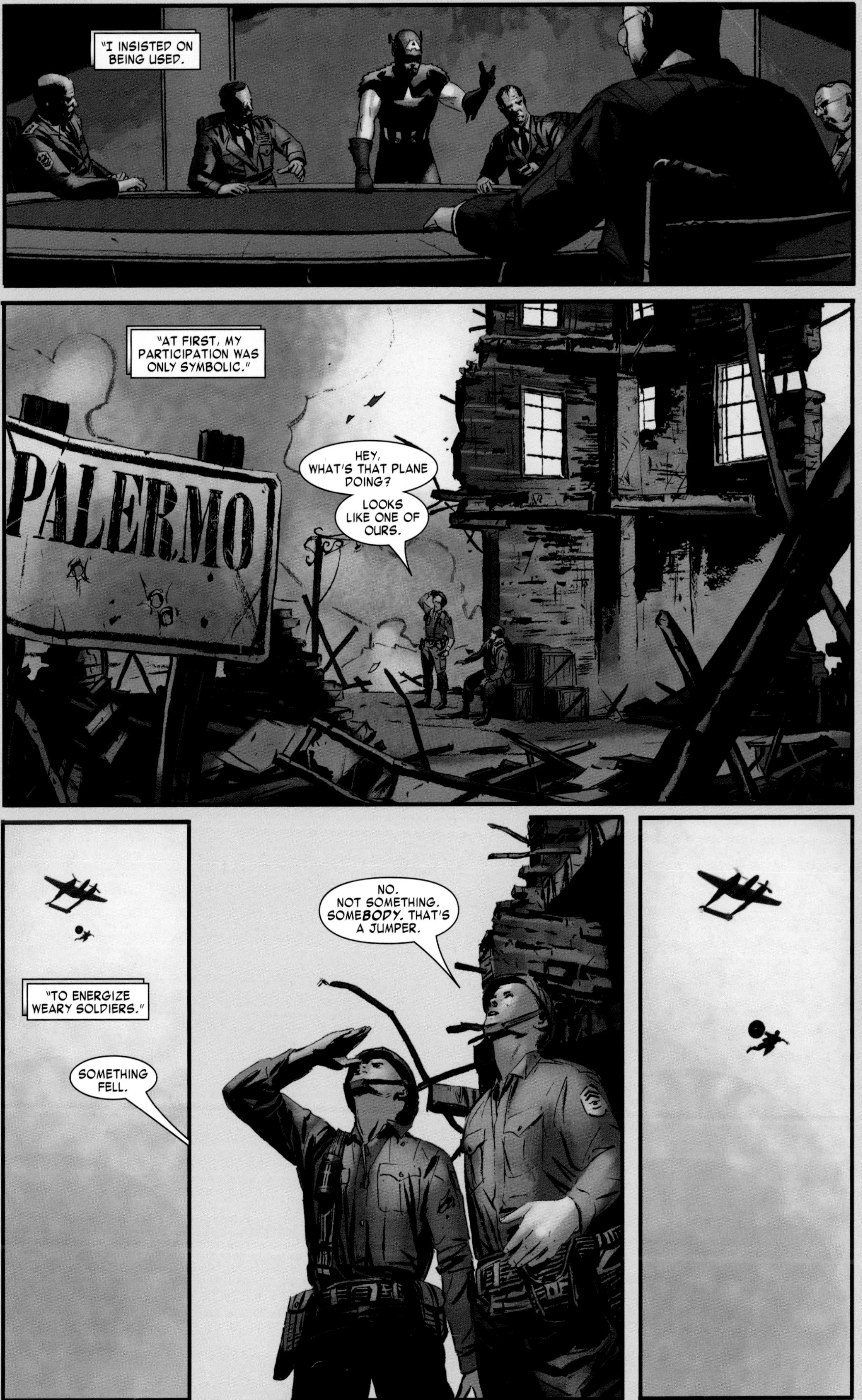
"I INSISTED ON BEING USED.
"AT FIRST, MY PARTICIPATION WAS ONLY SYMBOLIC."
PALERMO
HEY, WHAT'S THAT PLANE DOING?
LOOKS LIKE ONE OF OURS.
"TO ENERGIZE WEARY SOLDIERS."
SOMETHING FELL.
NO. NOT SOMETHING. SOMEBODY. THAT'S A JUMPER.

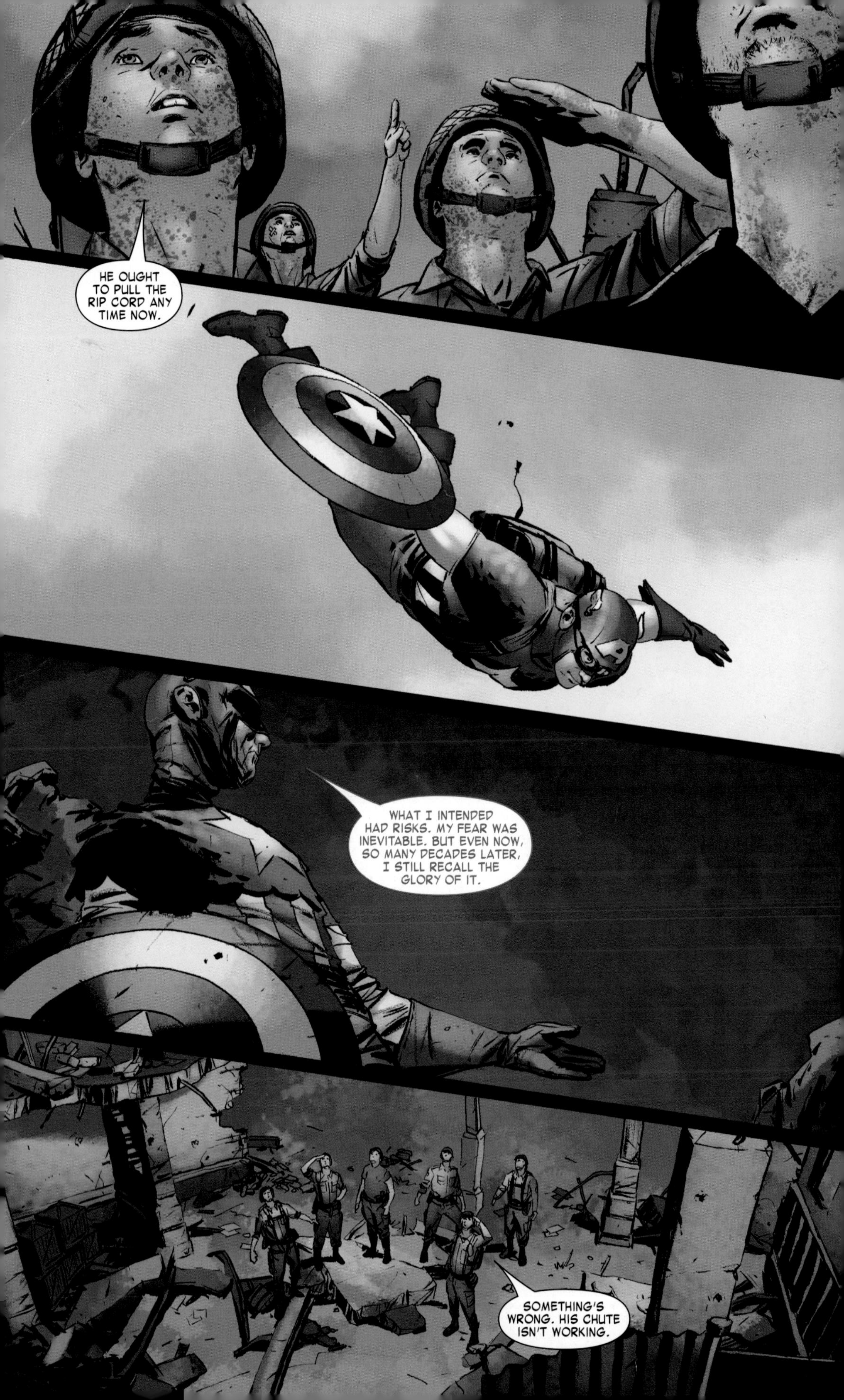
HE OUGHT TO PULL THE RIP CORD ANY TIME NOW.
WHAT I INTENDED HAD RISKS. MY FEAR WAS INEVITABLE. BUT EVEN NOW, SO MANY DECADES LATER, I STILL RECALL THE GLORY OF IT.
SOMETHING'S WRONG. HIS CHUTE ISN'T WORKING.

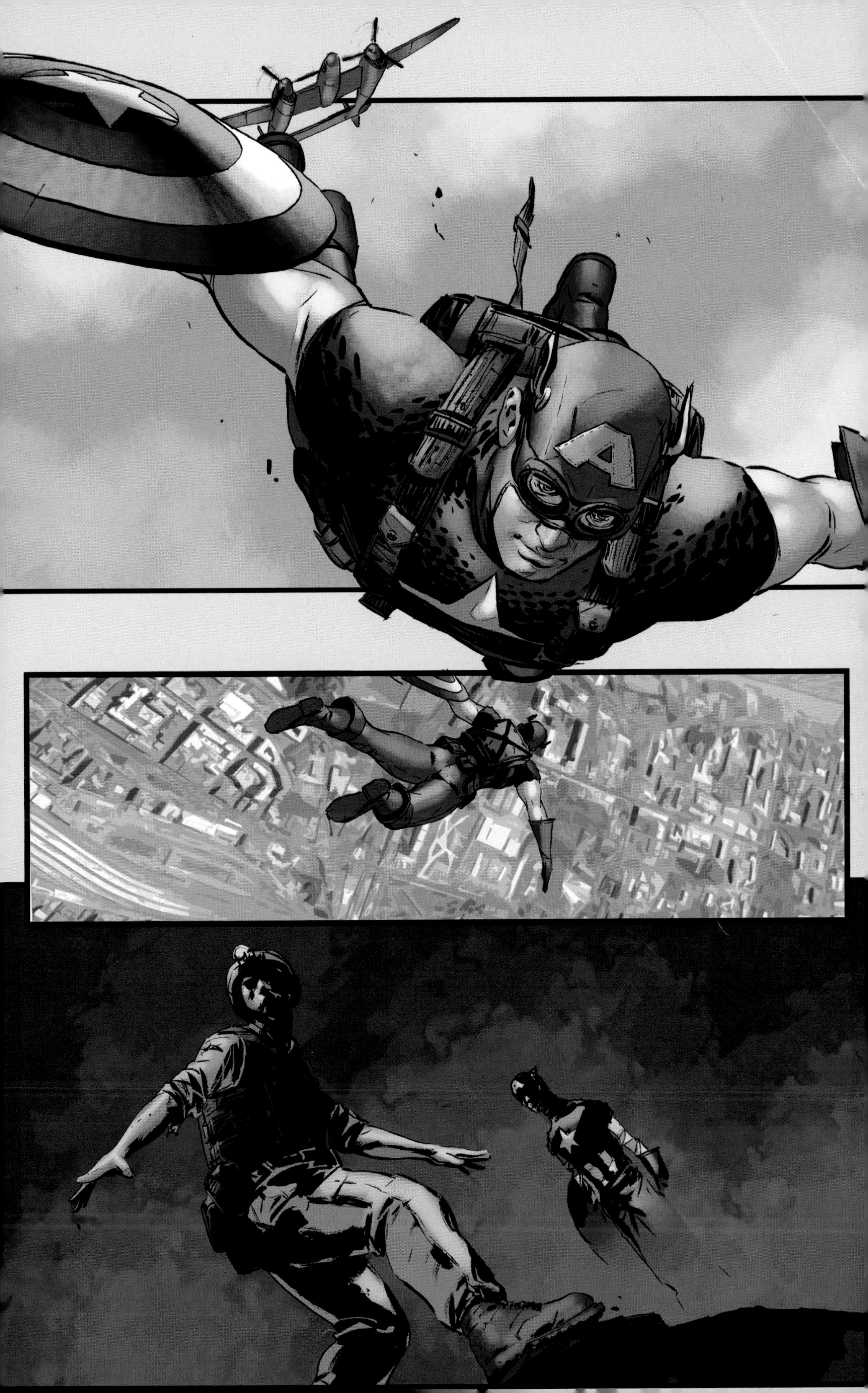

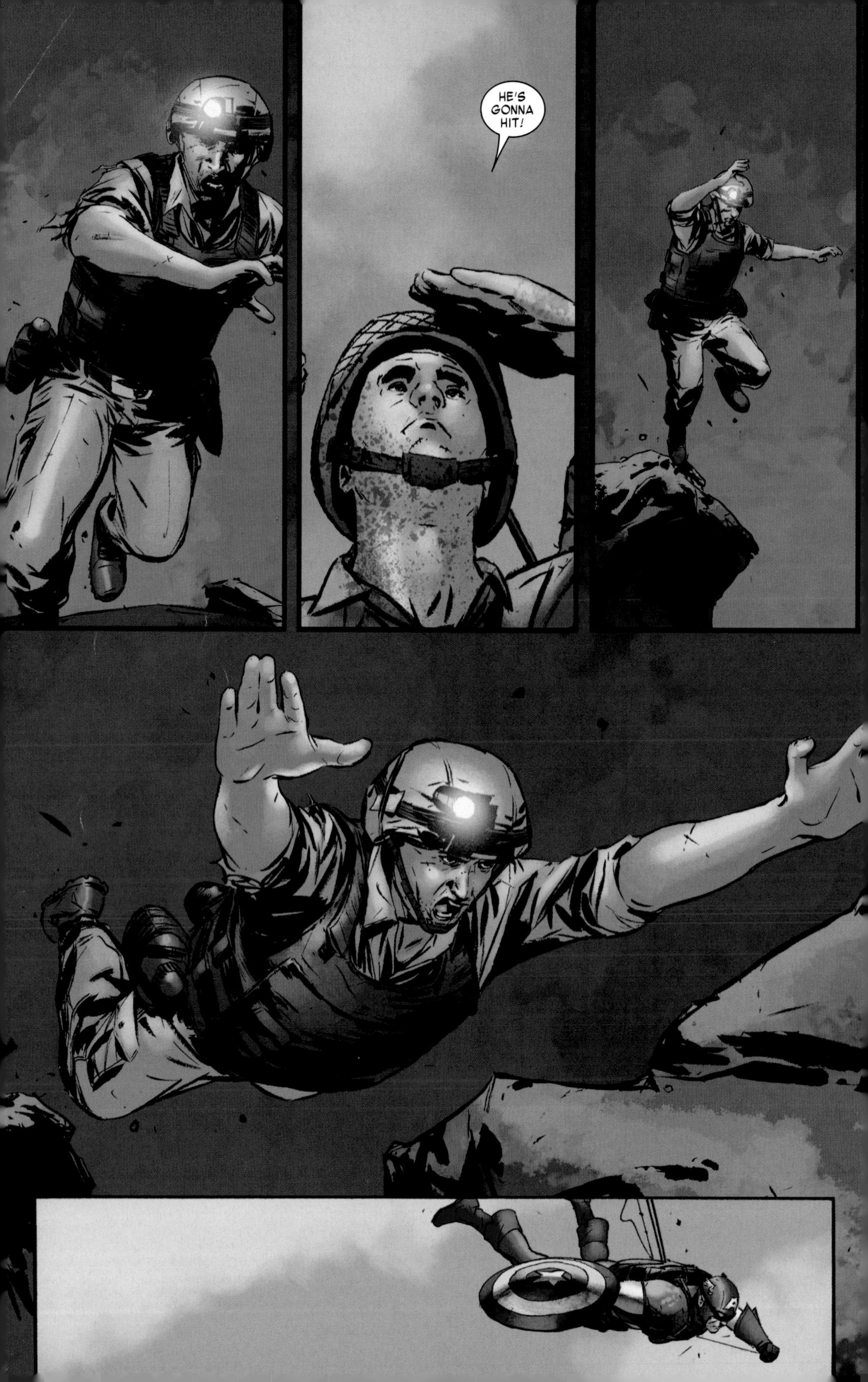
HE'S GONNA HIT!

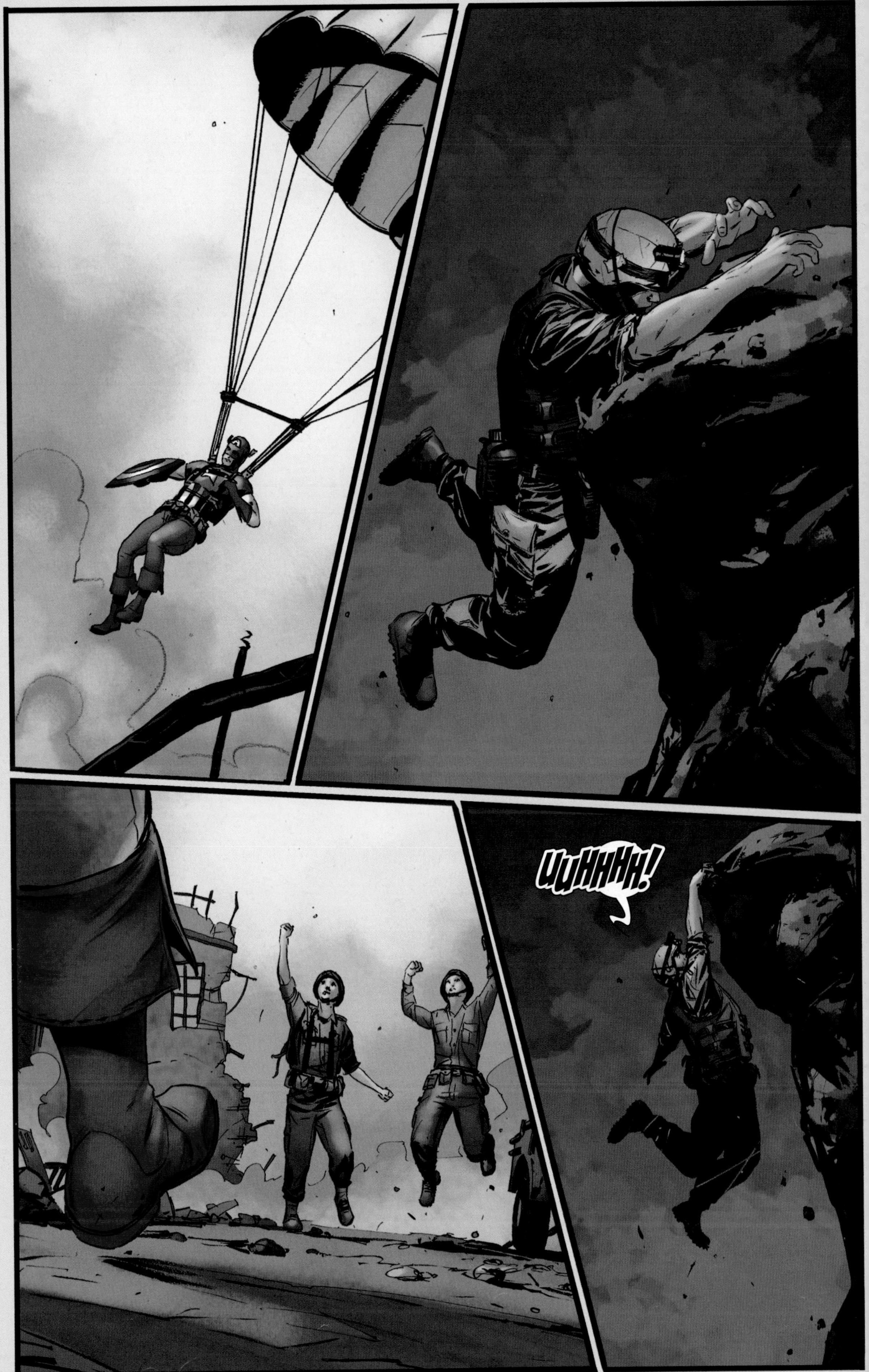
UUHHHH!

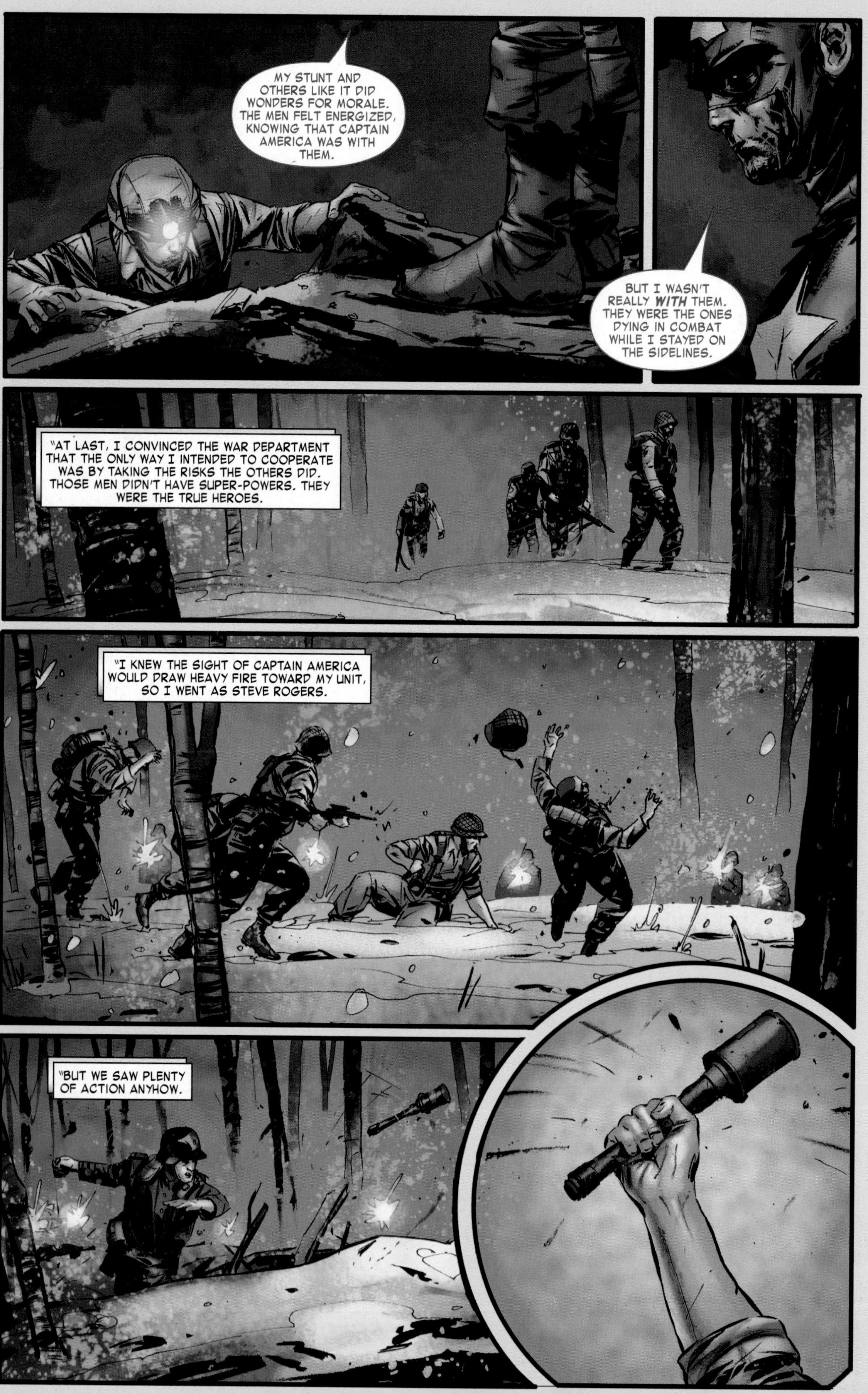
MY STUNT AND OTHERS LIKE IT DID WONDERS FOR MORALE. THE MEN FELT ENERGIZED, KNOWING THAT CAPTAIN AMERICA WAS WITH THEM.
BUT I WASN'T REALLY WITH THEM. THEY WERE THE ONES DYING IN COMBAT WHILE I STAYED ON THE SIDELINES.
"AT LAST, I CONVINCED THE WAR DEPARTMENT THAT THE ONLY WAY I INTENDED TO COOPERATE WAS BY TAKING THE RISKS THE OTHERS DID. THOSE MEN DIDN'T HAVE SUPER-POWERS. THEY WERE THE TRUE HEROES.
"I KNEW THE SIGHT OF CAPTAIN AMERICA WOULD DRAW HEAVY FIRE TOWARD MY UNIT, SO I WENT AS STEVE ROGERS.
"BUT WE SAW PLENTY OF ACTION ANYHOW.

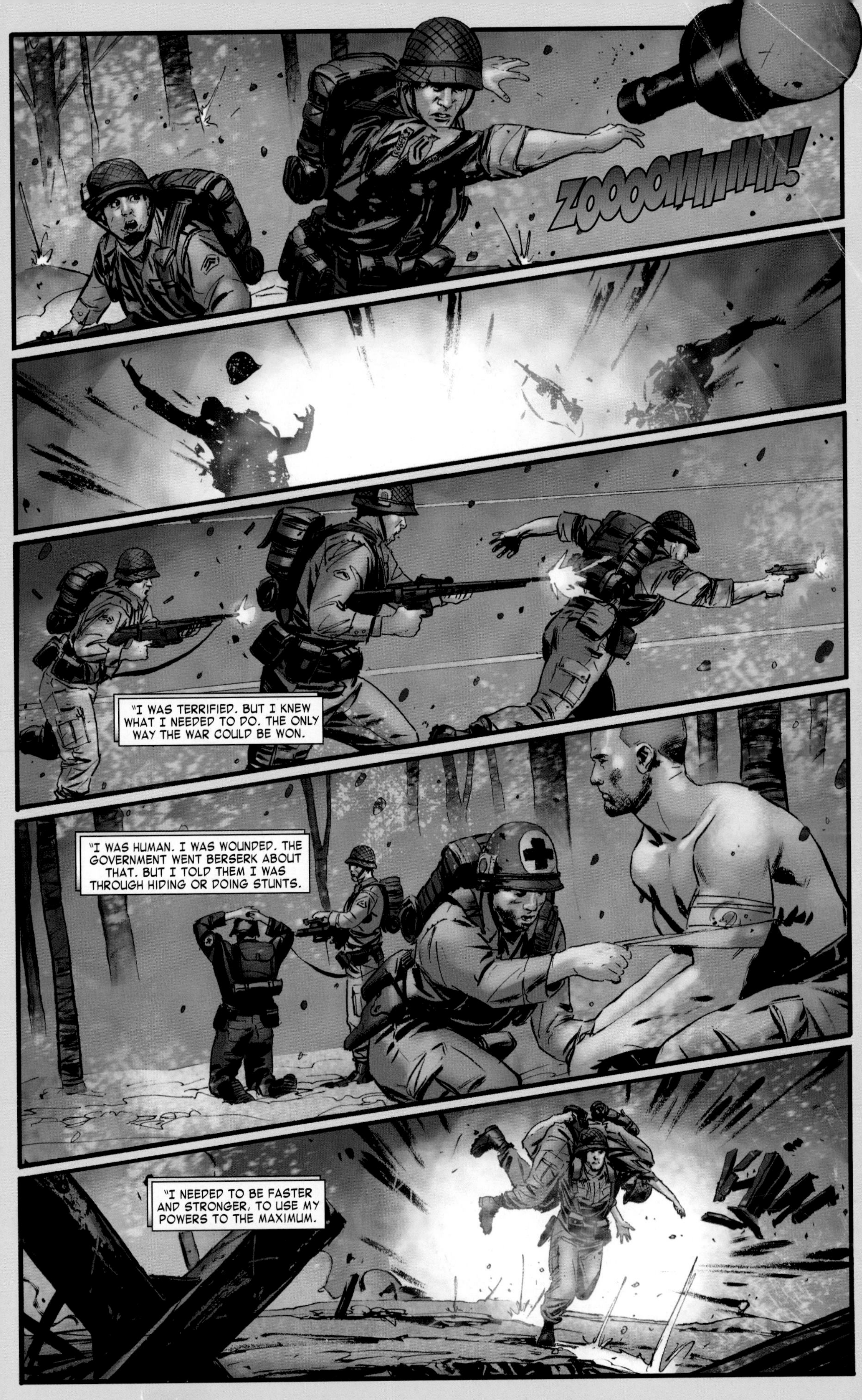
ZOOOOMMMM!
"I WAS TERRIFIED. BUT I KNEW WHAT I NEEDED TO DO. THE ONLY WAY THE WAR COULD BE WON.
"I WAS HUMAN. I WAS WOUNDED. THE GOVERNMENT WENT BERSERK ABOUT THAT. BUT I TOLD THEM I WAS THROUGH HIDING OR DOING STUNTS.
"I NEEDED TO BE FASTER AND STRONGER, TO USE MY POWERS TO THE MAXIMUM.

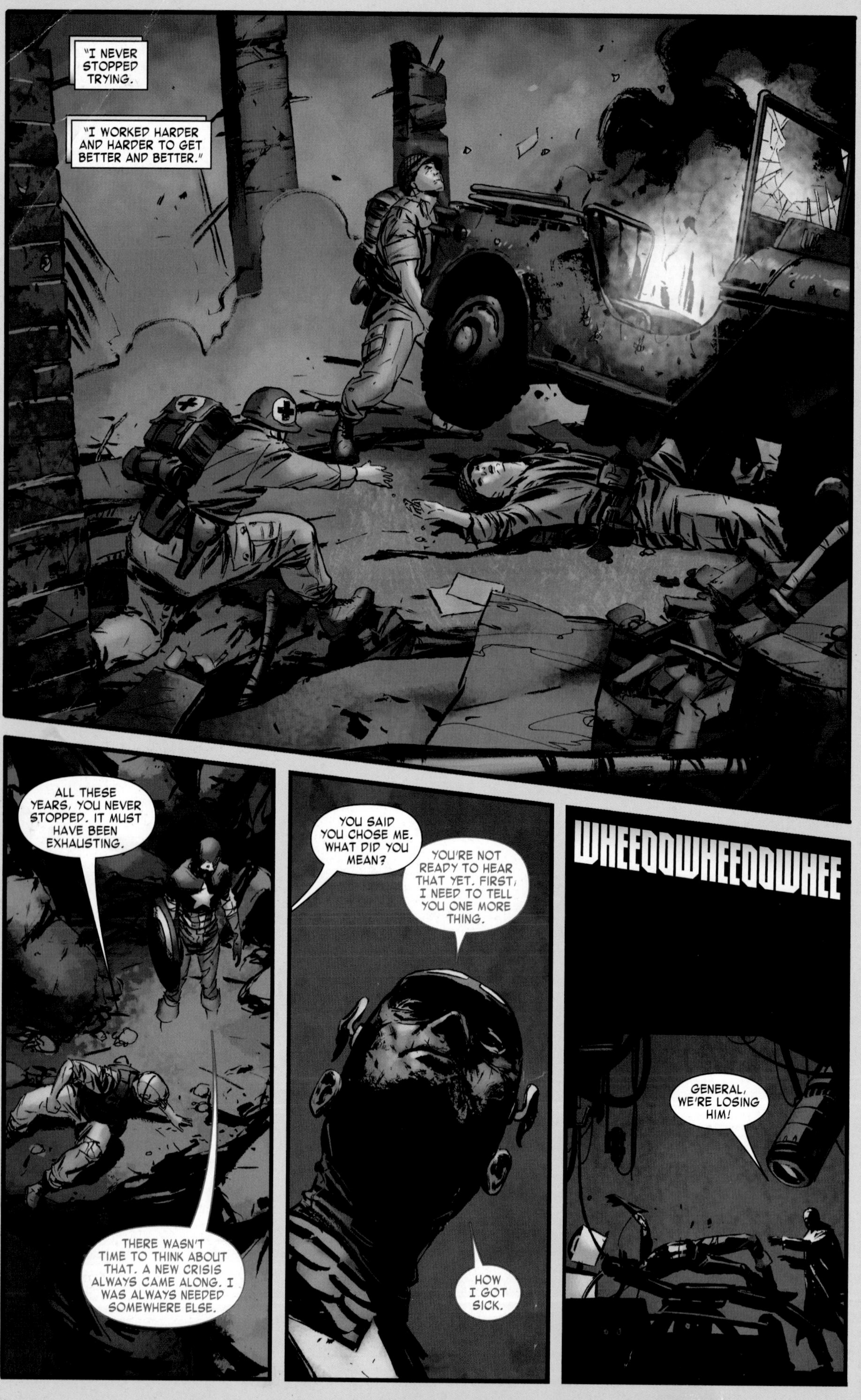
"I NEVER STOPPED TRYING.
"I WORKED HARDER AND HARDER TO GET BETTER AND BETTER."
ALL THESE YEARS, YOU NEVER STOPPED. IT MUST HAVE BEEN EXHAUSTING.
THERE WASN'T TIME TO THINK ABOUT THAT. A NEW CRISIS ALWAYS CAME ALONG. I WAS ALWAYS NEEDED SOMEWHERE ELSE.
YOU SAID YOU CHOSE ME. WHAT DID YOU MEAN?
YOU'RE NOT READY TO HEAR THAT YET. FIRST, I NEED TO TELL YOU ONE MORE THING.
HOW I GOT SICK.
WHEEOOWHEEOOWHEE
GENERAL, WE'RE LOSING HIM!

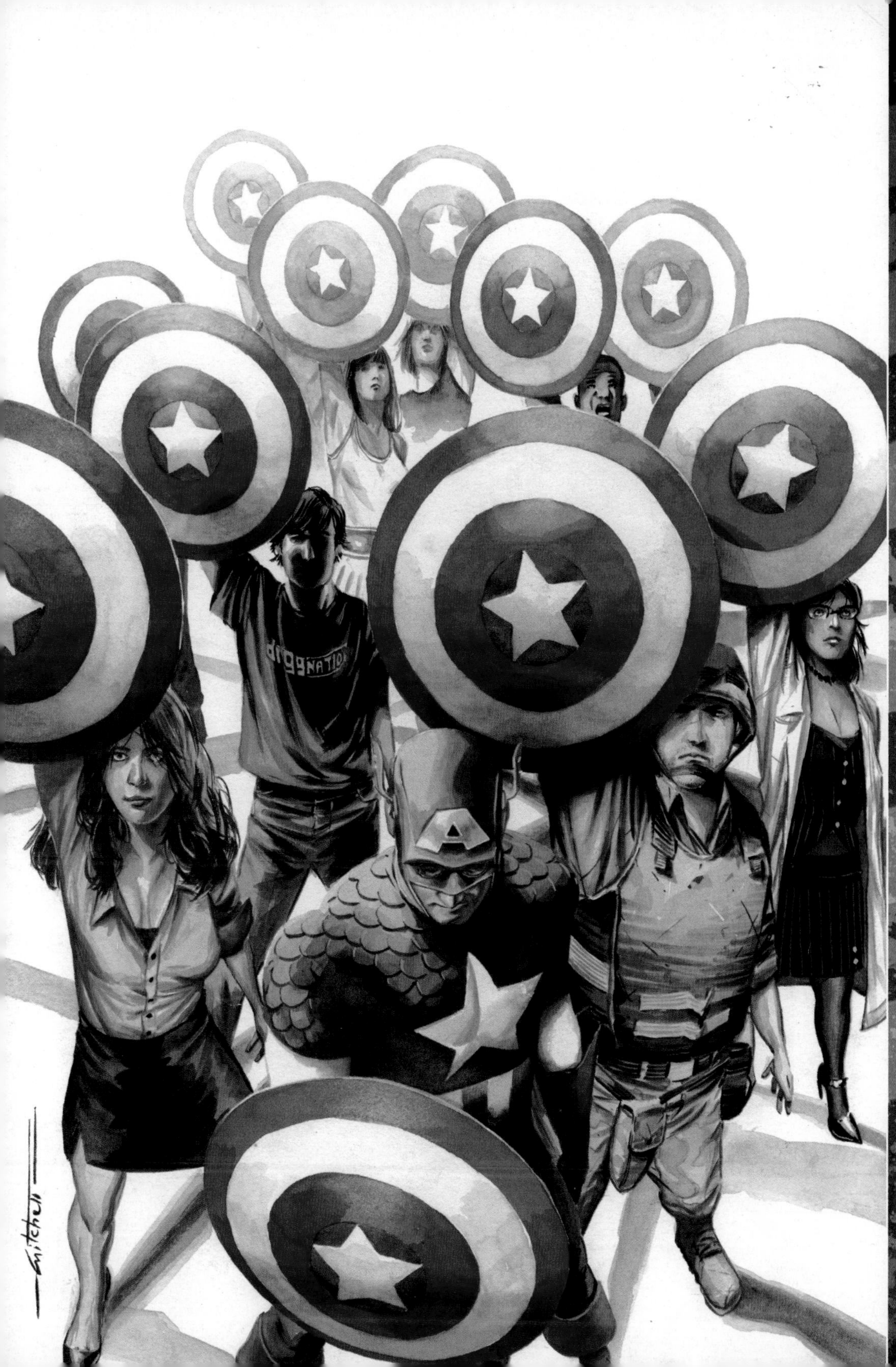

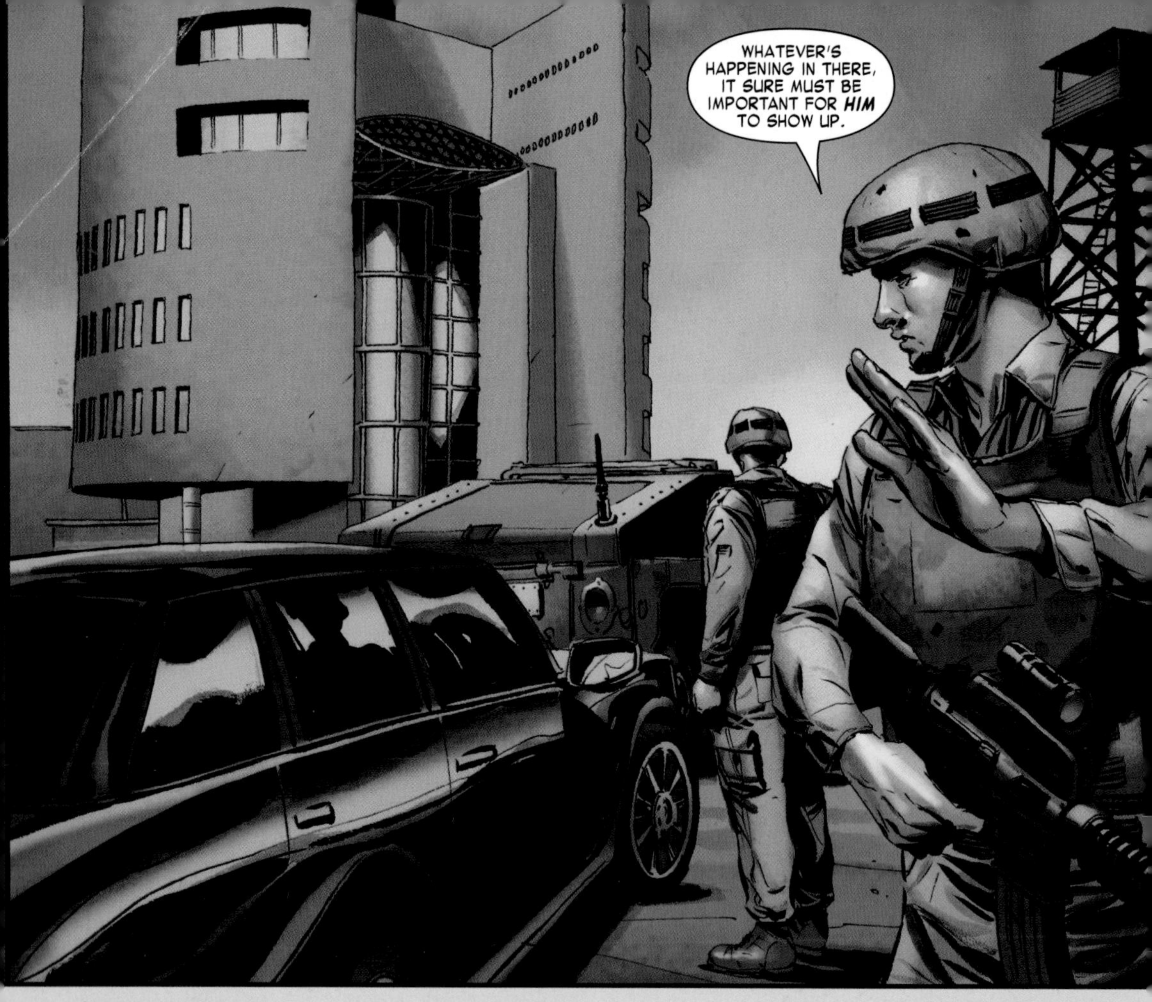
WHATEVER'S HAPPENING IN THERE, IT SURE MUST BE IMPORTANT FOR *HIM* TO SHOW UP.

CAPTAIN AMERICA: THE CHOSEN
CHAPTER 6:
MULTITUDE

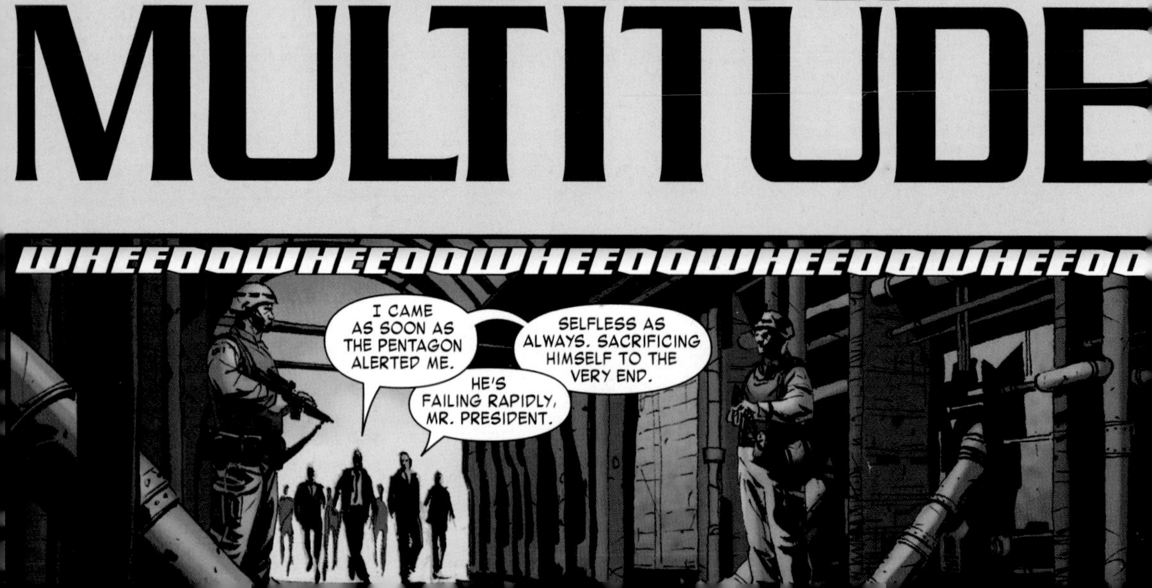
WHEEOOWHEEOOWHEEOOWHEEOOWHEEOO
I CAME AS SOON AS THE PENTAGON ALERTED ME.
HE'S FAILING RAPIDLY, MR. PRESIDENT.
SELFLESS AS ALWAYS. SACRIFICING HIMSELF TO THE VERY END.

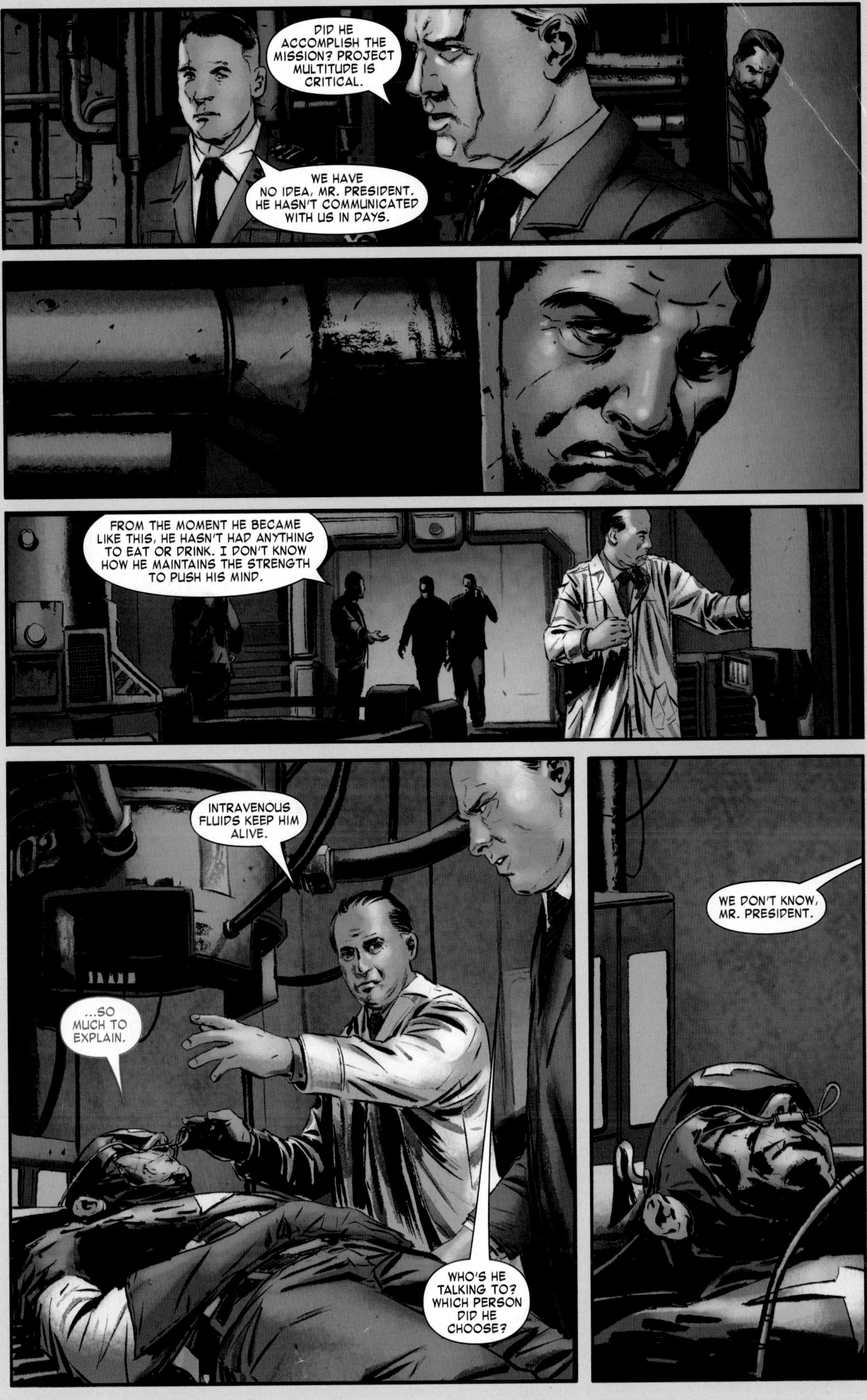
DID HE ACCOMPLISH THE MISSION? PROJECT MULTITUDE IS CRITICAL.
WE HAVE NO IDEA, MR. PRESIDENT. HE HASN'T COMMUNICATED WITH US IN DAYS.
FROM THE MOMENT HE BECAME LIKE THIS, HE HASN'T HAD ANYTHING TO EAT OR DRINK. I DON'T KNOW HOW HE MAINTAINS THE STRENGTH TO PUSH HIS MIND.
INTRAVENOUS FLUIDS KEEP HIM ALIVE.
...SO MUCH TO EXPLAIN.
WHO'S HE TALKING TO? WHICH PERSON DID HE CHOOSE?
WE DON'T KNOW, MR. PRESIDENT.

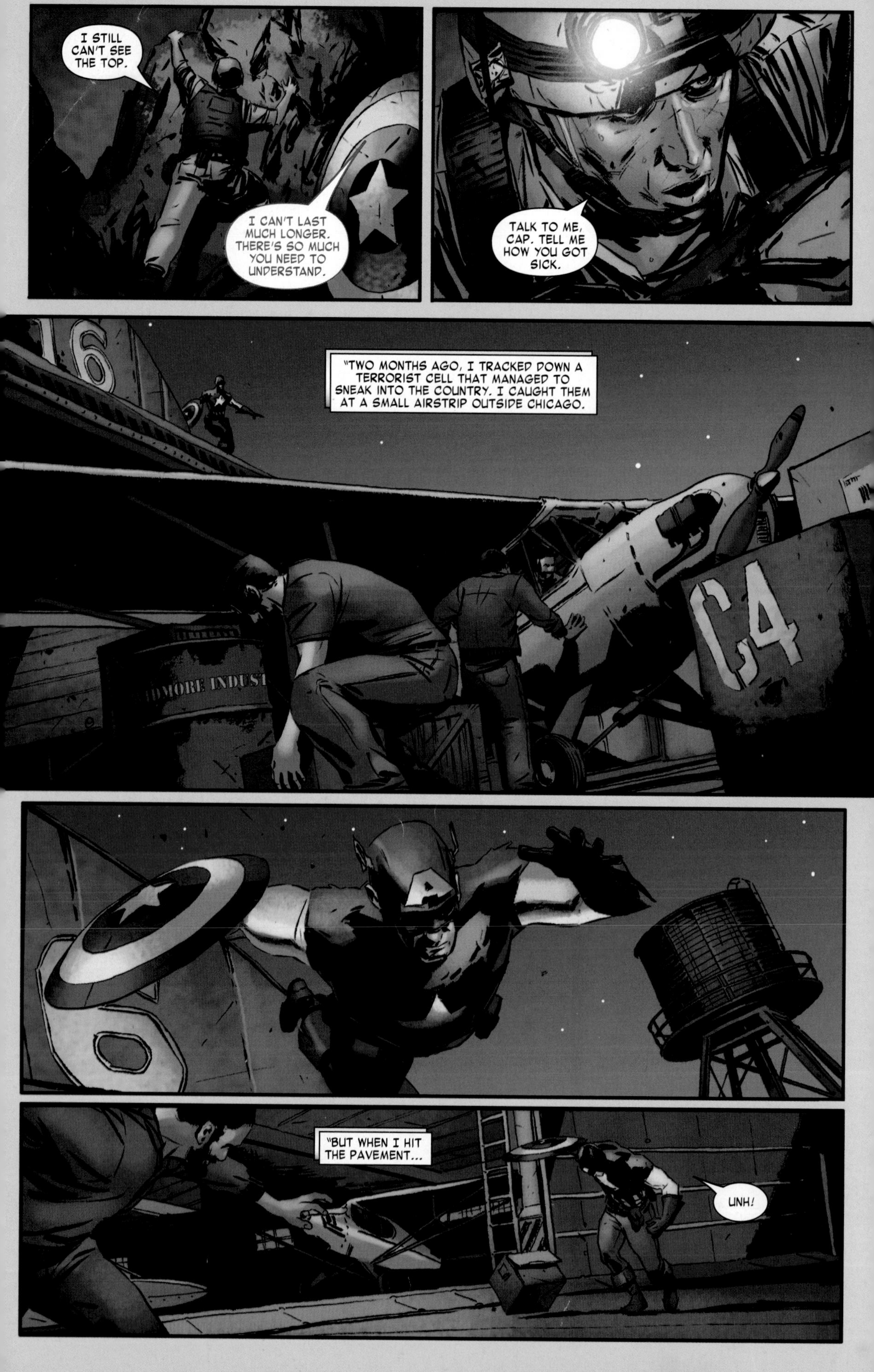

I STILL CAN'T SEE THE TOP.
I CAN'T LAST MUCH LONGER. THERE'S SO MUCH YOU NEED TO UNDERSTAND.
TALK TO ME, CAP. TELL ME HOW YOU GOT SICK.
"TWO MONTHS AGO, I TRACKED DOWN A TERRORIST CELL THAT MANAGED TO SNEAK INTO THE COUNTRY. I CAUGHT THEM AT A SMALL AIRSTRIP OUTSIDE CHICAGO.
C4
"BUT WHEN I HIT THE PAVEMENT...
UNH!

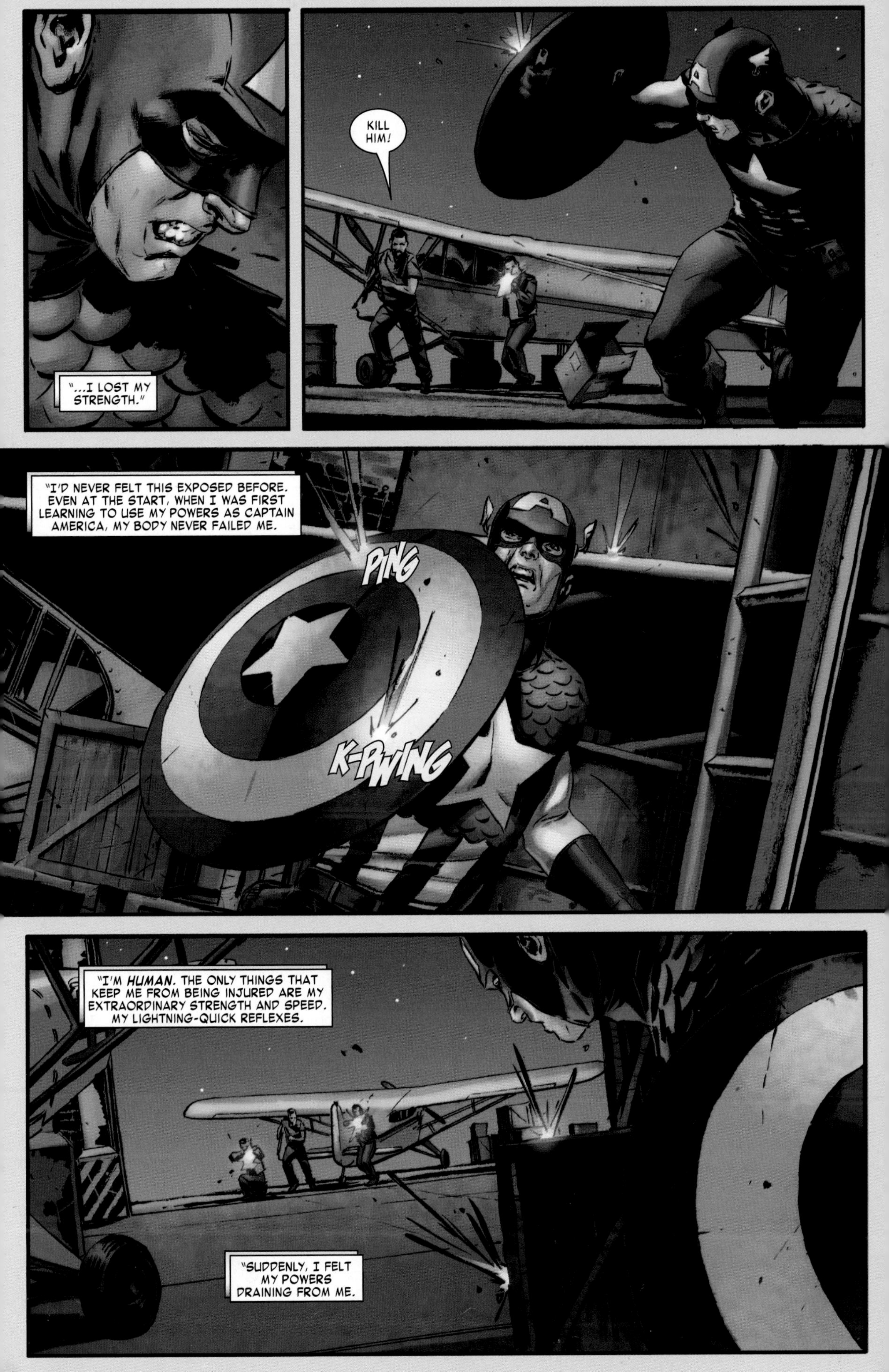
"...I LOST MY STRENGTH."
KILL HIM!
"I'D NEVER FELT THIS EXPOSED BEFORE. EVEN AT THE START, WHEN I WAS FIRST LEARNING TO USE MY POWERS AS CAPTAIN AMERICA, MY BODY NEVER FAILED ME.
PING
K-PWING
"I'M *HUMAN*. THE ONLY THINGS THAT KEEP ME FROM BEING INJURED ARE MY EXTRAORDINARY STRENGTH AND SPEED. MY LIGHTNING-QUICK REFLEXES.
"SUDDENLY, I FELT MY POWERS DRAINING FROM ME.

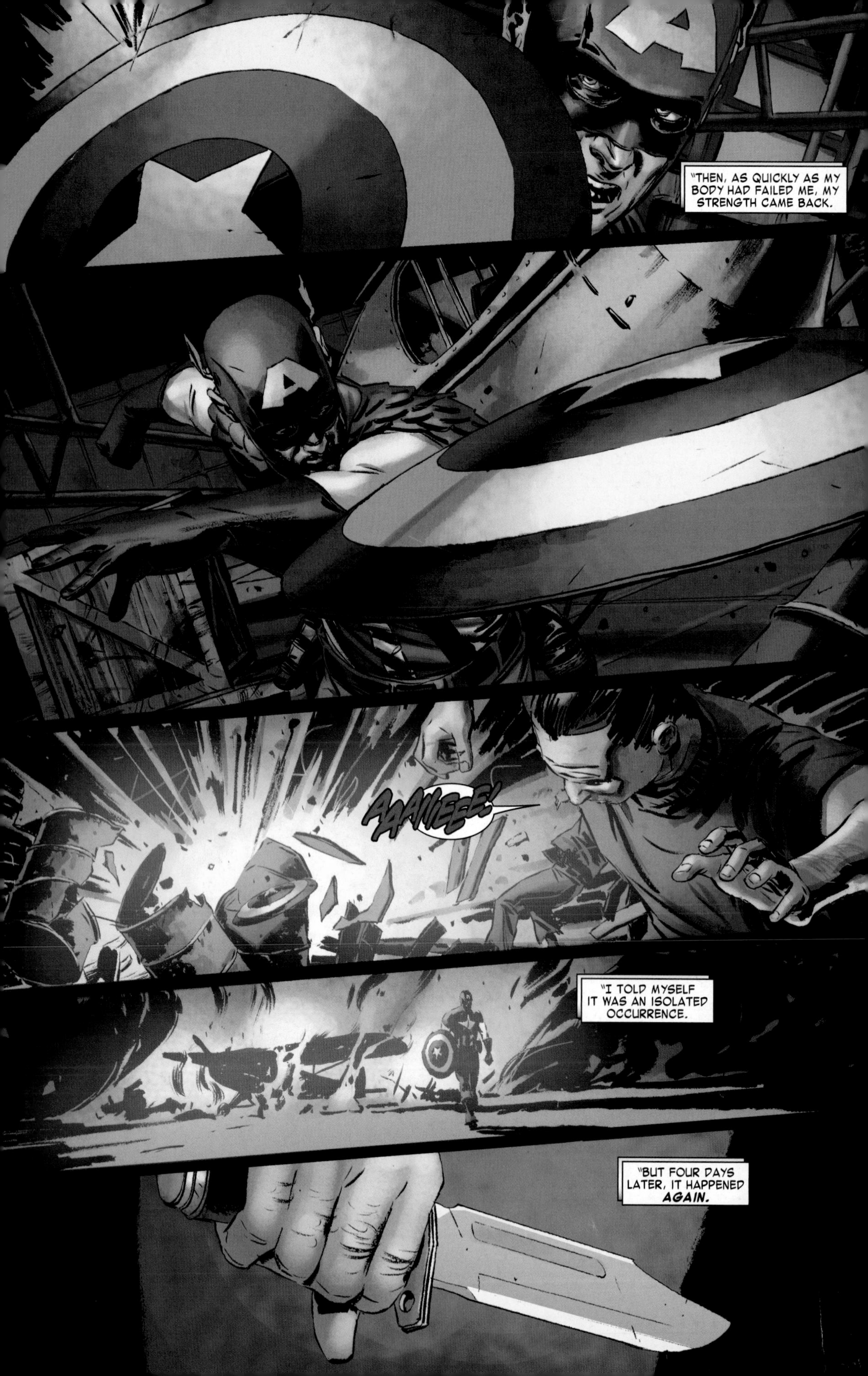
"THEN, AS QUICKLY AS MY BODY HAD FAILED ME, MY STRENGTH CAME BACK.
AAAIIEEE!
"I TOLD MYSELF IT WAS AN ISOLATED OCCURRENCE.
"BUT FOUR DAYS LATER, IT HAPPENED AGAIN.

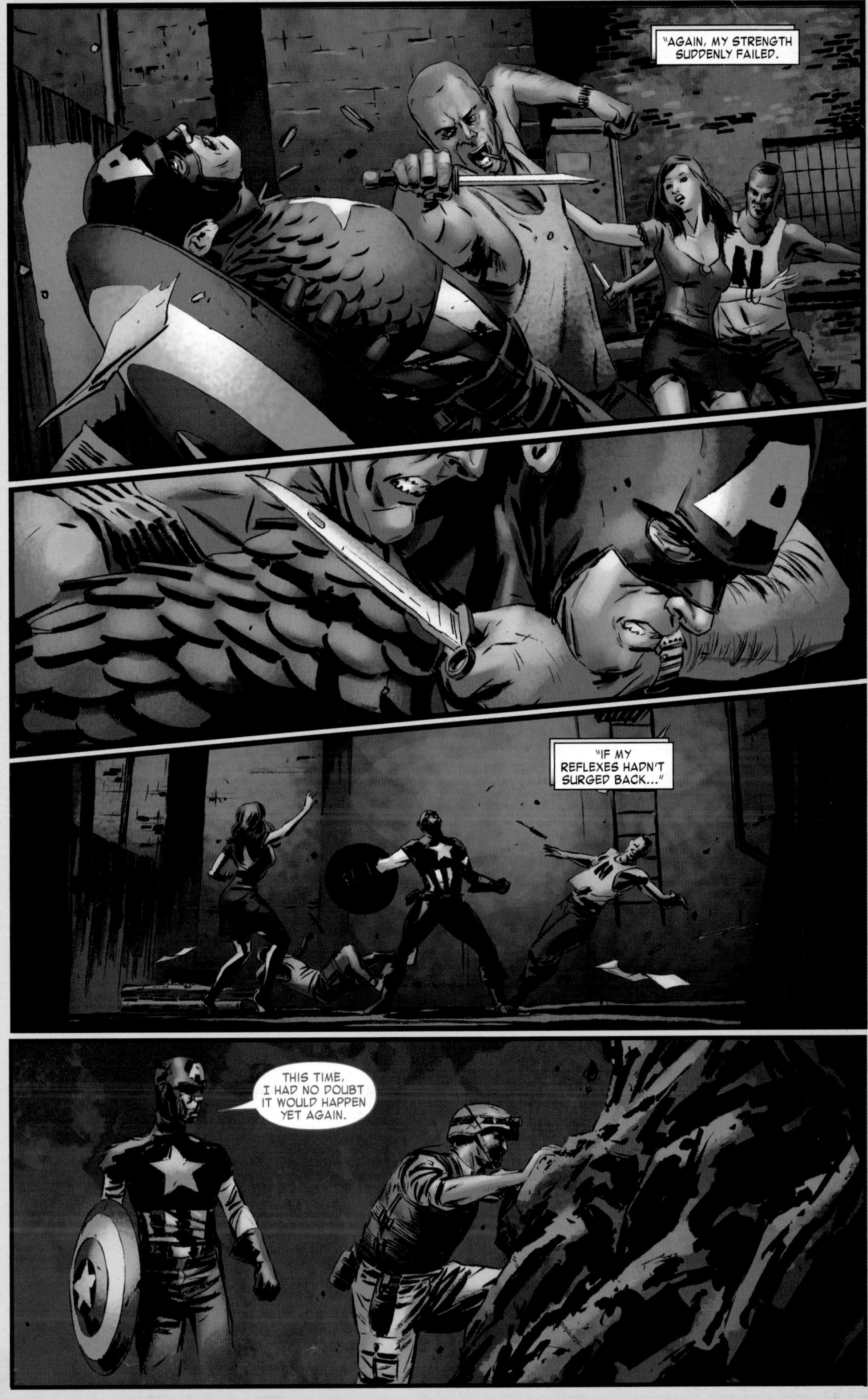
"AGAIN, MY STRENGTH SUDDENLY FAILED.
"IF MY REFLEXES HADN'T SURGED BACK..."
THIS TIME, I HAD NO DOUBT IT WOULD HAPPEN YET AGAIN.

"A TEAM OF MEDICAL SPECIALISTS GAVE ME EVERY TEST THEY COULD THINK OF."

HE'S LOSING MUSCLE DENSITY.

HE'S NOT PROCESSING OXYGEN AS EFFICIENTLY.

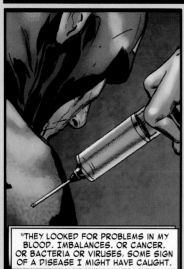

"THEY LOOKED FOR PROBLEMS IN MY BLOOD. IMBALANCES. OR CANCER. OR BACTERIA OR VIRUSES, SOME SIGN OF A DISEASE I MIGHT HAVE CAUGHT.

"IN THE END, THEY ALL REACHED THE SAME CONCLUSION."

ALL THESE YEARS AFTER PROJECT REBIRTH MADE ME CAPTAIN AMERICA, THE PROCESS WAS FAILING.

POSSIBLY, THE EXPERIMENTAL CHEMICALS AND HORMONES FINALLY LOST THEIR POTENCY. OR ELSE THE EFFECTS OF THE RAY MACHINE REACHED THEIR LIMIT. ALL WE KNOW IS, YOUR CELL STRUCTURE AND METABOLISM ARE REVERTING.

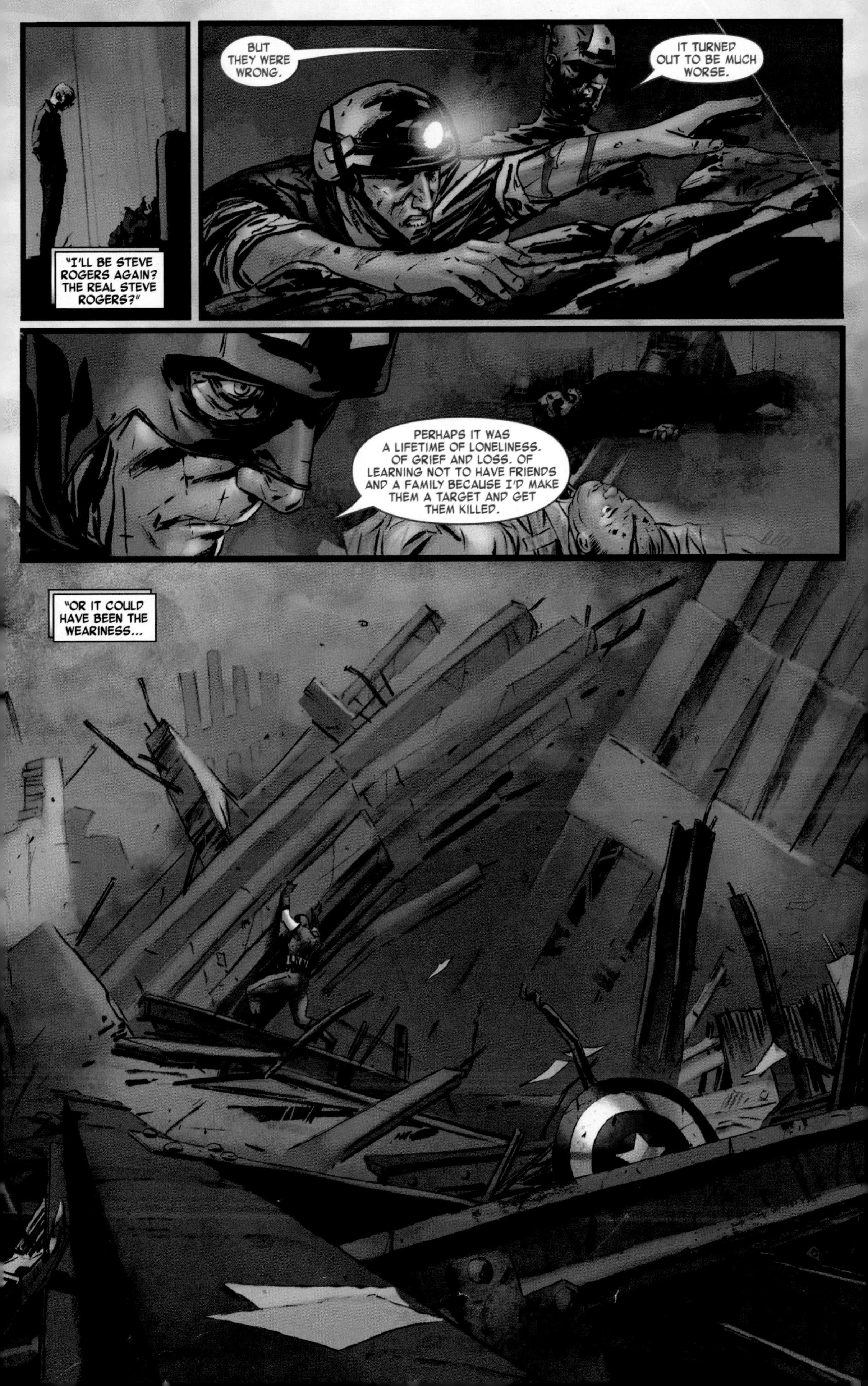
"I'LL BE STEVE ROGERS AGAIN? THE REAL STEVE ROGERS?"
BUT THEY WERE WRONG.
IT TURNED OUT TO BE MUCH WORSE.
PERHAPS IT WAS A LIFETIME OF LONELINESS. OF GRIEF AND LOSS. OF LEARNING NOT TO HAVE FRIENDS AND A FAMILY BECAUSE I'D MAKE THEM A TARGET AND GET THEM KILLED.
"OR IT COULD HAVE BEEN THE WEARINESS...

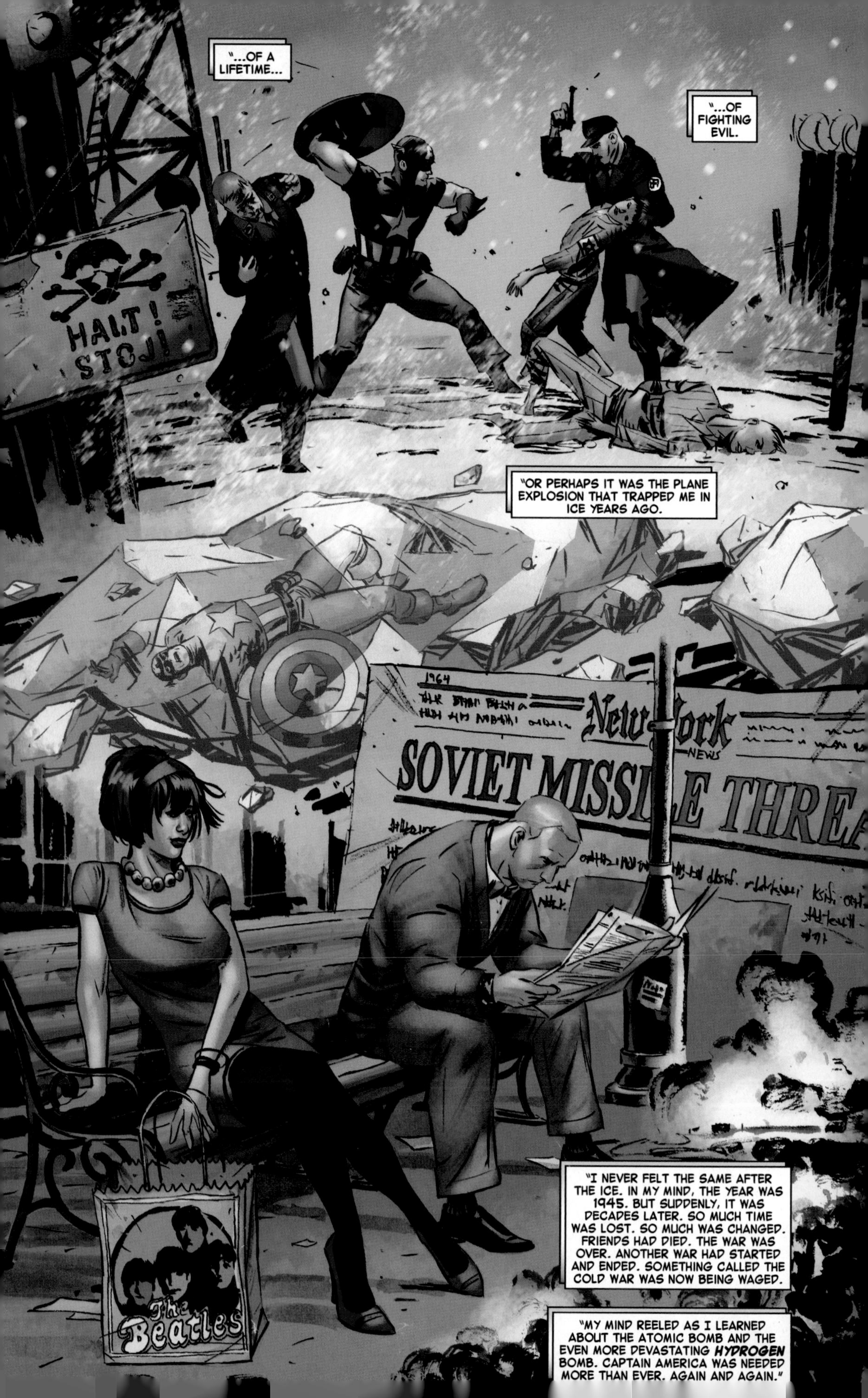
"...OF A LIFETIME...
"...OF FIGHTING EVIL.
HALT! STOJ!
"OR PERHAPS IT WAS THE PLANE EXPLOSION THAT TRAPPED ME IN ICE YEARS AGO.
1964
SOVIET MISSI LE THREA
"I NEVER FELT THE SAME AFTER THE ICE. IN MY MIND, THE YEAR WAS 1945. BUT SUDDENLY, IT WAS DECADES LATER. SO MUCH TIME WAS LOST. SO MUCH WAS CHANGED. FRIENDS HAD DIED. THE WAR WAS OVER. ANOTHER WAR HAD STARTED AND ENDED. SOMETHING CALLED THE COLD WAR WAS NOW BEING WAGED.
"MY MIND REELED AS I LEARNED ABOUT THE ATOMIC BOMB AND THE EVEN MORE DEVASTATING ***HYDROGEN*** BOMB. CAPTAIN AMERICA WAS NEEDED MORE THAN EVER. AGAIN AND AGAIN."
The Beatles

MAYBE BEING FROZEN ALTERED THE PROJECT REBIRTH CHEMICALS AND HORMONES IN MY SYSTEM. MAYBE THE DAMAGE FINALLY CAUGHT UP TO ME...OR MAYBE I JUST WORE DOWN.

"I BECAME AS FRAIL AS I'D ORIGINALLY BEEN-- BUT THEN I GOT FRAILER. IT BECAME OBVIOUS THAT THIS WASN'T ONLY A REGRESSION. I WAS THE VICTIM OF A RELENTLESS COLLAPSE."

HOW MUCH TIME DO I HAVE?

SIX MONTHS.

"BUT THAT WAS WRONG, TOO. IT HAPPENED IN WEEKS, NOT MONTHS.

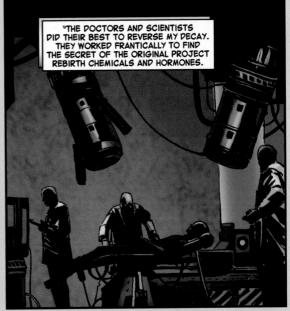

"THE DOCTORS AND SCIENTISTS DID THEIR BEST TO REVERSE MY DECAY. THEY WORKED FRANTICALLY TO FIND THE SECRET OF THE ORIGINAL PROJECT REBIRTH CHEMICALS AND HORMONES.

"THEY FAILED."

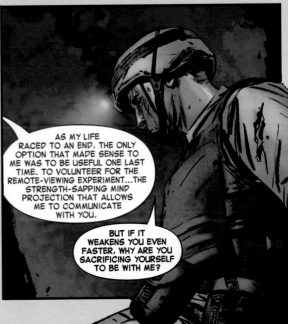

AS MY LIFE RACED TO AN END, THE ONLY OPTION THAT MADE SENSE TO ME WAS TO BE USEFUL ONE LAST TIME. TO VOLUNTEER FOR THE REMOTE-VIEWING EXPERIMENT...THE STRENGTH-SAPPING MIND PROJECTION THAT ALLOWS ME TO COMMUNICATE WITH YOU.

BUT IF IT WEAKENS YOU EVEN FASTER, WHY ARE YOU SACRIFICING YOURSELF TO BE WITH ME?

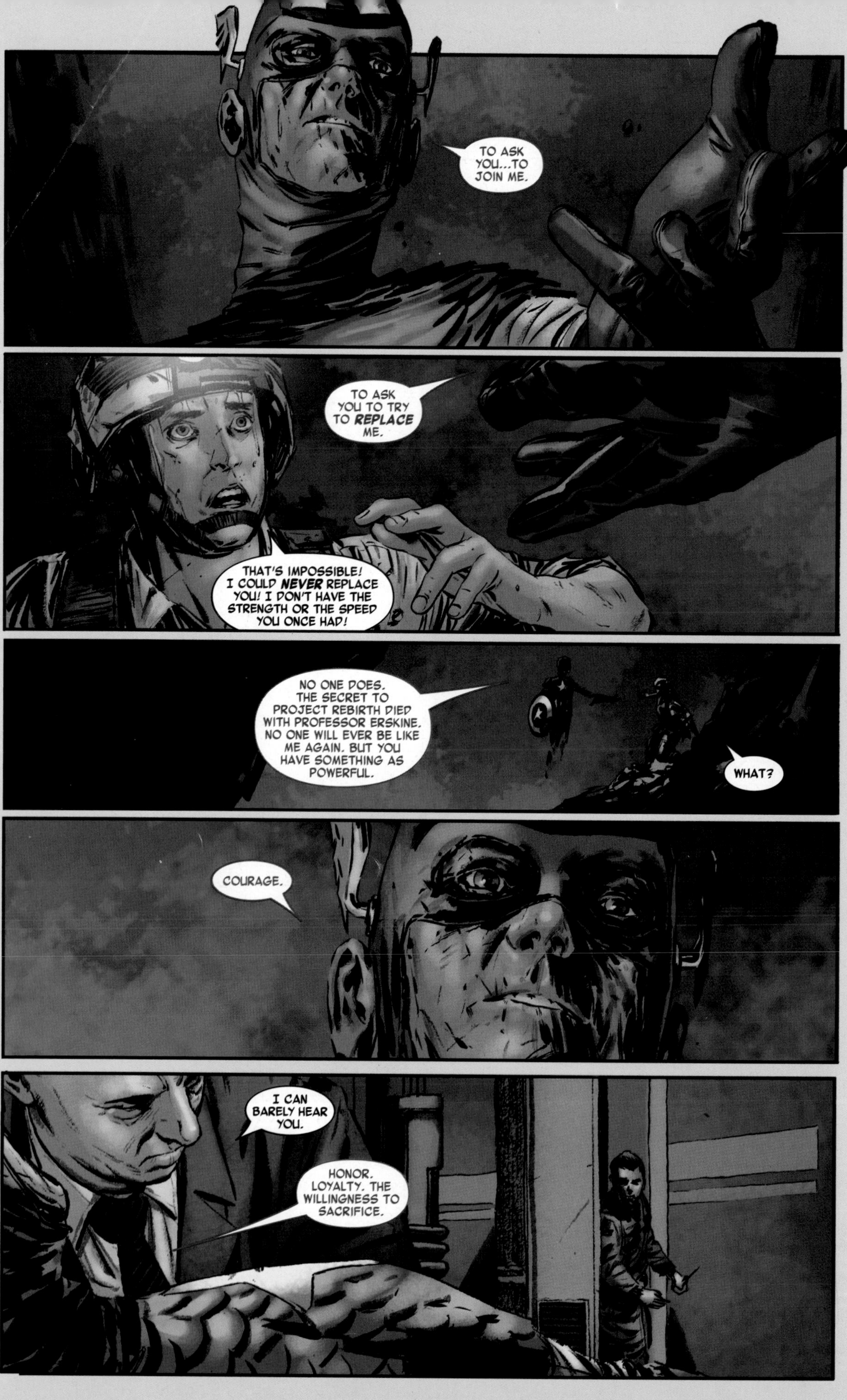
TO ASK YOU...TO JOIN ME.
TO ASK YOU TO TRY TO REPLACE ME.
THAT'S IMPOSSIBLE! I COULD NEVER REPLACE YOU! I DON'T HAVE THE STRENGTH OR THE SPEED YOU ONCE HAD!
NO ONE DOES. THE SECRET TO PROJECT REBIRTH DIED WITH PROFESSOR ERSKINE. NO ONE WILL EVER BE LIKE ME AGAIN. BUT YOU HAVE SOMETHING AS POWERFUL.
WHAT?
COURAGE.
I CAN BARELY HEAR YOU.
HONOR. LOYALTY. THE WILLINGNESS TO SACRIFICE.

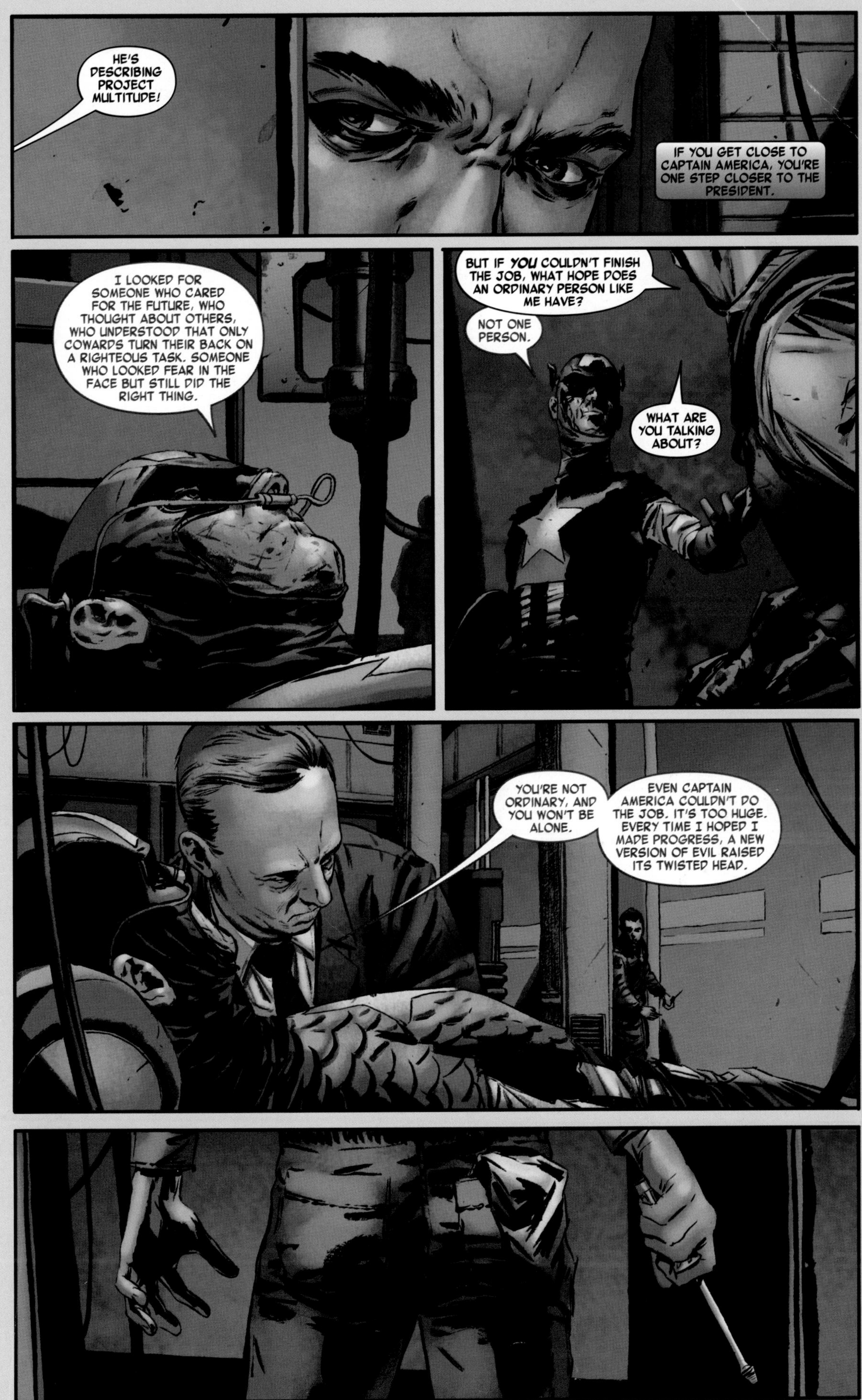
HE'S DESCRIBING PROJECT MULTITUDE!
IF YOU GET CLOSE TO CAPTAIN AMERICA, YOU'RE ONE STEP CLOSER TO THE PRESIDENT.
I LOOKED FOR SOMEONE WHO CARED FOR THE FUTURE, WHO THOUGHT ABOUT OTHERS, WHO UNDERSTOOD THAT ONLY COWARDS TURN THEIR BACK ON A RIGHTEOUS TASK. SOMEONE WHO LOOKED FEAR IN THE FACE BUT STILL DID THE RIGHT THING.
BUT IF YOU COULDN'T FINISH THE JOB, WHAT HOPE DOES AN ORDINARY PERSON LIKE ME HAVE?
NOT ONE PERSON.
WHAT ARE YOU TALKING ABOUT?
EVEN CAPTAIN AMERICA COULDN'T DO THE JOB. IT'S TOO HUGE. EVERY TIME I HOPED I MADE PROGRESS, A NEW VERSION OF EVIL RAISED ITS TWISTED HEAD.
YOU'RE NOT ORDINARY, AND YOU WON'T BE ALONE.

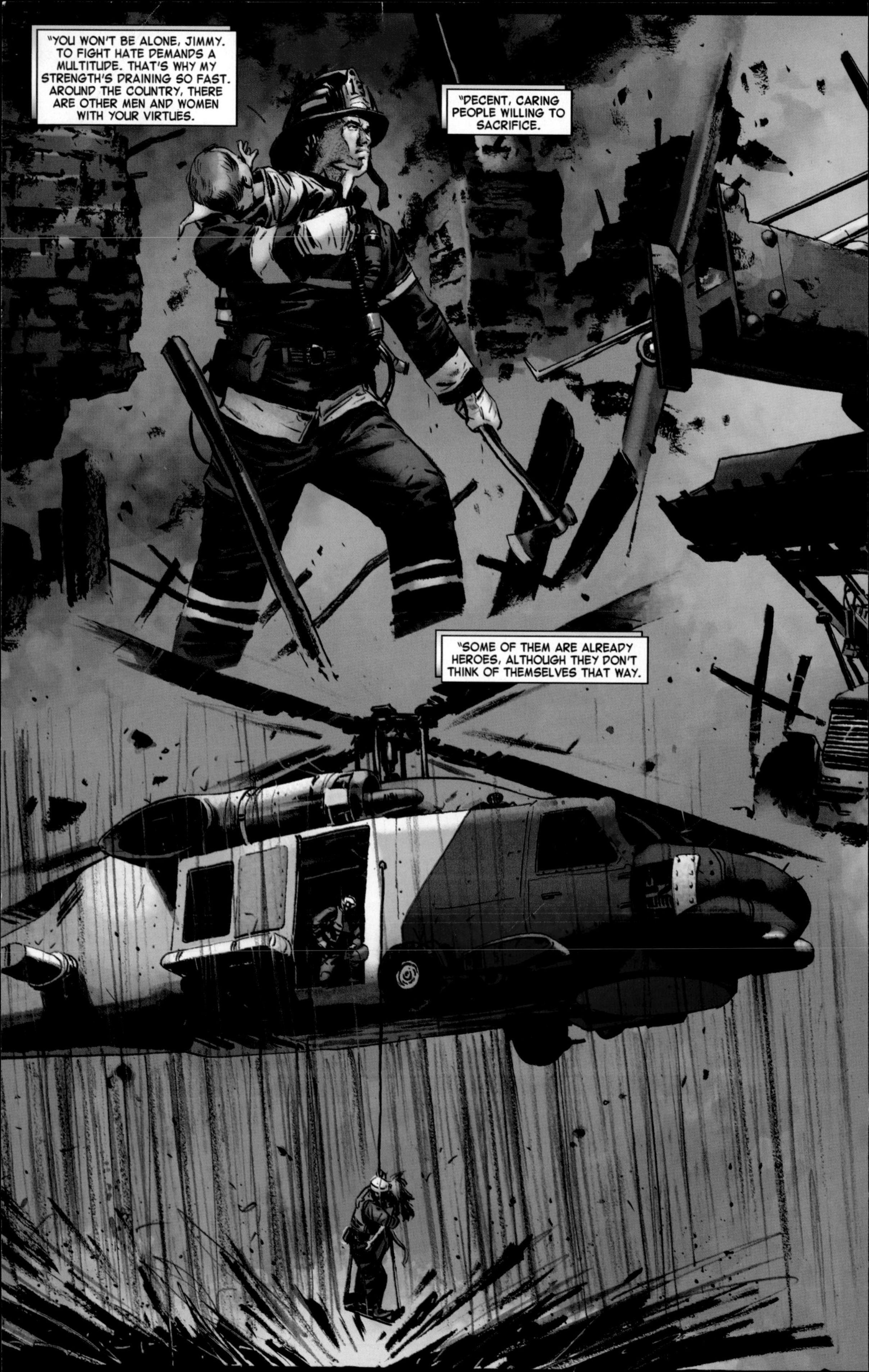
"YOU WON'T BE ALONE, JIMMY. TO FIGHT HATE DEMANDS A MULTITUDE. THAT'S WHY MY STRENGTH'S DRAINING SO FAST. AROUND THE COUNTRY, THERE ARE OTHER MEN AND WOMEN WITH YOUR VIRTUES.
"DECENT, CARING PEOPLE WILLING TO SACRIFICE.
"SOME OF THEM ARE ALREADY HEROES, ALTHOUGH THEY DON'T THINK OF THEMSELVES THAT WAY.

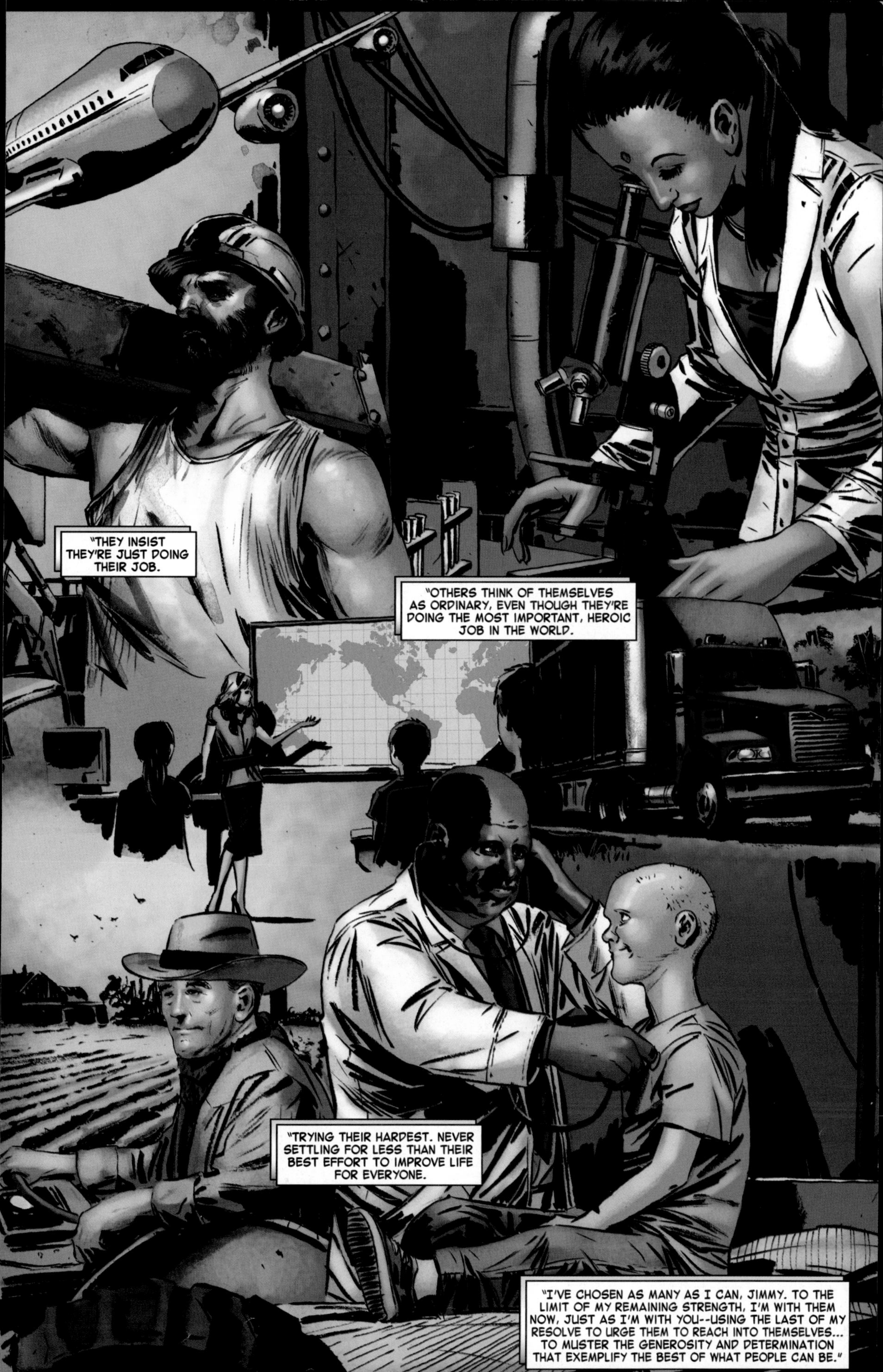
"THEY INSIST THEY'RE JUST DOING THEIR JOB.
"OTHERS THINK OF THEMSELVES AS ORDINARY, EVEN THOUGH THEY'RE DOING THE MOST IMPORTANT, HEROIC JOB IN THE WORLD.
"TRYING THEIR HARDEST. NEVER SETTLING FOR LESS THAN THEIR BEST EFFORT TO IMPROVE LIFE FOR EVERYONE.
"I'VE CHOSEN AS MANY AS I CAN, JIMMY. TO THE LIMIT OF MY REMAINING STRENGTH, I'M WITH THEM NOW, JUST AS I'M WITH YOU--USING THE LAST OF MY RESOLVE TO URGE THEM TO REACH INTO THEMSELVES... TO MUSTER THE GENEROSITY AND DETERMINATION THAT EXEMPLIFY THE BEST OF WHAT PEOPLE CAN BE."

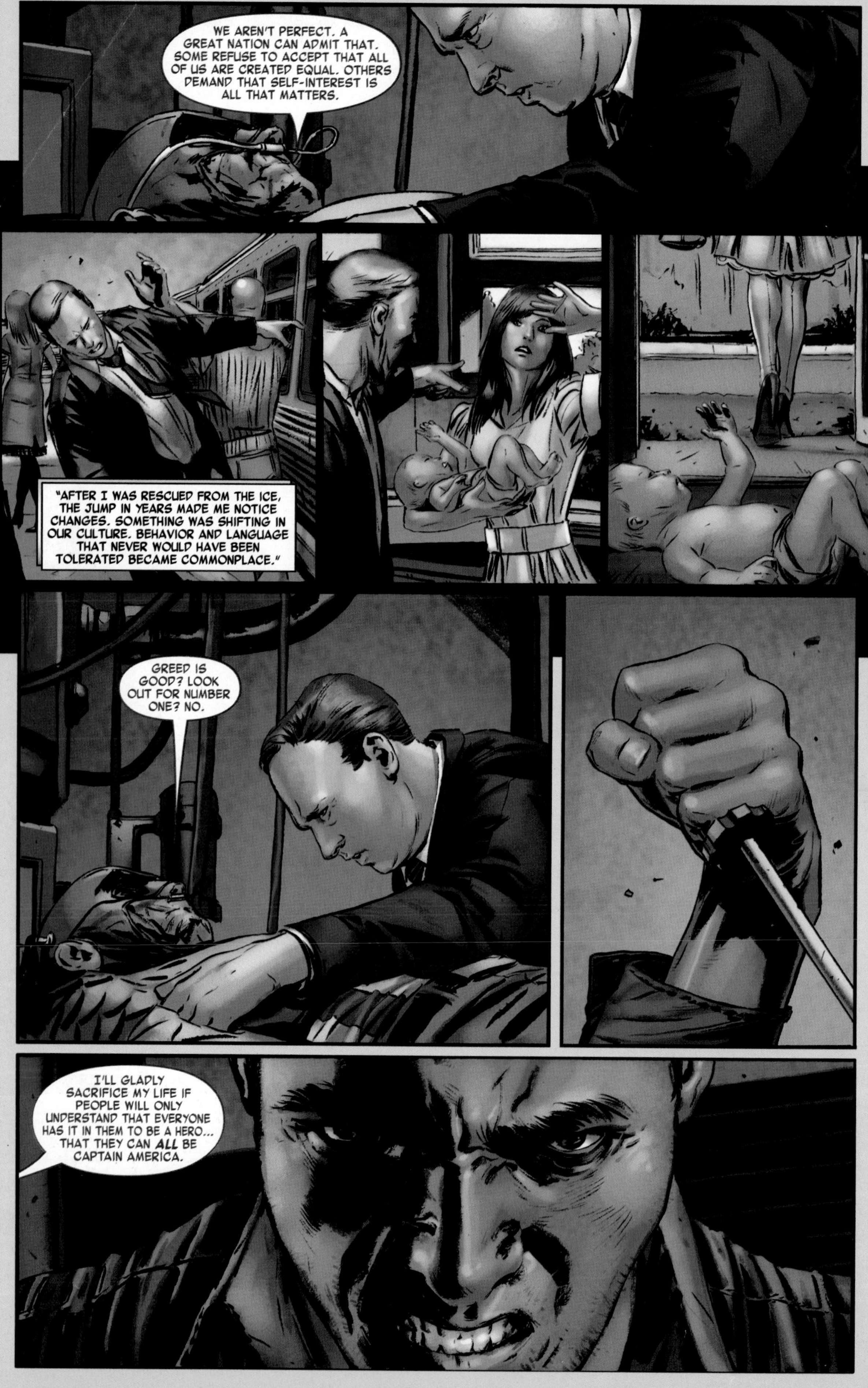
WE AREN'T PERFECT. A GREAT NATION CAN ADMIT THAT. SOME REFUSE TO ACCEPT THAT ALL OF US ARE CREATED EQUAL. OTHERS DEMAND THAT SELF-INTEREST IS ALL THAT MATTERS.
"AFTER I WAS RESCUED FROM THE ICE, THE JUMP IN YEARS MADE ME NOTICE CHANGES. SOMETHING WAS SHIFTING IN OUR CULTURE. BEHAVIOR AND LANGUAGE THAT NEVER WOULD HAVE BEEN TOLERATED BECAME COMMONPLACE."
GREED IS GOOD? LOOK OUT FOR NUMBER ONE? NO.
I'LL GLADLY SACRIFICE MY LIFE IF PEOPLE WILL ONLY UNDERSTAND THAT EVERYONE HAS IT IN THEM TO BE A HERO... THAT THEY CAN *ALL* BE CAPTAIN AMERICA.

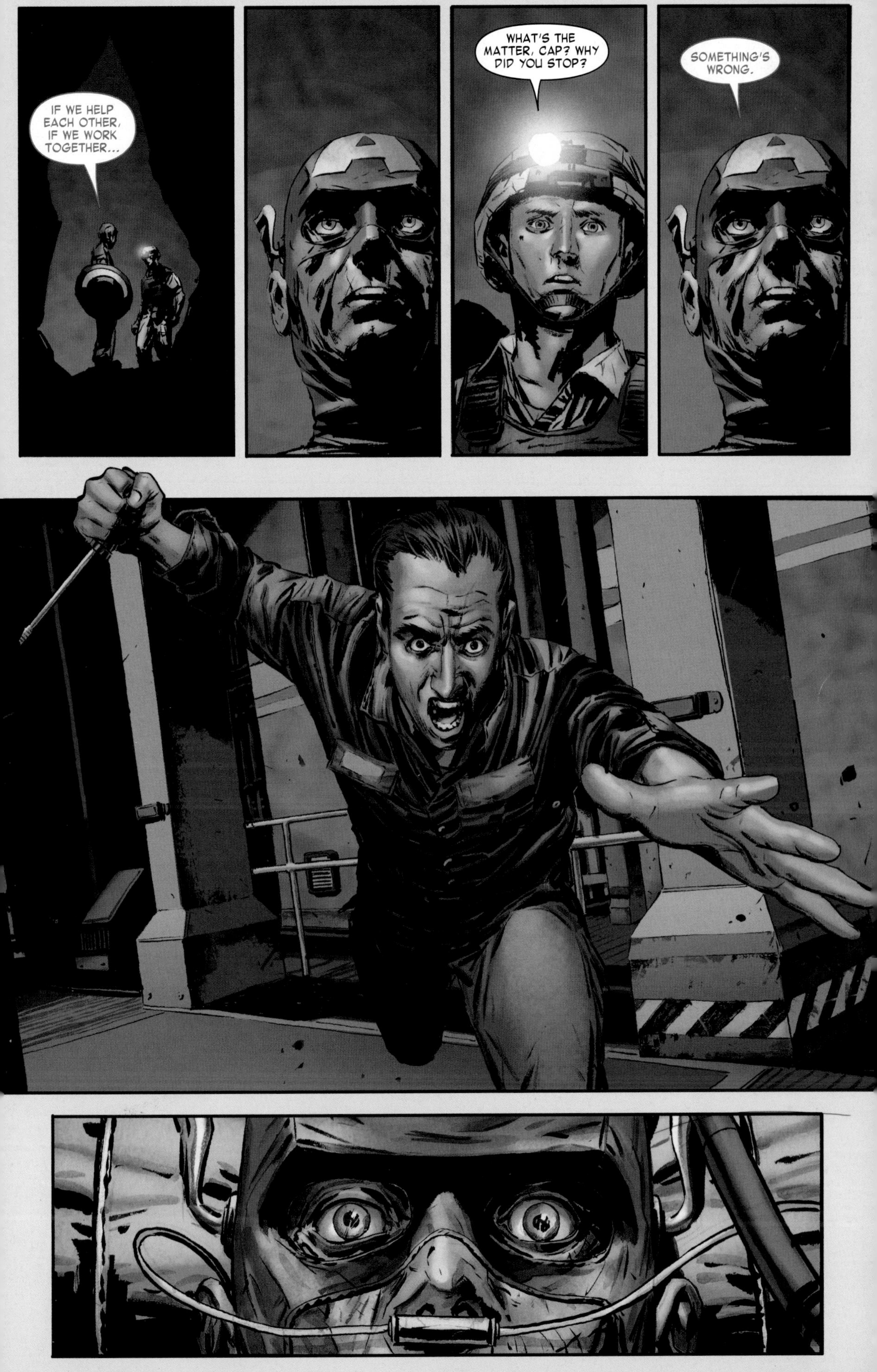
IF WE HELP EACH OTHER, IF WE WORK TOGETHER...
WHAT'S THE MATTER, CAP? WHY DID YOU STOP?
SOMETHING'S WRONG.

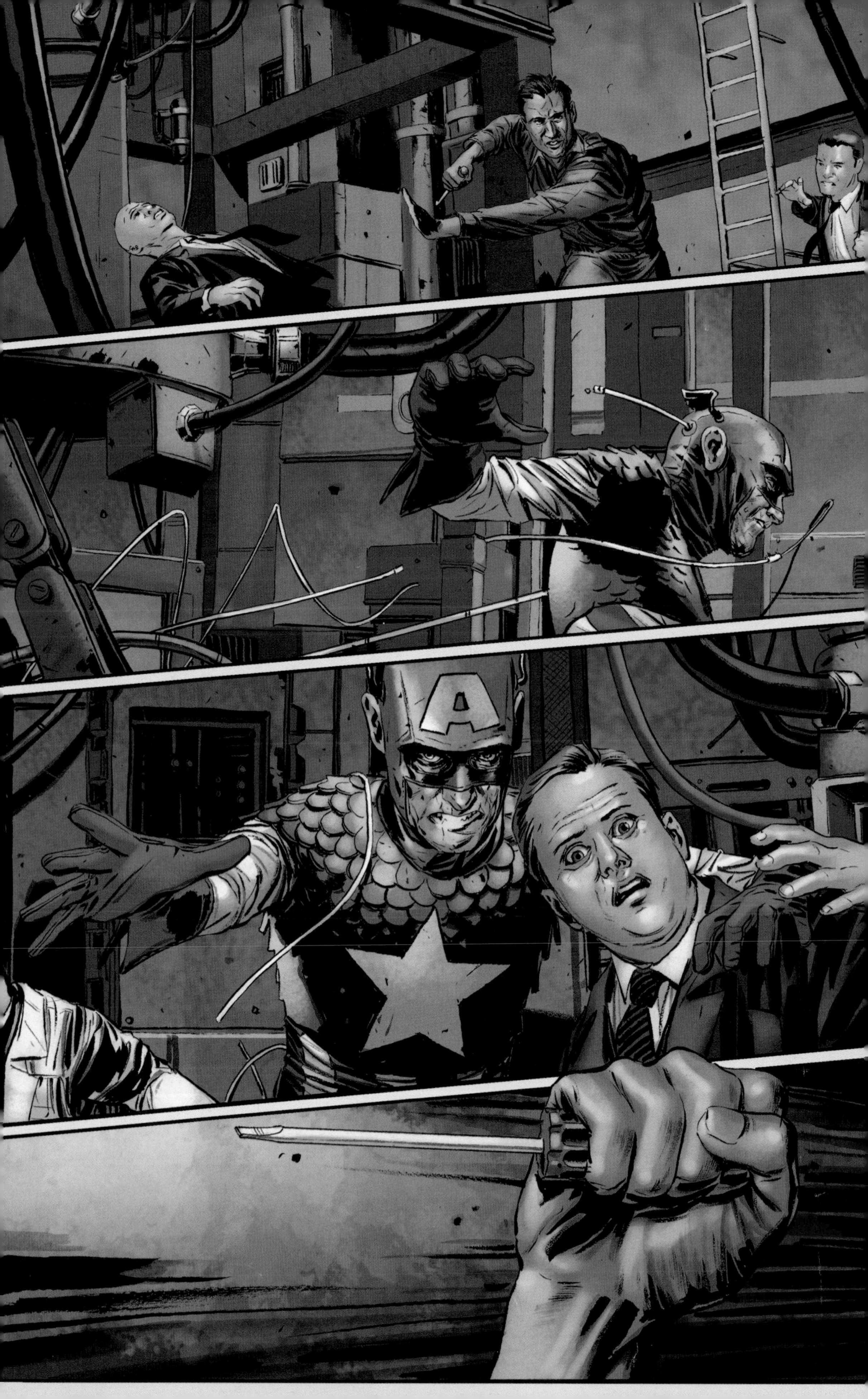

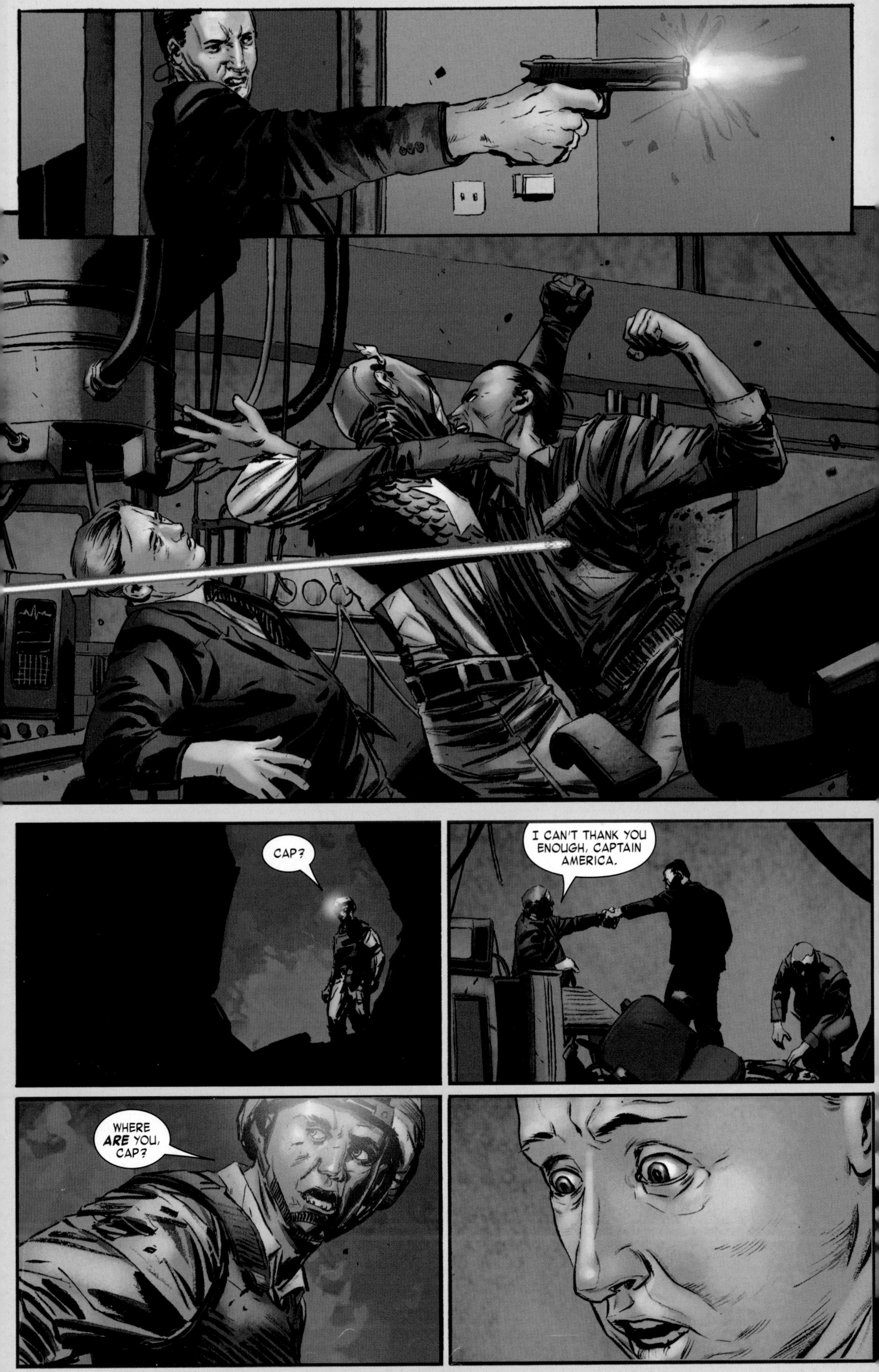
CAP?
I CAN'T THANK YOU ENOUGH, CAPTAIN AMERICA.
WHERE ARE YOU, CAP?

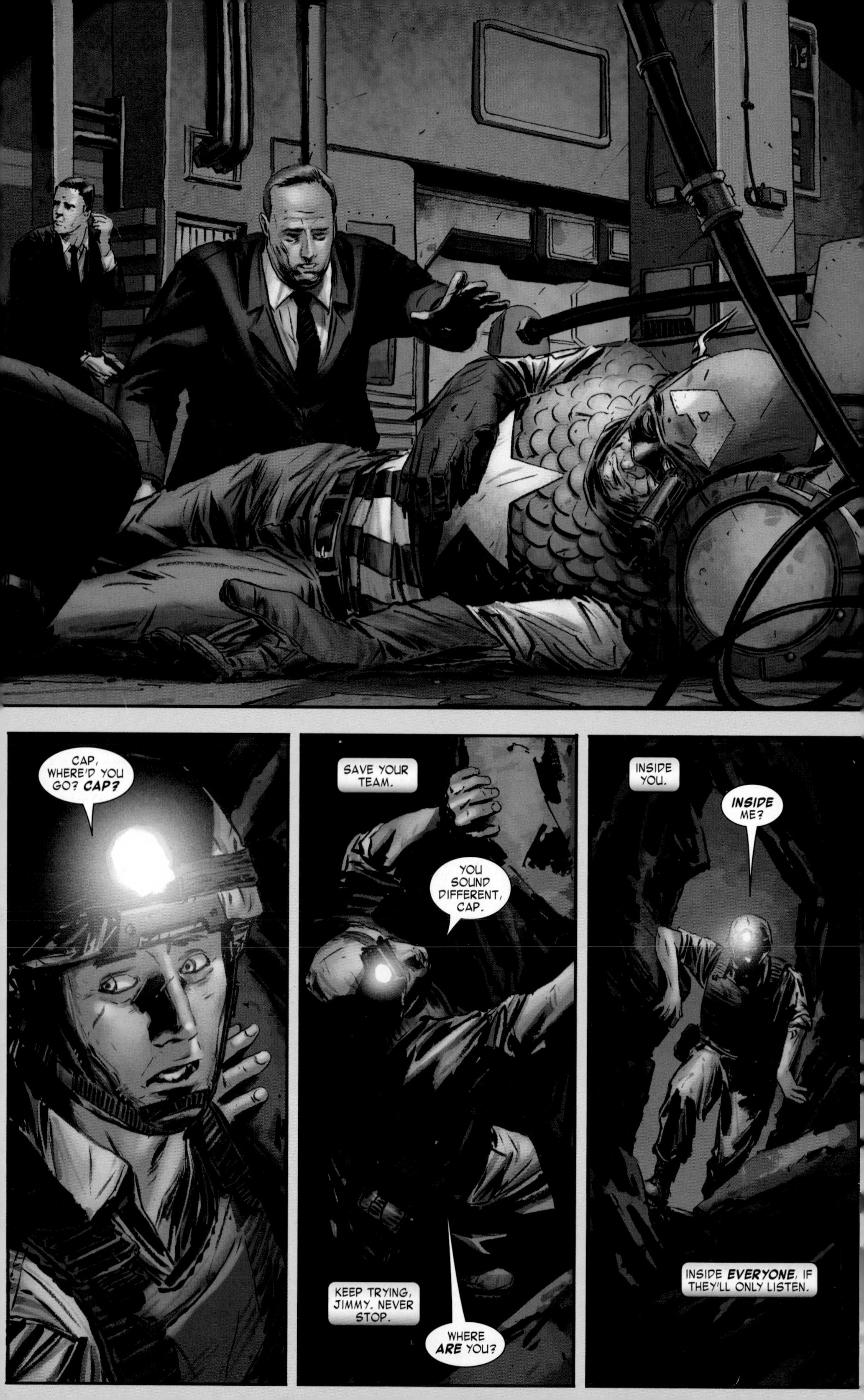
CAP, WHERE'D YOU GO? **CAP?**
SAVE YOUR TEAM.
YOU SOUND DIFFERENT, CAP.
KEEP TRYING, JIMMY. NEVER STOP.
WHERE **ARE** YOU?
INSIDE YOU.
INSIDE ME?
INSIDE **EVERYONE**, IF THEY'LL ONLY LISTEN.

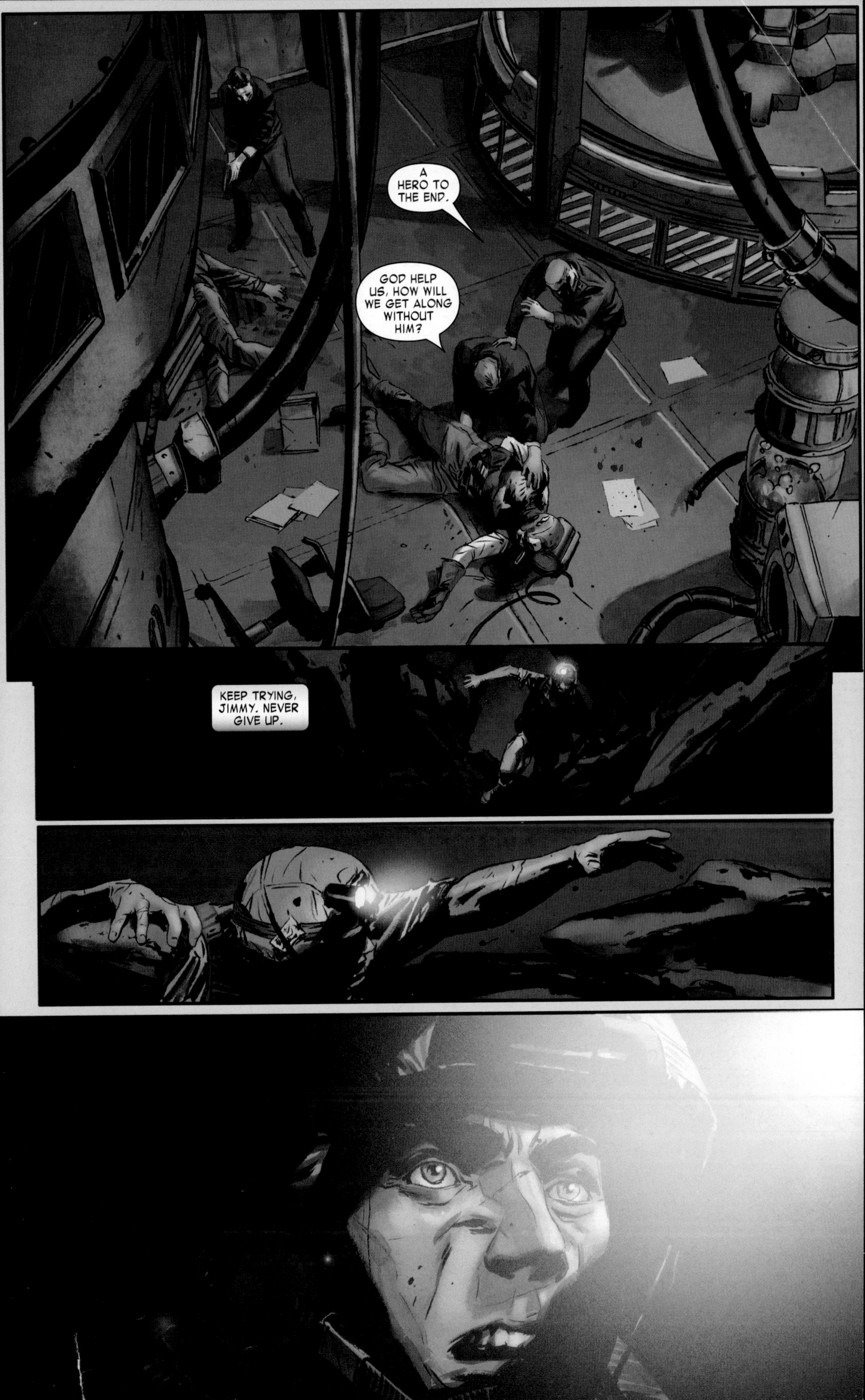

A HERO TO THE END.
GOD HELP US, HOW WILL WE GET ALONG WITHOUT HIM?
KEEP TRYING, JIMMY. NEVER GIVE UP.

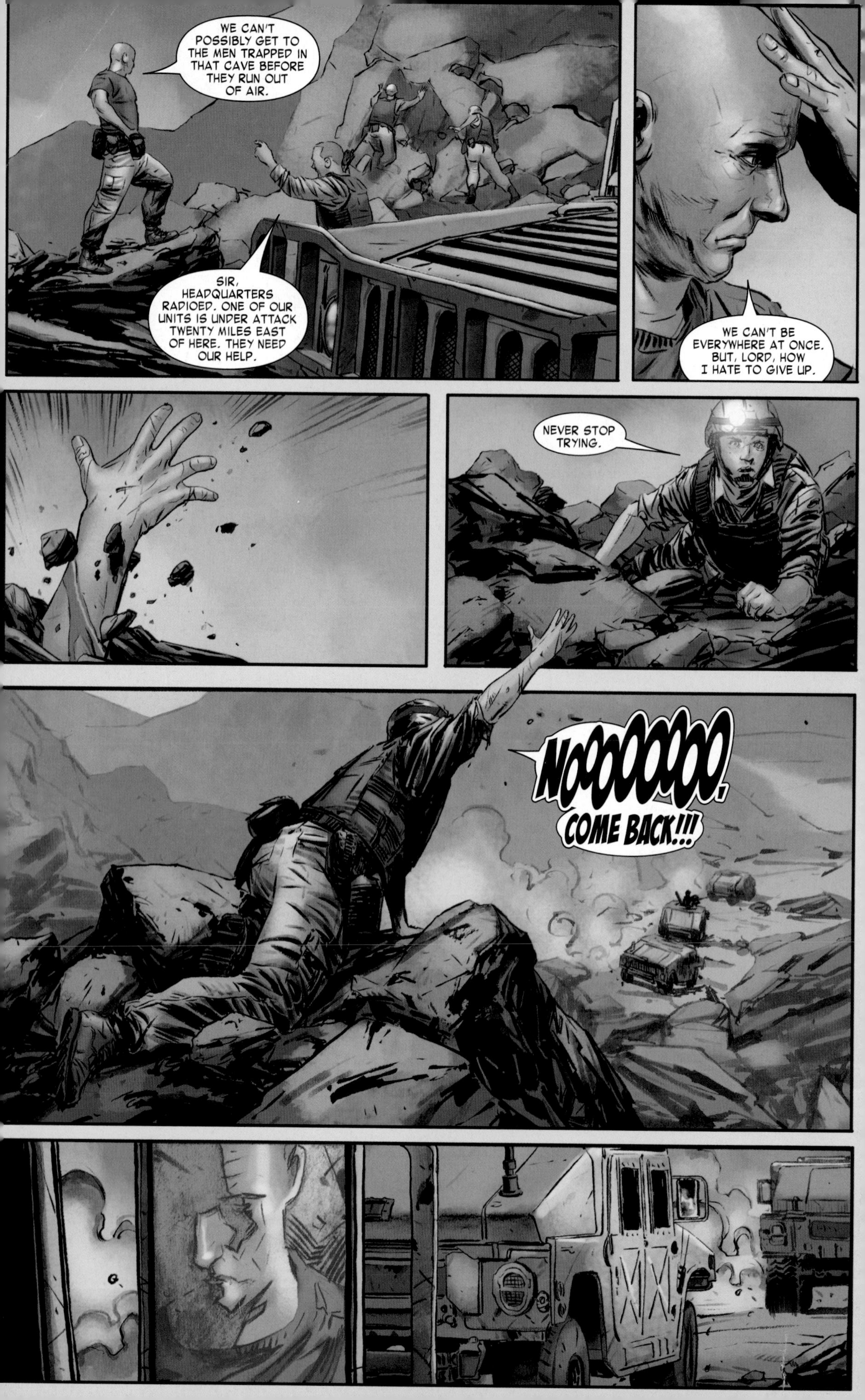
WE CAN'T POSSIBLY GET TO THE MEN TRAPPED IN THAT CAVE BEFORE THEY RUN OUT OF AIR.
SIR, HEADQUARTERS RADIOED. ONE OF OUR UNITS IS UNDER ATTACK TWENTY MILES EAST OF HERE. THEY NEED OUR HELP.
WE CAN'T BE EVERYWHERE AT ONCE. BUT, LORD, HOW I HATE TO GIVE UP.
NEVER STOP TRYING.
NOOOOOOO, COME BACK!!!

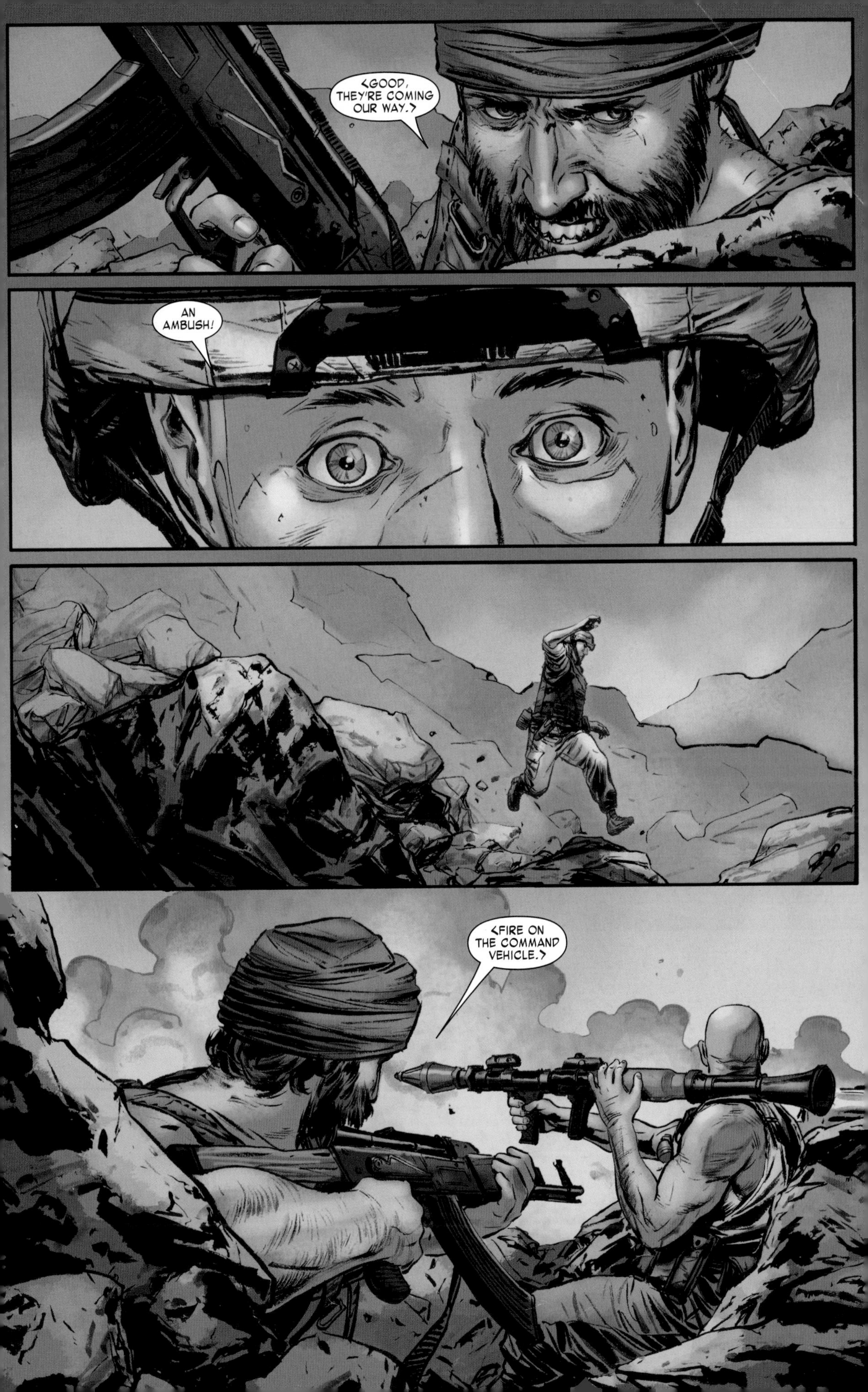

<GOOD, THEY'RE COMING OUR WAY.>
AN AMBUSH!
<FIRE ON THE COMMAND VEHICLE.>

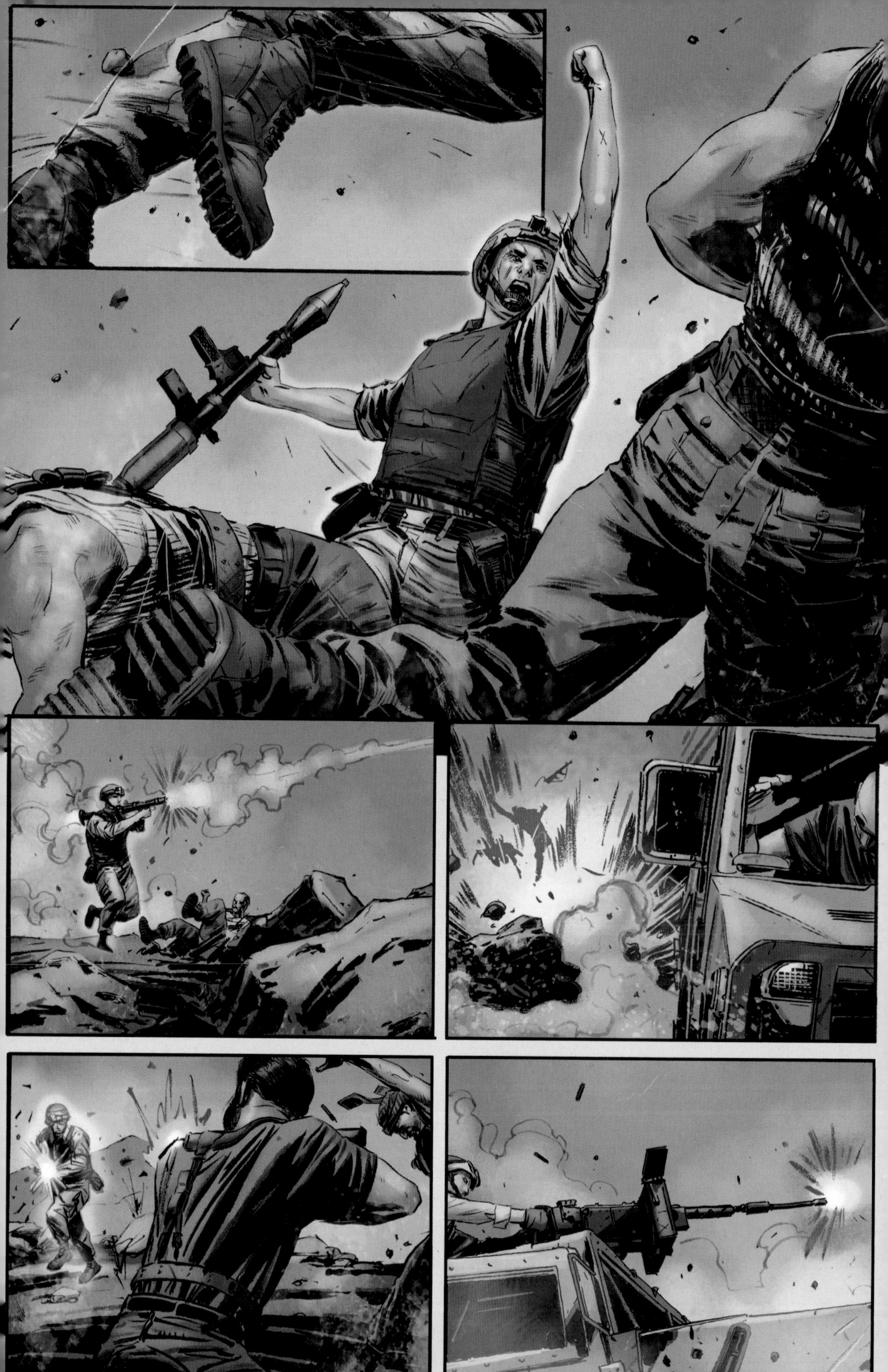

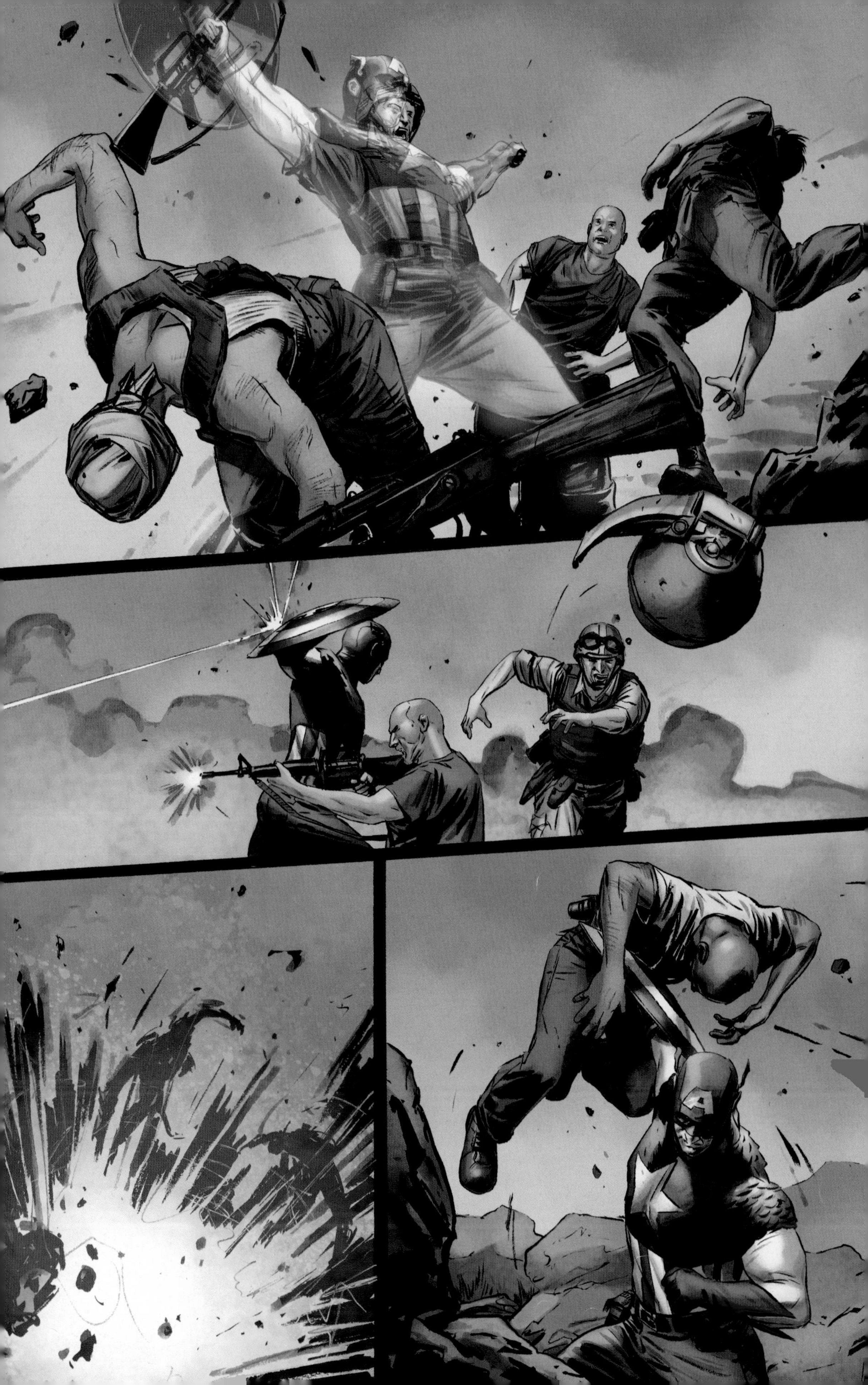

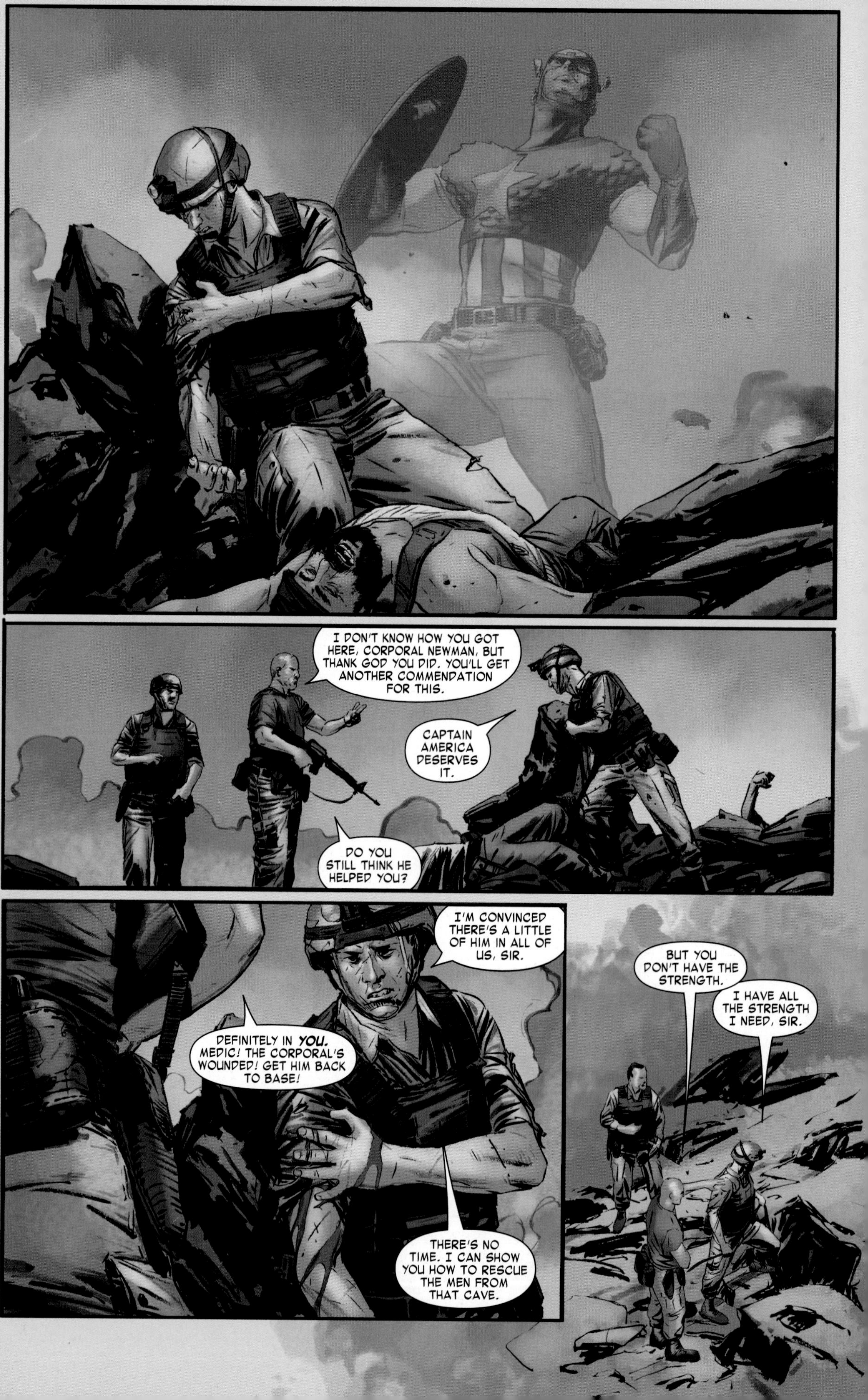

I DON'T KNOW HOW YOU GOT HERE, CORPORAL NEWMAN, BUT THANK GOD YOU DID. YOU'LL GET ANOTHER COMMENDATION FOR THIS.
CAPTAIN AMERICA DESERVES IT.
DO YOU STILL THINK HE HELPED YOU?
I'M CONVINCED THERE'S A LITTLE OF HIM IN ALL OF US, SIR.
DEFINITELY IN YOU. MEDIC! THE CORPORAL'S WOUNDED! GET HIM BACK TO BASE!
THERE'S NO TIME. I CAN SHOW YOU HOW TO RESCUE THE MEN FROM THAT CAVE.
BUT YOU DON'T HAVE THE STRENGTH.
I HAVE ALL THE STRENGTH I NEED, SIR.

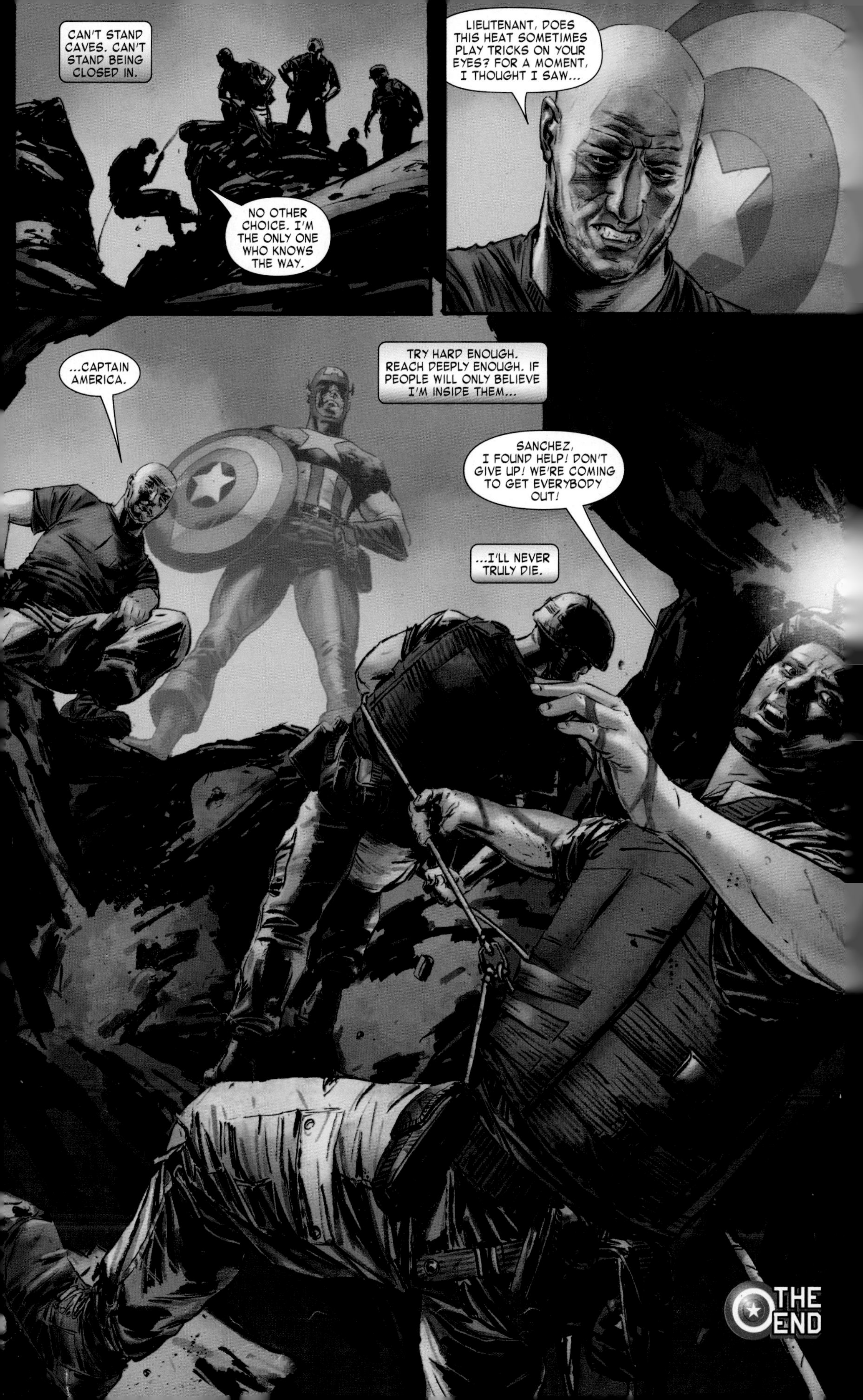
CAN'T STAND CAVES. CAN'T STAND BEING CLOSED IN.
NO OTHER CHOICE. I'M THE ONLY ONE WHO KNOWS THE WAY.
LIEUTENANT, DOES THIS HEAT SOMETIMES PLAY TRICKS ON YOUR EYES? FOR A MOMENT, I THOUGHT I SAW...
...CAPTAIN AMERICA.
TRY HARD ENOUGH. REACH DEEPLY ENOUGH. IF PEOPLE WILL ONLY BELIEVE I'M INSIDE THEM...
SANCHEZ, I FOUND HELP! DON'T GIVE UP! WE'RE COMING TO GET EVERYBODY OUT!
...I'LL NEVER TRULY DIE.
THE END

AFTERWORD

In March of 2004, a Marvel Comics editor named Andy Schmidt sent an email to my website, wondering if I'd be interested in writing a story for them. He explained that he was a fan of my novels, particularly of *First Blood* and *The Brotherhood of the Rose*, and the thought had occurred to him that the creator of Rambo might make a good pairing with another military icon, Captain America.

For me, this was a totally new idea. I'm always looking for different ways to tell a story, but I had never thought about writing a comic book. As a boy in the 1950s, I'd been addicted to them. Once a week, I had put on my roller skates and headed toward a comic-book store ten blocks away. It specialized in trade-ins. Stacks and stacks of used comics stretched along a counter. If I brought back three, I was allowed to choose one to take home. If I wanted more, I needed to pay a nickel or a dime or whatever, depending on how many I wanted.

My favorites were creepy EC series like *The Haunt of Fear*, *The Vault of Horror* and *Tales from the Crypt*. I can't tell you how much I enjoyed going to that store. But after a while, I noticed that it was hard to find any of the series I liked and that the choices available all seemed the same — cute and dull. Eventually, I lost interest.

What I didn't know was that the U.S. government decided that comic books were bad for me. Evidently if I read the really exciting ones, I would become a violent criminal. Years later, I learned that in the early 1950s, Dr. Fredric Wertham, the head psychiatrist for New York City's Department of Hospitals, had developed his anti-comic-book theory while working with violent children in Harlem. His 1954 book, *Seduction of the Innocent*, caused such a sensation that the U.S. Senate got involved, and the resulting Comics Code denatured comic books, basically banning anything that was interesting and essentially putting EC out of business (except for *Mad*, whose wonderfully subversive tone managed to survive because that publication was now classified as a magazine).

My interest in comics didn't return until the late 1970s when Russ Cochran began republishing the uncolored issues of my favorite EC series in attractive boxed sets that occupy a proud space on one of my bookshelves. Comics again caught my eye in 1986 with Frank Miller's *Batman: The Dark Knight Returns*, the grim gothic realism of which was groundbreaking. In 2001, another high point for me was *Spider-Man #36*, the 9/11 issue, with its stark black cover. Written by J. Michael Straczynski and illustrated by John Romita Jr., it showed how powerfully a comic book could develop character and have an important theme.

Still, comics seemed an alien world until Andy contacted me. The easy, enthusiastic answer to his question was,

"Yes. I'd love to write a comic-book series." But it had been decades since I'd looked at Captain America stories, and I told Andy that I'd need to be brought up to speed about the character's background. More important, I had no idea what a comic-book script looked like.

Thus began an education. Andy sent me a half-dozen scripts that demonstrated various formats. I learned that, years earlier, the traditional Marvel approach had been for a writer to provide an outline of the story and for the artist to fill in all the specifics, deciding which panels would show which information and where the dialogue would go. But that method had been superseded by a detailed script in which the writer described what happened in each panel and provided captions and dialogue. The artist then interpreted the author's words. There were slightly different script formats in which each panel could be described, but every format had one thing in common — they all emphasized the stop-action nature of comic-book narrative.

I immersed myself in comic-book theory. Will Eisner's *Comics and Sequential Art* was especially helpful, as was Scott McCloud's *Understanding Comics: The Invisible Art*. I was fascinated by the idea that what's skipped between the panels of a comic book can be as important as what's shown in the panels themselves, providing the dynamic of the stop-action quality that so intrigued me. A close-up of a face, juxtaposed with a panel that showed a hole in the ground, didn't need dialogue or even much detail in the face, in order to communicate the dread the character felt. Lack of detail in the close-up could even be an advantage, allowing the same image to be used several times throughout a story, and each time, the face would convey a different emotion, depending on the image with which it was juxtaposed. I also paid attention to the physical act of reading a comic, something I'd never done before. I began to think of each page as the equivalent of a paragraph in a novel. I became aware of how much I looked forward to the drama and surprise of what I would find when I turned a page.

The possibilities became more interesting as I read the core Captain America stories that Andy sent me. As created by Joe Simon and Jack Kirby in 1941, an orphaned skinny kid named Steve Rogers volunteered to be a soldier in World War II but was turned down because he was a runt. However, his determination caught the attention of three important men, who chose Steve to be part of a secret government program to create super soldiers to battle the Germans. In his new incarnation, he became Captain America. Years later, he was imprisoned in a block of ice in the North Atlantic until he was resurrected for the modern phase of his adventures.

Several things struck me. First, even though Cap's a super hero, he's still human. In extreme circumstances, he could be killed. But again and again, he pursues his mission. How does constantly confronting danger affect him?

Second, an awful lot of death surrounds him: his parents, Professor Erskine, Colonel Fletcher, his sidekick Bucky Barnes, several friends, including female ones. It doesn't pay to get close to him, and he's smart enough to realize that. What are the psychological costs of being forced to be a loner?

Third, he was imprisoned in that block of ice for a terribly long time. Surely, there were further psychological costs. What did it feel like to regain consciousness and discover how profoundly the world had changed, that he would forever be trying to catch up?

Fourth, during his creation, a Nazi spy infiltrated the experiment and shot Professor Erskine in order to prevent an army of Captain Americas from being created. Cap's furious reaction was to grab the assassin and hurl him across the laboratory, inadvertently destroying the ray machine that was part of the process that created him. The other part of the process was the serum that Professor Erskine invented. Only the professor knew its secrets. They died with him. But the ray machine might have provided clues about further ways to create more Captain Americas. That became impossible when Cap let his anger control him and threw the assassin against the machine, smashing it. In effect, Cap's loss of discipline doomed him to being alone. What were the psychological effects of *that*?

Basically, I wanted to examine Captain America as if he were a real person. I wanted to try to understand the weaknesses that he tried his hardest to suppress. I wanted the reader to be enthralled by Cap's exploits, but I also wanted the reader to be aware of Cap's inner turmoil and to feel for the character as much as to be in awe of him. In effect, I wanted to dramatize the burden of being a super hero in today's troubled world, especially a super hero named after the United States. Andy welcomed the approach and added that he'd also like more of Cap's backstory, particularly what Cap did in World War II, something that had seldom been written about.

By then, five months had passed. It was July. I worked on an outline, but outlines are not my strength, and I finally decided to write the first episode. It's important to note that Marvel and I were only at the discussion phase. They hadn't offered a contract. An untried comic-book writer, I made the choice to audition.

In August, I heard back about the script I'd submitted. The response turned out to be favorable, but Marvel still wanted a sense of the scope of the project, so I sent Andy a lengthy analysis of the theme and how I wanted to explore it. At that point, the project idled for several more months. But Captain America now possessed me. My passion for the project can't be overstated. As a consequence, near the end of 2004, I wrote the second issue, still without a contract and without any guarantee that the project would receive the go-ahead.

Andy was surprised, to put it mildly. This had never happened to him before, and he emphatically cautioned me that I might be wasting my time, that Marvel had no obligation to me.

"I know, but it doesn't matter," I told him. "I'm so committed to this story that I'll write all six issues without a contract, just for the satisfaction of telling it."

Marvel's reaction to the second script was again favorable. Perhaps my determination tipped the balance, or perhaps the way I wanted to develop Captain America's character was now clear. For whatever reason, early in 2005, Andy contacted me with the good news that the project, a six-part self-contained story, then titled *Captain America: The End*, was now a "go."

Immediately, I followed Andy's revision suggestions and made changes to the first two scripts. Then I set to work on the remaining issues. But my contribution was only a portion of what the project required. This was, after all, an illustrated story. We needed an artist. In April of 2005, when I traveled to New York City to meet with my publisher about my upcoming novel, *Creepers*, Andy and I finally got together. It was a pleasure to shake hands with the man who had started me on this adventure. After a restaurant breakfast, Andy opened a portfolio and set various drawings next to the plates on the table.

The illustrations were by various artists, some of who had considerable experience in the comic-book world while others were at the start of their careers. Because my approach to the story was realistic, dramatizing events that take place during the current war in Afghanistan, Andy and I agreed that a comparable realistic approach was needed in the artwork. Illustrators who tended toward fantasy or glamour didn't seem appropriate. What the series needed was the visual feel of the grit of the sand in Afghanistan, of sharp rocks and dust, of fear and pain.

We went through a lot of images during that half hour, but the work of one particular artist, a breathtakingly talented newcomer, Mitch Breitweiser, kept attracting our attention. The drawings weren't only vivid. They were palpable. Their texture invoked touch as much as sight. From the moment, I saw Mitch's work, I had no doubt that my script would be in good hands, that he wouldn't merely illustrate my script but that he would interpret it.

That's one reason I wanted the script for the first issue to be included in this book — to show that ours was a genuine collaboration. For example, the second main character of the series is Corporal James Newman, a U.S. Marine who's determined to do his duty while at the same time he suffers from battle fatigue and longs to return home to his wife and infant son. I wrote a few panels in which his wife and son are depicted. Mitch, in turn, found a further way to dramatize how the son weighs on Newman's mind — he attached a photograph of the son to the side of Newman's helmet, and that photograph appears throughout the story. A comparison of my script to his depiction of it reveals his further contributions.

Another reason I wanted the script for issue one to be included is that some readers might be as uninformed as I was about the look of a script. When the first issue appeared, I showed it to a well-known crime-fiction editor, who turned several pages and looked puzzled.

"You didn't do much writing," he said. "There's hardly any dialogue."

I quickly explained that every panel of every page was scripted, that the process was a little like writing dialogue for a film while describing the image on each storyboard for the film. Just as directors prefer to minimize dialogue and develop their movies through visual elements, so I wanted the series to be primarily visual and to employ dialogue only when I couldn't find a visual way to communicate something. On occasion, several pages go by without any dialogue or captions at all.

In the summer of 2005, a year after I had sent Andy the first script, I finished writing issue six. Each of the episodes has twenty-two pages, a standard length, but because numerous plot elements needed to be resolved in the final installment, Marvel allowed me to add four more pages at the end. Meanwhile, Mitch immersed himself in research about Marine uniforms, assault weapons, armored vehicles, and all the other elements that would need to be depicted accurately in order to sustain the level of realism that we wanted.

Mitch's painstaking approach gave me time to revise my scripts. Even though they'd been accepted for publication, I couldn't stop tinkering with them. The process continued when I saw nearly final versions of the colored pages just before each issue was published. Some of the dialogue no longer seemed necessary while other dialogue needed elaboration. On occasion, a few panels needed to be added, but with no time for them to be drawn, sections of existing panels were magnified and inserted where clarity required them. For example, in issue three, look at the bottom of page five. The last panel was originally as wide as the page. But I felt the reader needed to be reminded about Newman's childhood trauma when he nearly suffocated in the trunk of a car. By then, I'd been assigned another editor, Alejandro Arbona, with whose help two images from issue two were cropped and then inserted as supposedly new images in this later issue. To make room for them, the right side of the wide image on page five (it showed details of the cavern) was eliminated. As I discovered, visual storytelling created new challenges and new methods for solving problems.

Colorist Brian Reber made a huge contribution to this project, also. My script describes the muted yellows and browns of a desert country. I wanted primary colors introduced gradually, such as the bright oranges and reds of the initial battle sequence. But not until two-thirds of the way through issue one does the reader see many brilliant colors as Captain America finally makes his appearance. That full-page image is devoted entirely to Cap, and Mitch's artwork is so impressive, Brian's colors so eye-popping that when Marvel decided to reprint issue one, that panel was selected for the new cover. One of Brian's techniques was to give each page a dominant color and then to highlight that color through the use of muted contrasting ones. Another of his techniques was to make the images look scratched and pitted to emphasize the gritty feeling the story required.

I mentioned that the original title of the series was *Captain America: The End*. Occasionally, Marvel applies that subtitle to one of its super heroes, providing a story in which that hero supposedly dies. In this case, (if you haven't yet read the series, stop right now), the whole point was that the burden of more than almost seventy years of being a super hero, the effort and responsibility, not to mention the grief and regrets, had been so great that they brought Captain America close to death. Despite his supercharged metabolism, he's only human, after all. But he was still so determined to help the world that he used his last strength to transport himself into ordinary people who were already heroes of a sort — teachers, doctors, farmers, and so on — but who had the capacity to be super heroes if they only reached deeply enough inside themselves. Ultimately, Cap dies — gruesomely while sacrificing himself to stop an assassin from killing the president — and yet as the concluding panels show, through Corporal Newman and other surrogates, he lives on. The final caption tells us that as long as we listen to Cap's voice within us, he can never truly die.

Despite this optimistic conclusion, *The End* seemed a fitting subtitle for the series. An early announcement appeared on influential comic-book Internet sites and in newspapers like *USA Today*, promoting it as such. But in March of 2007, Captain America died in another Marvel series, *Civil War*, shot down on the steps of a federal courthouse. The attention this event received was amazing. CNN and Fox News devoted discussions to it, as did radio call-in shows. People who knew about my *Captain America: The End* series began wondering how his end could be depicted there if he had already died in another series.

Consequently, my title needed to be changed to eliminate some of the confusion. I had called the fifth issue "The Chosen." Thematically, that worked for the entire series. Plus, its optimism fit the series better than the negativity of *The End*. As for the different ways in which Captain America supposedly dies, in my series the reader is meant to get the impression that, under the proper circumstances, Captain America's spirit is eternal. I'm not sure, then, that the two series are incompatible. The Marvel Universe is vast and varied, with many surprises.

In September of 2007, two and a half years after Andy Schmidt contacted me, issue one of *Captain America: The Chosen* finally appeared. It had been a long journey, but the satisfaction of seeing my story in print, of admiring Mitch's illustrations and Brian's coloring, was worth the wait. When I held the first issue in my hands, I felt again like that little boy on roller skates who set out each week toward the comic-book store.

DAVID MORRELL
SANTA FE, NEW MEXICO

CAPTAIN AMERICA: THE CHOSEN

by

David Morrell

CHAPTER ONE

NOW YOU SEE ME-NOW YOU DON'T

Page 1

PANEL A: Across the top of the page, gusting yellow grit fills the entire panel.

PANEL B: The grit is less thick.   There's a hint of an American flag tugged by the wind.

PANEL C: As the grit dissipates, we see a windblown tent-big, military, camouflaged to blend with the desert.

PANEL D: A Marine peers from the flap of the tent. Twenty years old. Cropped hair. Good looking. But his face, particularly around his eyes, is strained with tension.

CAPTION: Corporal James Newman, US Marine.

NEWMAN: Looks like the storm's moving on.

OFF-PANEL MARINE: Finally. Roared so loud, I couldn't sleep.

OFF-PANEL OFFICER: Saddle up, everybody.

PANEL E: Close on hands cleaning an M-16.

OFF-PANEL NEWMAN: Damned sand gets in everything.

Page 2

PANEL A: Half the page, which includes TITLE and CREDITS ... Huge panorama. Craggy mountains at the top, desert in the middle, a mud-brick village at the bottom.

Beyond the village, ominous smoke rises.

CAPTION 1:   AFGHANISTAN.

PANEL B: The village. A US military convoy enters.

UNSEEN MARINE IN ONE OF THE ARMORED VEHICLES: Heads
up, everybody. I just got word on the radio. See that
smoke rising past the village?

INSERT—TOP RIGHT CORNER OF PANEL B: A flaming truck.
A Red Cross insignia on it. A blood-spattered American
civilian writhes in flames on the ground.

PANEL C: Newman, helmeted now, peers warily from a
window in an armored vehicle, his rifle at the ready.
His eyes show even more strain. A tag on the chest of
his fatigues notes his last name.

CAPTION 2: Sometimes I wonder.

Page 3

PANEL A: Newman's POV. Robed villagers stare from
half-closed doors and shutters. A child races for
cover.

CAPTION 1: I want to help my country.

PANEL B: Looking ahead past the lead vehicle. A
furrowed dirt road. Dismal mud-brick dwellings, some
of them in ruin, the result of explosions. A woman
hurries a frightened child into a doorway.

CAPTION 2: I want to help THIS country.

PANEL C: From a flat roof angling down toward the
convoy. A Mideastern man kneels out of sight, holding
a missile launcher. Two men crouch next to him,
clutching rifles.

CAPTION 3: But how can I help ANYBODY ...

PANEL D: On the mud floor of a building, a robed man
and woman huddle with a child between them, staring in
terror at something.

CAPTION 4: If everybody looks THE SAME ... If I can't
tell ...

PANEL E: Fuller angle inside the building. In the
background, the frightened family stares at two men
with rifles in the foreground, crouching next to a
window. A third man aims his gun at the family.

CAPTION 5: The people I want to help from the people I
need to fight?

PANEL A: An alley as the convoy passes. Two gunmen hide behind rubble.

CAPTION 1: I know why I'm here.

PANEL B: Panorama of a desert training camp. Hate-faced gunmen practice shooting and blowing up vehicles. The targets look like Americans.

CAPTION: Al Qaeda.

INSTRUCTOR: Death to America! Death to Satan! Death to Zionists!

PANEL C: Furious, robed, bearded men whip a teenaged boy. A radio lies smashed beside him. Other furious men hurl stones at a woman. Her face is uncovered. Blood flies from her head as she falls.

ATTACKER 1: I caught him listening to music!

ATTACKER 2: She isn't wearing a veil!

PANEL A: The Manhattan skyline. The trade towers. A 747 hurtles into one.

CAPTION 1: Zealots crazy enough to believe that ...

PANEL B: The USS Cole, a gaping hole blasted out of its side.

CAPTION 2: Hate ...

PANEL C: A battered SUV. A fanatical bearded Mideastern man orders a teenager to load a crate into the back. The crate is marked EXPLOSIVES. The teenager strains from its weight.

CAPTION 3: ... is the same thing as believing in God.

PANEL D: A government-style building. A sign says US EMBASSY. A lot of Mideastern civilians and a few US soldiers stand in front of it. The truck hurtles toward them.

CAPTION 4: But what they really believe in ...

UPPER RIGHT CORNER OF PANEL D: Close on the young driver's face. The boy's eyes look ecstatic.

DRIVER: I get to be a martyr! I'll go to paradise! Virgins wait for me!

PANEL E: A massive explosion. Wreckage, bodies, and blood erupt.

CAPTION 5: ... is pain and death.

Page 6

PANEL A: The convoy moves through the village. We see Newman watching warily from his armored vehicle.

CAPTION 1: I know why I came here. If I help make this country safe, I hoped to help make AMERICA safe.

PANEL B: Looking past the front vehicle. A battered truck blocks the road.

CAPTION 2: But I've been fighting for what seems forever.

PANEL C: From the flat roof looking down. The final vehicle of the convoy passes. The robed gunmen aim, one of them with a missile launcher.

CAPTION 3: I'm so used to being scared that I'm numb.

PANEL D: Behind the truck blocking the road. Another gunman aims a missile.

CAPTION 4: Five months ago, my wife gave birth to our baby girl.

Page 7

PANEL A: An attractive young woman holds a pretty baby. The woman shows the baby a framed photograph of Newman in uniform. They're sitting in a park, the green trees of which contrast with Afghanistan's bleak terrain. In the background, we see the Golden Gate bridge.

CAPTION 1: My wife's name is Lori. My son's name is Brad. I love them so much I ache.

LORI (SHOWING PHOTOGRAPH): That's your daddy.

PANEL B: Newman's armored vehicle in the village.

CAPTION 2: I pray I'll live to reach home and hold them.

PANEL C: From the blockade, a missile streaks toward us.

PANEL D: From the alley, shots blaze, bullets hurtling toward us.

PANEL E: From the roof, a missile streaks toward us.

Page 8

PANEL A: High overhead shot, the convoy obscured by smoke, explosions, and gunfire.

CAPTION 1: Freezing in the winter. A hundred degrees in the summer. The air's so dry, you normally don't sweat.

PANEL B: A truck blows apart.

PANEL C: A Marine falls from a Humvee, blood spraying.

PANEL D: Newman furiously shoots his M-16. Moisture flies from his face.

CAPTION 2: But believe me, when you're in a fire fight, you sweat till your uniform's soaked.

PANEL E: His viewpoint. At an open window, two gunmen hurtle back, blood on their faces.

Page 9

PANEL A: The convoy. Another vehicle explodes.

PANEL B: A Bradley Fighting Vehicle fires a shell.

PANEL C: The blockade explodes.

PANEL D: His vehicle on fire, Newman jumps to the road. Other Marines leap down behind him. All are shooting.

CAPTION: I carry fifty pounds of gear. My body armor feels like a load of bricks. At the very start, when we were getting organized, there was such a shortage, Lori had to buy the armor and send it to me.

PANEL E: The alley. Two gunmen are torn apart by gunfire.

Page 10

PANEL A: Newman staggers from the impact of a bullet hitting his chest. Fabric erupts from a hole in his uniform. As his head jerks back, his helmet flips away. The pain on his sweat-dripping face is manifest.

SOUND EFFECT: THUNK!

CAPTION: Thank heaven, Lori sent it.

PANEL B: A different angle on Newman as he recovers and angrily returns fire.

PANEL C: A rooftop. A gunman crouches behind a parapet as Newman's bullets take chunks from it.

PANEL D: A Bradley vehicle fires another shell.

PANEL E: The roof blows apart, the gunman hurtling through the air.

Page 11

PANEL A: Newman (helmet-less) and his fellow Marines race, firing, toward the cover of a building.

CAPTION 1: There's no time to think. You're just in it. Training. Instinct. Determination to stay alive. That's all you've got.

PANEL B: Behind Newman, two Marines drop, blood spraying from their heads.

CAPTION 2:   And the loyalty of your buddies.

PANEL C: Running, Newman fires. His eyes are fierce. He's hardly recognizable as the man we saw on page 1.

CAPTION 3: And your fury.

PANEL D: In the smoke-filled alley, another gunman drops.

PANEL E: Outraged, Newman races through a doorway, firing.

PANEL A: In the building, a gunman lurches back, bleeding.

PANEL B: Newman spins angrily, aiming at another target.

PANEL C: His viewpoint. The Mideastern man and woman huddling frightened on the floor, the child between them.

PANEL D: Newman aims, sweat, grime, and blood on his face.

PANEL E: His finger is on the trigger.

CAPTION 1: Can I trust them? Is there a rifle under their robes? A grenade?

PANEL F: CLOSE ON THE FACE OF THE TERRIFIED FATHER.

CAPTION 2: Are they the people I'm helping or the people I'm fighting?

PANEL A: Newman lowers his rifle

CAPTION 1: God ...

PANEL B: Ravaged by emotions, he leans against the wall.

CAPTION 2: Got to hold it together.

PANEL C: His tortured face.

CAPTION 3: Tired. Bone tired. Don't know how long I can keep doing this ... how long I can muster the strength ... the courage ... the determination ...

PANEL D: Through the smoke at the open door, we see a glimmer of a blue suit.

UNSEEN SPEAKER: To fight the enemies of freedom? To fight hate?

PANEL E: Newman's face reveals his stunned emotions. His eyes are wide in surprise.

UNSEEN SPEAKER: You want to know how long we can keep doing this?

Page 14

FULL PAGE: Captain America stands in the doorway, blindingly brilliant. Red, white, and blue. His shield is like a talisman. There's more color than in any other panel so far. Huge. Dramatic. Bullets from outside tear at the doorjamb.

CAPTAIN AMERICA: As long as we're able to lift a finger. As long as we can draw a breath.

UNSEEN NEWMAN: Captain America??!!

Cap's right hand offers Newman's helmet to us, as if we're Newman.

CAPTAIN AMERICA: You're going to need this, Corporal Newman.

Page 15

PANEL A (OUTSIDE THE BUILDING): A burning armored vehicle. A wounded Marine is trapped beneath rubble next to it. Smoke. Bullets kick up dirt.

WOUNDED MARINE: Help!

CAPTAIN AMERICA: We're coming!

PANEL B: Captain America and Newman rush from the building. Cap raises his shield, protecting them as bullets whack into it. Their eyes blaze with determination.

CAPTAIN AMERICA: Courage. Honor.

PANEL C: Gunmen on a roof shoot at them.

PANEL D: Amid smoke, Newman reaches the wounded Marine, pulling rubble from him. Cap continues to use his shield to block the bullets.

Page 16

PANEL A: Newman drags the wounded Marine from the

burning vehicle.

PANEL B: Close on Captain America's hand picking up a huge chunk of rubble.

PANEL C: Cap hurls the chunk through the air.

CAPTAIN AMERICA: Loyalty. Sacrifice.

PANEL D: The chunk hits the roof's parapet. Fragments of mud-brick erupt, knocking the gunmen back, exposing them.

PANEL E: Newman kneels beside the wounded Marine, firing his M-16 toward the roof.

PANEL F: The gunmen lurch back, bleeding from the impact of his shots.

UNSEEN MARINE: Help!

Page 17

PANEL A: A wounded Marine strains to try to get out of a Humvee. Smoke rises behind him.

MARINE: My right leg's broken! Can't move it!

PANEL B: Newman and Captain America race toward him, their eyes more determined. Again, Cap uses his shield to protect Newman from the hail of bullets.

CAPTAIN AMERICA: We'll get you!

PANEL C: Newman leaps onto the smoking Humvee.

PANEL D: Newman braces himself behind a mounted machine gun, shooting in a fury.

PANEL E: Attackers drop.

Page 18

PANEL A: Newman pulls the wounded Marine from the hatch of the burning vehicle.
WOUNDED MARINE: The soles of my boots are melting!

PANEL B: On the road, Newman hurries, carrying the Marine.

PANEL C: The smoking vehicle explodes.

PANEL D: Newman crouches behind rubble. With the
wounded Marine next to him, Newman raises his M-16,
looking for targets, determined to protect the man he
saved.

NEWMAN: Captain! Do you see anybody else we need to
help? CAPTAIN? DO YOU HEAR ME, CAPTAIN?

PANEL E: Behind Newman as he aims toward the smoke in
the street.

OFF-PANEL SPEAKER: I hear you, Corporal Newman.

Page 19

PANEL A: Newman whirls, gaping in surprise.

PANEL B: His viewpoint. A captain and a lieutenant
face him.

OFF-PANEL NEWMAN: Captain???

PANEL C: Close on the captain, his insignia and a name
on his uniform (Harrigan) clearly identify him.

CAPTAIN HARRIGAN: What's the matter, Corporal? You
look surprised. What other captain did you expect to
see? I'm the only captain here.

PANEL D: Newman (his face streaked with dirt, sweat,
and blood) looks shocked.

NEWMAN: But ... he was here. Cap was HERE!

PANEL E: Angle down past the captain and the
lieutenant toward Newman, who stares to the side in
confusion.

CAPTAIN HARRIGAN: "Cap"? You sound like you're
talking about Captain America.

NEWMAN: I saw him! He was next to me!

LIEUTENANT: Corporal, think about it. He's got better
things to do than pay attention to what happens to a
forgotten patrol in a village in the middle of nowhere.

PANEL A: Through smoke toward Newman as he stares frantically toward the rubble in the street. In the background, two medics attend to the injured Marine.

NEWMAN: Next to me. Captain America was NEXT to me. He helped me save these men!

PANEL B: The captain and the lieutenant look puzzled.

CAPTAIN HARRIGAN: No, Corporal. We saw everything that happened. You saved these two Marines all by yourself.

LIEUTENANT: I've been over here eighteen months. I survived a lot of firefights. I've never seen such bravery.

PANEL C: Newman stares toward us. In the background, the medics carry the injured man away in a stretcher.

OFF-PANEL CAPTAIN HARRIGAN: You'll get a commendation for this, Corporal.

NEWMAN: Captain America deserves the commendation.

OFF-PANEL LIEUTENANT: Did anybody else see Captain America?

PANEL D: Several weary Marines covered with dirt and sweat emerge from rubble and bullet-riddled buildings.

MARINE: No, sir. All we saw was the corporal saving those men. The way he was fighting, he didn't need Captain America to help him.

PANEL E: Close on Newman's strained face. He looks like he fears he's gone insane.

NEWMAN: You didn't see him? That's impossible! Cap was next to me! Captain America was HERE!

OFF-PANEL OFFICER: Sometimes, a firefight can twist your imagination. Take it easy for a while, Corporal. Lord knows, you've earned the rest.

PANEL A: Overhead shot, looking down toward Newman who stares frantically toward the smoke, debris, and bodies in the street.

NEWMAN: Have I been fighting here so long I've lost my mind?

PANEL B: Same overhead shot, but now there's a border of blue.

NEWMAN: Cap??

PANEL C: Same overhead shot, but now the border of blue is larger.

NEWMAN: CAPTAIN AMERICA??

PANEL D: Same overhead shot, but now we see that the border of blue is Captain America's helmet. His face is haggard. Electrodes and wires are attached to him.

CAPTAIN AMERICA: Courage. Honor. Loyalty. Sacrifice.

Page 22

FULL PAGE: The overhead shot of Newman is small, surrounded by a large shot of the following:

1. Captain America is tilted back in a medical chair with all kinds of electronic gadgets attached to him, including wires to his helmet. The contrast with his usual appearance is shocking. He looks frail, thin, pale, and sick. His face is withered.

2. High-ranking military officers and lab-coated scientists study him.

3. All kinds of sophisticated electronic apparatus fill the background.

4. A sign in the background says: TOP SECRET RESTRICTED AREA.

The small image of Newman amid the wreckage floats above Captain America.

NEWMAN (IN THE HOLOGRAPH): CAPTAIN?!

CAPTAIN AMERICA: You're braver than you think.

TO BE CONTINUED

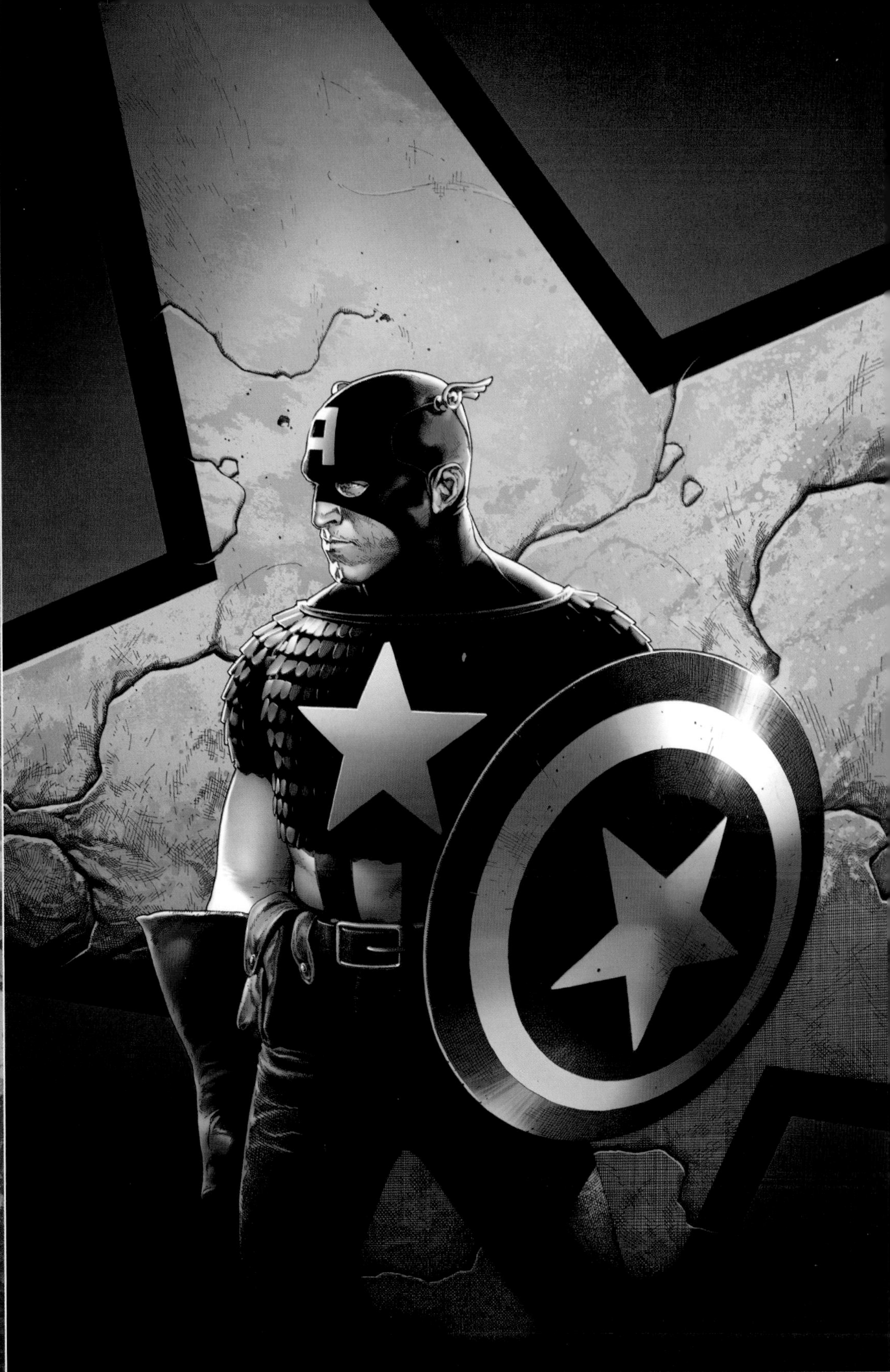

ISSUE #1 VARIANT

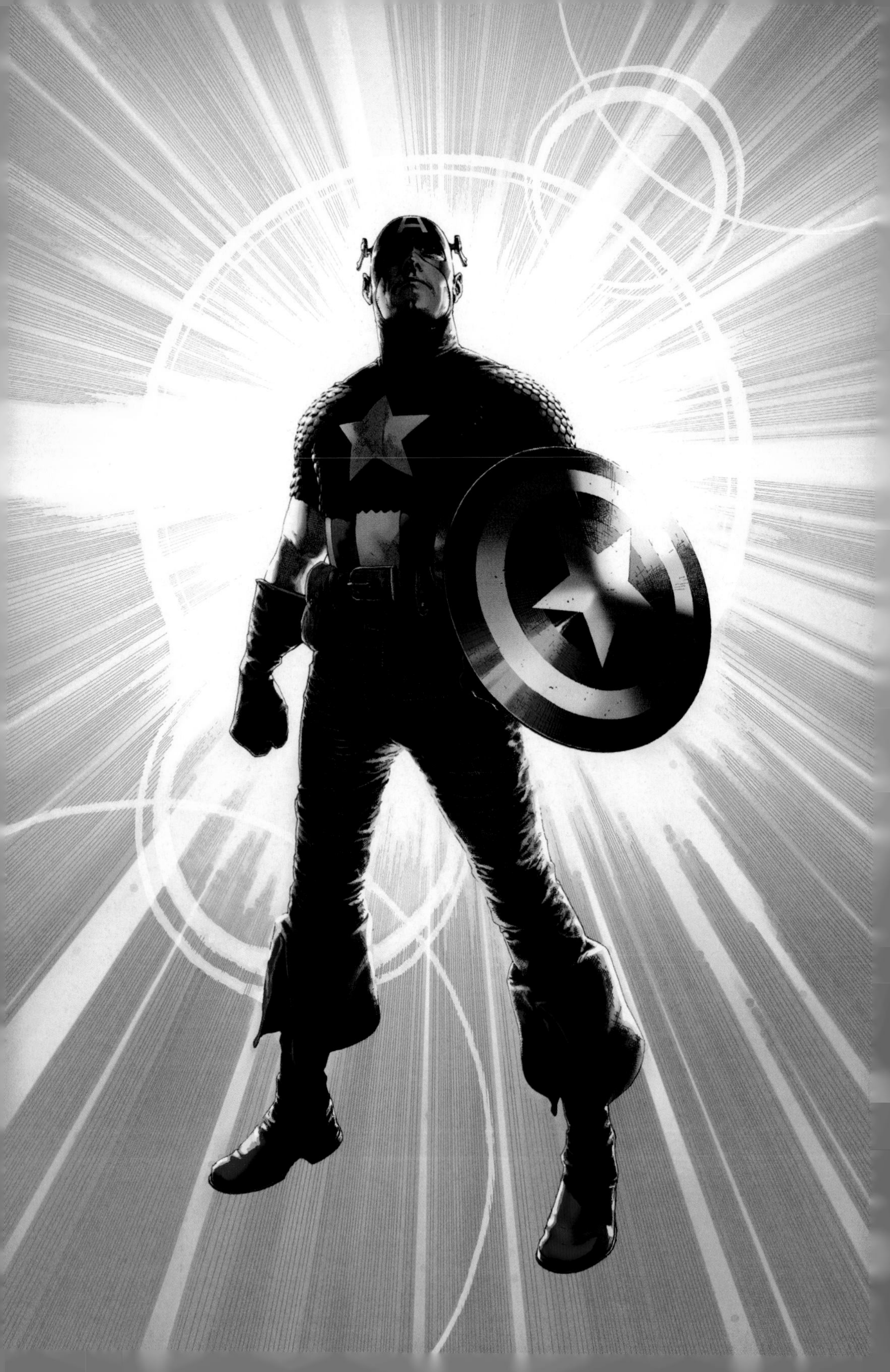

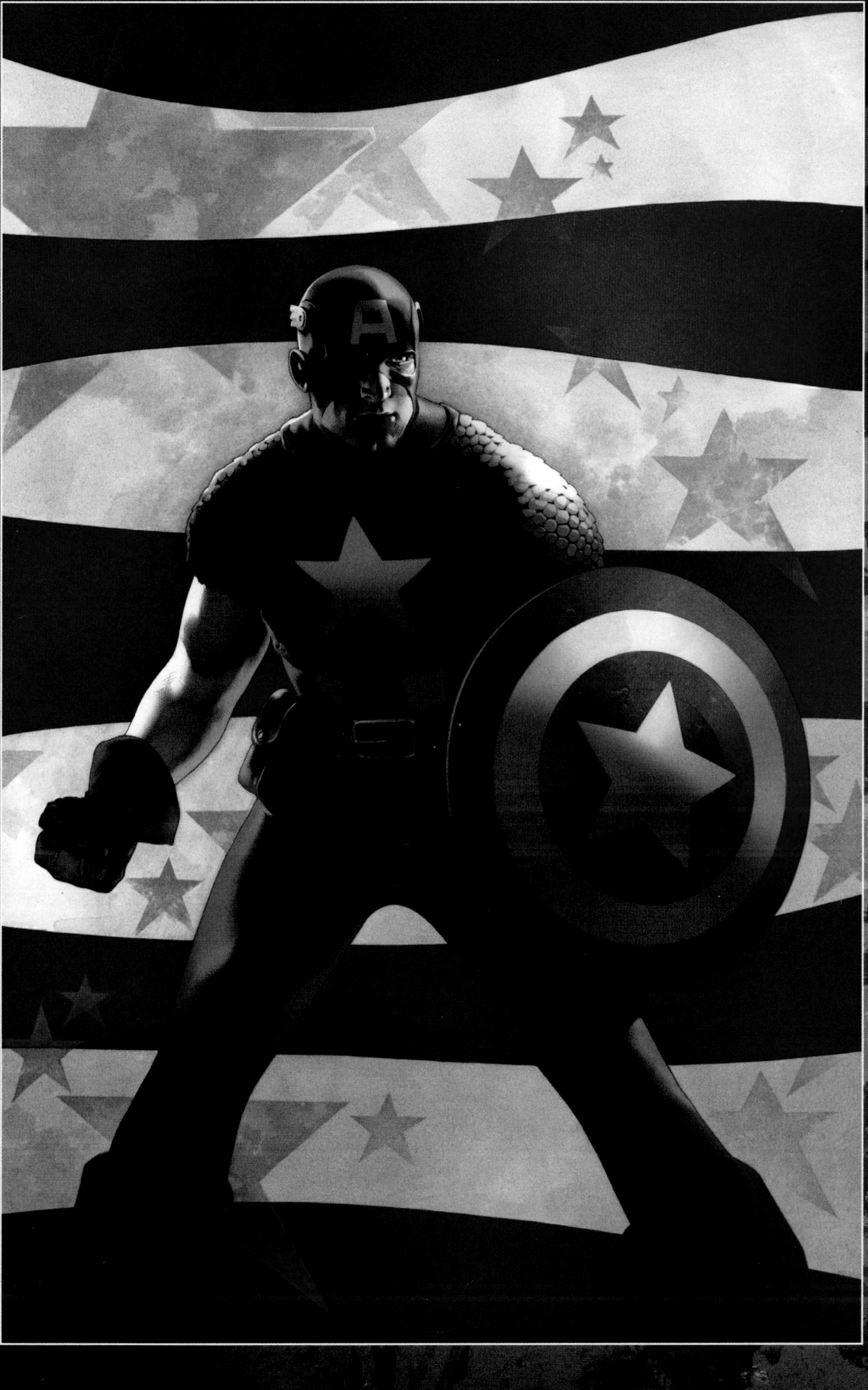

ISSUE #3 VARIANT

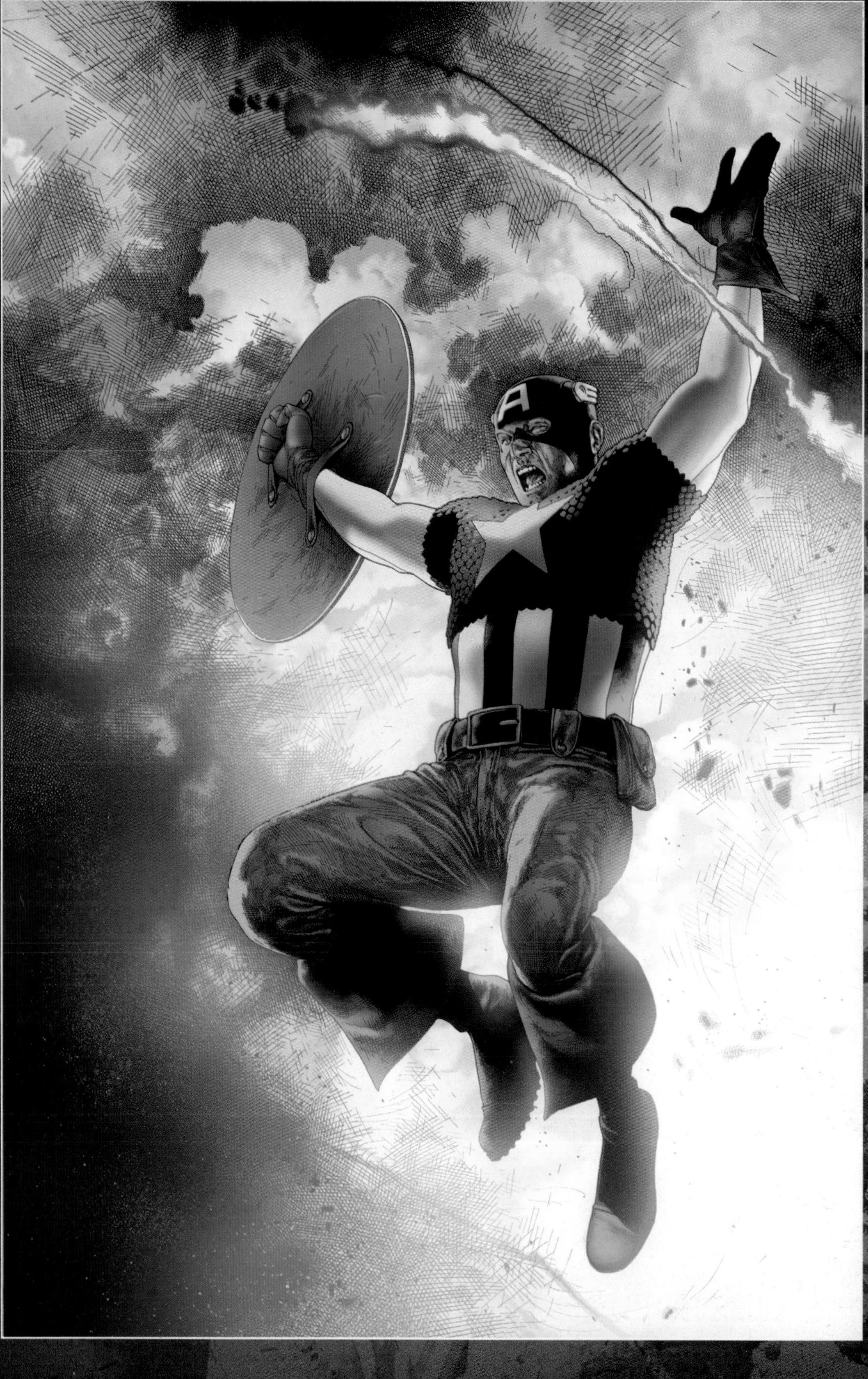

ISSUE #4 VARIANT

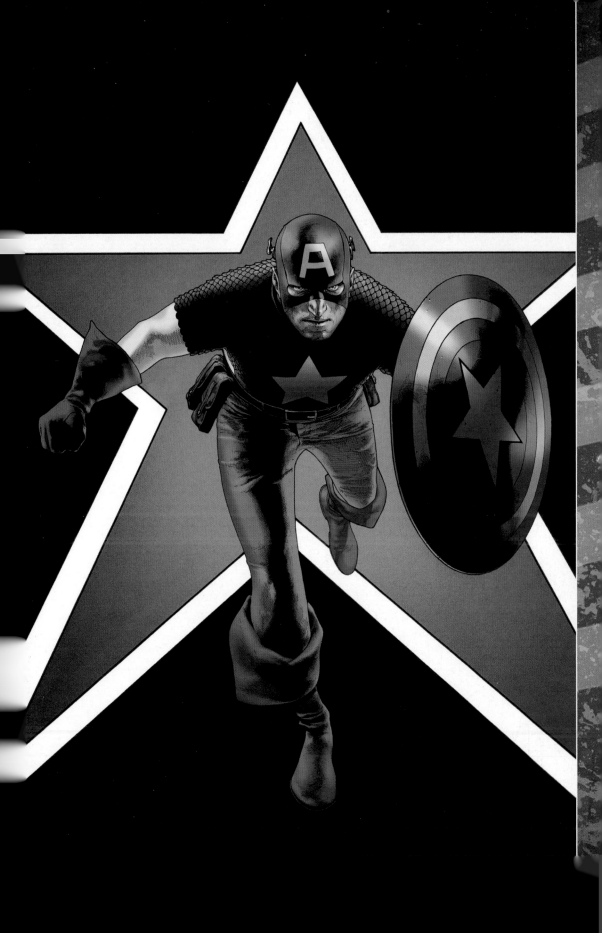

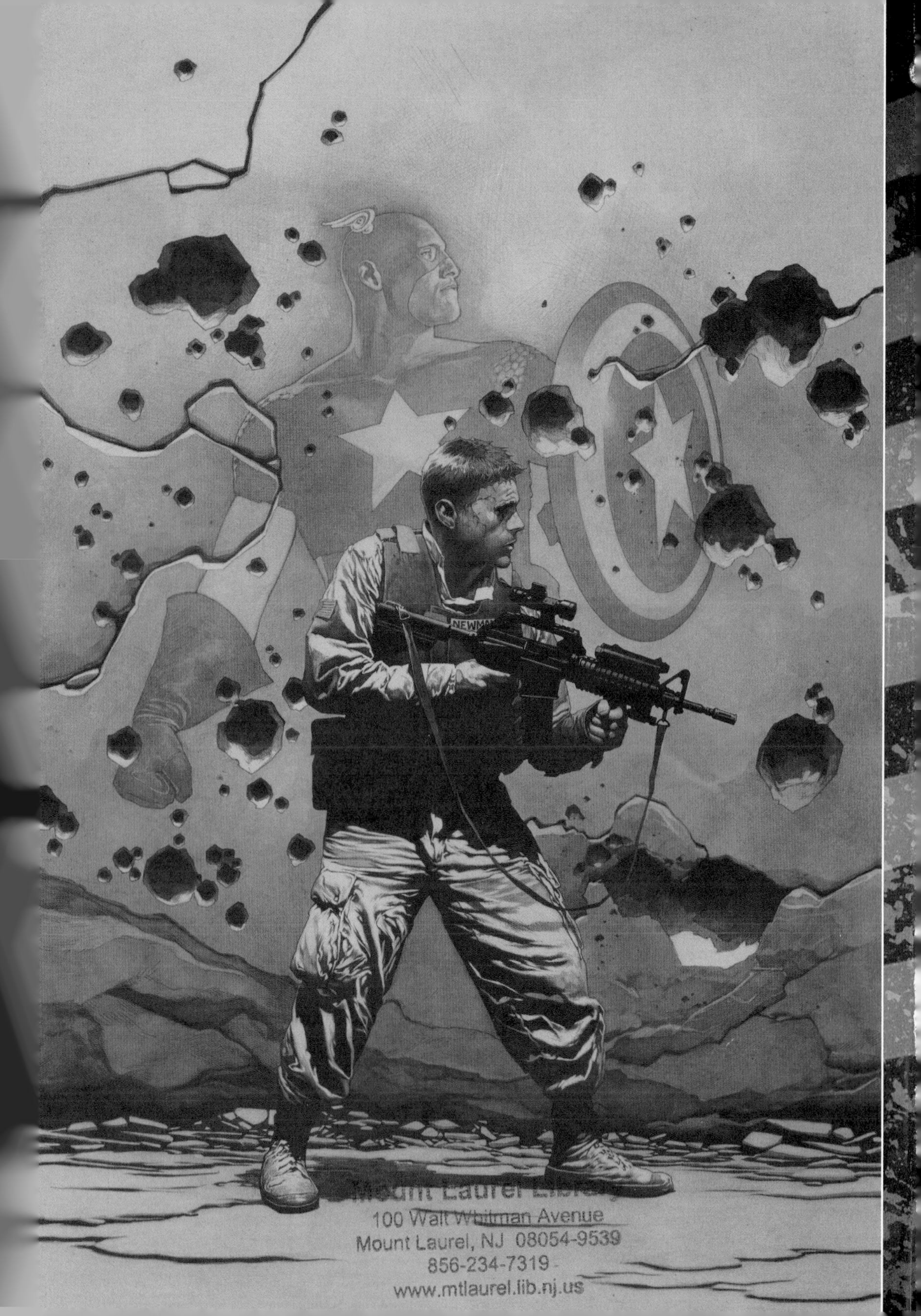